DETECTIVE DUPIN READS WILLIAM FAULKNER

Solutions to Six Yoknapatawpha Mysteries

CHARLES CHAPPELL

For Kathy and Sam,

in appreciation of your friendship and in gratitude for our festive times in Memphis and Little Rock.

Chuck

DETECTIVE DUPIN READS WILLIAM FAULKNER

Solutions to Six Yoknapatawpha Mysteries

CHARLES CHAPPELL

Charles Chappell
December 27, 1997

International Scholars Publications
San Francisco - London - Bethesda
1997

Library of Congress Cataloging-in-Publication Data

Chappell, Charles, 1942-
    Detective Dupin reads William Faulkner : solutions to six
    Yoknapatawpha mysteries / Charles Chappell.
      p. cm.
    Includes bibliographical references and index.
    ISBN 1-57309-166-9. -- ISBN 1-57309-165-0 (pbk.)
    I. Title.
    PS3553.H2976D47   1997
    813'.54—dc21   97-15671
                                                                                   CIP

Copyright 1997 by Charles Chappell

All rights reserved. Printed in the United States of America. No part of this book may be used or reproduced in any manner whatsoever without written permission except in the case of brief quotations embodied in critical articles and reviews.

                            Editorial Inquiries:
                            International Scholars Publications
                            7831 Woodmont Avenue, #345
                            Bethesda, MD 20814

                            To order: (800) 55-PUBLISH

For Carol,
Chris, Tim, and Michael

"Bud, no matter what you write, it's a mystery of one kind or another."

— William Faulkner to his friend
Albert I. Bezzerides

Oxford, Mississippi
July, 1947

Table of Contents

Chapter One: Introducing Dupin and Company

Meet Mister Narrator and His Burg	3
Plaint of the Perplexed Professor	7
Walking Across Murryville	15
Our Ratiocinist Revealed	31

Chapter Two: The Case of the Furtive Memphis Lawyer in *Sanctuary*

Bullish Back-Porch Boogie	53
Tapping the Stein and the Spine	65
Ballads at the Old Cafe	80

Chapter Three: The Case of Ms. Quentin's Second-Story Job in *The Sound and the Fury*

Campus Shaft	99
Blackboard Jumble	110
Take Me Out to the Mules' Game	118
Mysteries of One Kind or Another	122
Risky Business at Twilight Time	127

Chapter Four: The Case of Quentin Compson's Suicide Site in *The Sound and the Fury*

Hospital Street Blues	157
Bridge Over Tempting Waters	162
Tracking the Troubled Mississippian	177

Chapter Five: The Case of Addie Bundren's Mathematical Bequest in *As I Lay Dying*

    Bare-Chested Running Choir   199
    Count No Count   210
    New Slant on an Old Testament   227

Chapter Six: The Case of Faulkner's Arch-Villain in *Light in August*

    Neatsy Keen   257
    Head of the Crass   265

Chapter Seven: The Case of the Infatuated Final Narrator in *Light in August*

    Simple and Odd   299
    Gets Around, Gets Around, A Body Gets Around   310

Epilogue   341

Notes   343

Works Cited   357

Preface

The chapters in this book developed out of a longtime fascination with the fiction of William Faulkner and are based upon a series of articles which I have published during the past decade in a variety of journals. Readers who want to ponder a mystery's solution as it appears in its original expository form are welcome to seek any of the following:

"The Memphis Lawyer and his Spine: Another Piece in the *Sanctuary* Puzzle." *Essays in Literature* XIII (Fall 1986): 331-338.

"The Other Lost Woman of *The Sound and the Fury*." *Publications of the Arkansas Philological Association* 20 (Spring 1994): 1-18.

"Quentin Compson's Scouting Expedition on June 2, 1910." *Essays in Literature* XXII (Spring 1995): 113-122.

"The Mathematical Bequest of Addie Bundren." *The Faulkner Journal* I (Spring 1986): 69-74.

"Faulkner's Arch-Villain: Eupheus (Doc) Hines." *College Literature* XVI (Winter 1989): 66-74.

"The Infatuated Final Narrator of *Light in August*." *Publications of the Arkansas Philological Association* 14 (Spring 1988): 1-12.

All of the characters who appear in the following chapters as participants in my narrative are imaginary, and any resemblance between these characters and any actual persons, living or deceased, is purely a coincidence. Murryville, Arkansas, and Crowder County, Arkansas, as well as Crocodile, Butler County, Brookville, and Whisenhunt County, Arkansas, are fictional places and are based on no actual towns or counties in Arkansas or in any other state. Rivers, streets, businesses, schools, and other geographical or humanmade parts of Murryville, Crowder County, Crocodile, Butler County, Brookville, or Whisenhunt County are also imaginary. As author Donald Hays writes in the frontispiece to his splendid novel *The Dixie Association,* "This is all made up."

All references in these pages to Faulkner's novels *Sanctuary, The Sound and the Fury, As I Lay Dying,* and *Light in August,* and to any other Faulkner novel or story, adhere strictly to the printed passages in the cited works themselves. None of the Faulkner references are "made up."

In order to eliminate potential interruptions to the narrative, I have avoided placing numerals or other designations of scholarly citations within the text itself. Readers should feel free to turn to the "Notes" section for documentation of research sources and for further explanations of some of my interpretations of the four examined novels.

Chapter One

Introducing Dupin and Company

Meet Mister Narrator and His Burg

I suppose that this business of trying to make more sense of some of William Faulkner's books began when young Peter Prefont came to my office for an eye examination. Or perhaps it actually started when Augie and Mary Alice Dupree moved into town and settled into the old Baldwin place next door to where my wife Julianna and I have lived for over twenty years. Now that I think back on the many extensive discussions about Faulkner's novels that Pete, Augie, and I have enjoyed during the past year or so, I would have to conclude that we three ambitious readers made a firm commitment to this wild and crazy project when we first sat on my back porch during an early April afternoon in 1995, glanced around with mutual pleasure at the ghostly blooms of the Bradford pear trees lining my back fence, smelled the freshly cut grass of the season's first mowing, sipped fresh iced tea augmented with mint leaves, and opened our copies of *Sanctuary* to the first passages that baffled Professor Prefont and inspired him to solicit the help of Augie, a retired policeman, in digging out the clues necessary to the solution of a fictional puzzle. But before I attempt to recount some of the numerous arguments, cussings, and discussings that we eventually held over four of Mister Faulkner's masterpieces, perhaps I should introduce more fully the participants in this recurring exercise in literary detective work, beginning with yours truly, esquire, M. D.

My name is Archibald Fulmer Watkins, and I am a practicing ophthalmologist in the town of Murryville, Arkansas, which is the county seat and largest municipality (27,247 worthy souls) in Crowder County. Our fair town is located in the northeastern quadrant of this southern-southwestern state (erroneously referred to by President George Bush during the 1992 campaign as appearing on the map between Texas and Oklahoma). Although an occasional telephone solicitor might brassily refer to me as "Archibald" and Julianna often calls me "Archie," from my childhood years onward most people have hailed me by the use of my nickname "Speck." As you might imagine, I serve as a mobile billboard for my office's optical shop by always appearing in public in a pair of spectacles. When I was a callow youth of eight, I began wearing glasses to correct severe myopia, and blessedly the moniker of "Speck," shortened from first "Spectacles" and then "Specks," won out over "Four Eyes," "Goggle Head," and "Coke-Bottle Face" among the descriptions preferred by my notably uncharitable playground pals. During my college years some of my classmates attempted to hang titles such as "Baldy" and "Chrome Dome" on me, since by the age of twenty I had lost all but a lower fringe of my formerly curly locks. However, again the nickname "Speck" stuck, and of course now I am contentedly accustomed to it.

To complete your visual perception of the least significant player of the three in this series of literary investigations, I will add that I am five feet eight inches in height, can claim fifty-three years of riotous living, and am constantly battling to keep my weight below two hundred, especially since on occasion for lunch I order a greasy double cheeseburger with large fries and always seem to crave Rocky Road or Cherry Cordial ice cream at dessert time. No one could accurately call me handsome, but Julianna still finds me acceptable and makes certain that at work I wear fashionable charcoal or gray suits, subtly patterned sport coats, or blue blazers, all usually purchased straight off the rack at our local Dillard's, before I switch to my green surgical suit in the operating room or my white lab coat at the office. I don a colorful Nike exercise suit of purple, pink, and white for my frequent early morning brisk walks, and I try to keep a pleasant smile on my round face with its downsliding triple chins. My dear spouse has also convinced me to wear trendy blended bifocals with thin silver outer bands instead of my decades-old thick lenses housed in large dark frames, since she believes that my patients derive confidence from, as she puts it, "the constantly shining twinkle in your baby blues." Julianna has little trouble in persuading me that she is right on this issue as well as on many others, since she is not only my heart's darling but also, all five feet two inches and one-hundred-five pounds of her petite and energetic self, the authoritative and very successful mayor of Murryville, winning her second term with sixty-five per cent of the vote and exercising a firm control over the members of the Town Council, some of whom she very privately calls "Yahoos" and "Donkey Heads."

Julianna Murry Watkins is a native of this burg. Her ancestor John Wesley Murry was one of the original Scottish and English settlers who migrated westward from Kentucky to this fertile land on the Churchill River at the transition between the abundantly rich topsoil of the Mississippi Delta on the east and south and the meandering foothills of the Ozarks on the west and north. In 1821 J. W. Murry convinced his fellow pioneers of the wisdom of staking out a settlement on the higher ground above the Churchill's formation of a swooping bend, and our town witnessed its rough-hewn nascence.

The Churchill originally was named the Ozark River and was retitled during a fit of Allied and Anglophilic patriotic fervor in 1942. The river begins amidst the Arkansas Ozark Mountains in the northwestern part of the state, at the level of 3,000 feet in Lake Juan Brazos, named for an intrepid 17th-century Spanish explorer, brigand, and map forger. The Churchill then flows across northern Arkansas through the Ozarks, where it has become nationally famous as a scenic and challenging stream ideal for canoeing and rafting. As it continues its southeastward journey, it becomes wider, slower, and deeper, curving majestically past Murryville and then generously fulfilling its roles as a major navigable stream for commercial vessels and large pleasure craft as well as a source of irrigation for hundreds of farmers in the Delta, until it flows into the Mississippi River south of West Memphis and north of Helena.

Our town was first called Bend-in-the-river, then River Bend, and finally Murryville when John Wesley Murry's fellow founders persuaded Julianna's reticent ancestor to lend the town his sonorous surname. By the end of the nineteenth century the population had grown to 6,000, and today Murryville serves as the financial, legal, commercial, and medical center of a five-county region of this part of Arkansas. Soybeans, rice, and cotton are dependable annual crops for the planters in the contiguous Delta, and wheat, dairy cattle, and poultry dominate the agriculture in the rolling terrain north and west of town. Tyson Corporation has built a large processing plant just past the northwestern city limits, Monsanto long has managed a fertilizer factory on the eastern stretch of the river front, and several grain silos serve the barges that make constant round trips on the Churchill through the flat lands of eastern Arkansas to the confluence of our river with the Mississippi.

Murryville can boast of being home to twenty-one attorneys, five of whom are judges; thirty-seven physicians, more than half of them specialists; several civil, mechanical, and electrical engineers; three busy architects; and a slew of Ph.D. professors, since Moffatt College, an undergraduate liberal arts school with 1,300 mostly pre-professional students, has existed in Murryville since 1884. When Dr. Peter Edward Prefont, then 27, joined the faculty of the Department of English at Moffatt in the fall of 1994, he brought with him a newly awarded doctorate in American literature from Indiana University, a stunningly beautiful blonde wife named Ellie, and a reputation for teaching with contagious enthusiasm his courses in literature and writing. And when Professor Pete came to my office late on a Monday afternoon in the middle of March, 1995, with complaints of blurry vision and headaches, our trio's adventures in literary sleuthing experienced their spontaneous beginnings.

Plaint of the Perplexed Professor

I moved the slit lamp away from Pete's face, increased the dim lighting in the examination room, and rolled my stool away from the patient's chair into which Pete earlier had folded his lanky body.

"Mister Prefont—excuse me, Doctor Prefont, since I see by your chart that you have a Ph.D.—your eyes are in excellent condition. Your vision is 20-20, and I found no evidence of any ocular disorders."

Pete brushed a clump of his unruly sandy hair away from his forehead, cracked two of his knuckles, and then stretched his arms and shoulders, first in front of himself and then behind. He was wearing what I came to learn was a variation of his standard attire for days on which he was teaching: loosely fitting Oxford broadcloth shirt with button-down collar; a tie with maroon, blue, and beige depictions of Tabasco sauce and life in the Louisiana bayou country; khaki Docker pants; and thick-soled tan Bass shoes. His L. L. Bean gray sweater, size extra-large, lay haphazardly over an extra chair set against the back wall of the examining room.

"Thanks, Doctor Watkins. I'm relieved to know that my eyes are doing okay. But what about my blurry vision and my headaches?"

On my examining stool I rolled backward two feet and then, with left index finger placed vertically in front of my lips, I studied my new patient. "Have you had a general physical exam recently?"

"As a matter of fact, yeah. I just took out a small life insurance policy and had to go to a doctor for a checkup, so I picked Doctor Zeigler; do you know him?"

"Peter—may I call you by your first name?"

"Sure, Doctor, but please make it 'Pete.'"

"Pete, then. I have practiced ophthalmology here in Murryville since 1974, so I am acquainted with all members of the medical community. What did

Pablo Zeigler say about your physical condition?"

"Said I was fine; as he put it, in superb health. I told him about the blurry vision and the headaches, and he suggested that I come to you."

"Did he ask you about stress in your life?"

"Sure did. And when I talked to him, I denied that I was under any inordinate pressure. But since then I've asked Ellie—my wife—what she thinks, and she said that I have been sleeping too little, reading and studying even more than usual, and not exercising often enough."

I stared at Pete and replied, "Sounds like a typical graduate school regimen to me. Is this how you lived while you were working on your doctorate?"

Pete stood up and stretched all of his limbs this time. He leaned forward, clasped his hands behind his back, and began to pace in measured steps around the small room, dodging medical equipment as he strode.

"At first I did, but by my fourth and fifth years I settled into a pattern that worked well for me. Am I taking too much of your time, Doctor? I sense that this conversation is helping me, although I'm not really sure just how."

"Go ahead, Pete," I replied, as I leaned back on my stool. "I'm curious about your daily pattern, and you're my final patient of the day. My staff well knows my fondness for chatting with my patients."

As if on cue, May Ellen Adair, my jewel of an office manager, opened the door slightly, leaned in, and said, "Doctor Watkins, I'm leaving now. It's past 5:30."

"Fine, May Ellen. See you tomorrow. I'll close up shop."

"Good evening, then. Have a pleasant remainder of the day, Professor."

Silence from Pete.

"Professor. . . ."

"Oh, sorry, ma'm. I'm still getting used to being a professor, much less to being called one. Thanks, and good-bye to you, also."

As the door closed quietly, I swung my rotating stool in Pete's direction.

"Now back to your daily routine."

"Yes, of course. By my fourth year at Indiana I was working steadily on my dissertation, teaching two undergraduate classes in introduction to fiction, and serving as a dutiful househusband. Each morning at six I would run at least five miles. . . ."

"Excuse me," I interrupted, "five miles every morning?" Since I had begun only the previous summer to walk for exercise, a daily five-mile jaunt sounded as formidable to me as a marathon, and I told Pete of my admiration for his dedication to running.

"Actually, Doctor Watkins, when I was playing soccer and running track at Wittenberg—that's my undergrad school—I ran much farther than five miles on many days. I played midfielder on the soccer team in the fall and then ran the mile and the two-mile in meets during the spring."

"So you resumed your running toward the end of your graduate school days?"

"Yes, and I followed a sensible routine of teaching my classes, grading papers and preparing for my lectures, working afternoons and evenings on my epic tome of a dissertation, and hanging around Ellie all that I could. I also slept soundly, and usually for six to seven hours per night."

"What about this year, since you have joined the faculty at Moffatt?"

"Now that we talk about it, sir, I'm beginning to understand that Ellie may be right when she said that I am neglecting my health. I spend so much time preparing for my new courses that I'm avoiding nutritious food, missing sleep, and finding excuses not to run. Could my frantic schedule be causing my vision problems?"

Pete stopped his pacing and stared pleadingly at me, the alleged authority. All of us physicians get called upon to practice some minor office psychiatry now and then, and I decided to apply some common-sense therapy to Pete's present dilemma.

"Here's my recommendation, Pete. First, try to get back to your pattern of running every day and sleeping for a decent amount of time. Probably your normal appetite will return quickly. Stay away from a steady diet of junk food." I spouted that last dictum with a twinge of guilt as the supreme Mexican dinner from Margarita's Corner Cantina continued to play a raucous version of "La Cucaracha" in my digestive tract.

Pete stretched his arms until he touched the ceiling. "Great advice, Doctor. I will do what you say. What else do you recommend?"

I found myself distracted by the sight of Pete's fingertips touching my overhanging acoustical ceiling tiles. Glancing quickly at Pete's chart, I noticed that his height was listed as six feet, five inches.

"You're taller than I first noticed, Pete. You say that you played soccer and not. . . ."

Pete finished my sentence. "Basketball. That's right. I couldn't dribble, shoot, or pass. Other than those three handicaps, I was average. But I could jump, contrary to the racial stereotype, so I was a decent rebounder. I quickly discovered that soccer was my game and that my specialty could be using my big old head to pass the ball or to try to place it into the net and score a goal. And I'm surely glad that I stuck with soccer, because that's how I met Ellie. Did I tell you that she was the team captain at Indiana? I met her when I worked out with the women's team, and now she's coaching the Silver Streaks here at Moffatt."

The hour was late, everyone else had left the office, and I realized that I had promised Julianna that I would serve as her smiling escort at a Chamber of Commerce banquet at seven. "Pete, I'm enjoying our conversation, but I need to draw it to a close. Let me try to get to the root cause of your current stress."

Pete plopped resoundingly back into the patient's chair. I grimaced as my instruments vibrated and a mirror tilted sideways on the wall.

With anguish evident in his voice, Pete responded, "My Faulkner course—that's what's causing me to lose sleep and to forget to eat. And also to rob me of my time for running."

I recognized the name of the eminent and enigmatic author from our neighboring state of Mississippi. "Does your Faulkner course take more time than your other—how many courses?"

"Three. And hell yes, it does. Oops, excuse me, Doc. A mere slip of the profane tongue."

"No problem," I replied. "Sometimes emphatic verbiage is appropriate. But why this course?"

Pete bounced up and began anew his pacing. "I've been scrambling all semester with this monster course. I took a Faulkner seminar at Indiana during my master's year, and I wrote a small part of my doctoral examinations on Faulkner's short novel *The Bear*. But my major field of concentration is modern American poetry; my dissertation is on William Carlos Williams. I inherited this Faulkner course from Patrick Faris, the longtime Moffatt teacher who retired last spring. My chairman told me that the course was so popular I would need to teach it this year, even though I had asked for a year to prepare for the challenge."

Pete's anxiety was evident, and I tried to be helpful with my reply. "I read some Faulkner during my undergraduate days at Moffatt in the early sixties, and all I can remember is that the damned stuff confused me endlessly. I sympathize with your problem. Are you at the point where you can see the end of the semester coming?"

Long arms flailed upward. "Yes, thank God. I'm teaching *Sanctuary* now, and I'm trying to prepare for the final assignments of the term, *Spotted Horses, Old Man, The Bear,* and *The Sound and the Fury*. So I think I'll make it. But I am staying up late every night stewing over the questions that my students ask about the novels. I HATE to appear unprepared, but sometimes I just can't answer a perfectly legitimate question. I always dig through the critical studies of Faulkner's novels and once in a while find a plausible solution—or several—to a problem of interpretation, but sometimes I just can't find any helpful scholarly works. And then I really get pissed off—excuse me, mightily frustrated. May I take two more minutes and give you a quick example?"

I checked my watch—6:05—and told him please to proceed.

"Thanks, Doctor. Okay, to the point, and I'll be brief because I don't have the novel with me. In *Sanctuary* one of the minor characters is a Jewish lawyer from Memphis. This lawyer is first identified—and also denounced in bitter and highly racist language—by Clarence Snopes, the Mississippi state senator from Yoknapatawpha County, principal setting of most of the book's events. Later this same lawyer appears but doesn't speak at the pivotal trial near the novel's end. Now, it seems likely that this lawyer has been hired by a Memphis gangster named Popeye, who is the book's main villain, but I can't tell for certain. And also I can't understand why Snopes curses the lawyer so maliciously. By the way, at the time of his racist diatribe Snopes sports a black eye and a damaged nose and mouth. Last week a bright young woman in the class asked me about the Memphis lawyer, Snopes, and their possible connections, if any. Like the impressive scholar that I am supposed to be, I stood before the assembled young lambs and heroically replied, 'Er, uh, gee, gosh, well—I don't know.' AAARGH! How embarrassing!"

With the heel of his left hand Pete sharply pounded his forehead three times and then shook his head vigorously—six, eight, ten times. I stood and then tapped my teeth with my ball-point pen.

"Excuse me, Professor, but do you abuse your skull in that manner while standing in front of your classes, or perhaps when you are working alone in your office? Or even when you are studying at home?"

Pete ceased all motion. He then turned slowly and faced me.

"Well, shi—, uh, sheet rock and ship shape. I guess that I do, Doc. Several times a day, too."

"Is your vision blurry afterward? Does your head hurt?"

With a sheepish grin Pete fell backward into the chair, this time dislodging into a tumble a stuffed Barney the dinosaur from my back shelf, where I keep games and toys as distractions for young patients. "You're a sly investigator, Doctor Watkins, You must be right. I've been causing my own problems and then compounding them through worry and ceaseless fretting."

The time arrived for Hippocratic magnanimity on my part. "Don't be so hard on yourself, Pete. Sometimes it takes a little digging to solve a mystery."

I stood and escorted Pete to the front desk, where he graciously asked about my fee and quickly wrote out a check for the office visit. As he shook hands and thanked me for my time and advice, I gave in once more to what I like to call "curiosity" but a habit that Julianna insists is actually habitual and pernicious nosiness. "By the way, did you ever find the answers to that student's questions about *Sanctuary*?"

Pete's placid demeanor immediately dissolved into one of despair.

"Naaah, of course not. The critics have some theories, but I could find no definitive solutions. A couple of my most reliable printed sources conclude that we readers will never know the answers because Faulkner simply hasn't supplied enough facts for us to pursue."

At that instant the phantom genie residing in my chromium domium pulled the fabled chain to the proverbial light bulb. "Pete, you mentioned Memphis, a gangster, crimes, a trial, and a mysterious lawyer. Perhaps you could find some answers to your questions if you consulted a real-life detective. My next-door neighbor is Augustus Dupree, who happens to be retired from the Memphis police force, where he served for many years as a detective. I wonder if he could help you?"

Pete grabbed me by the shoulders and shouted in my face. "Do you think that he would? Just possibly? Man, that would be terrific! Will you ask him, Doctor Watkins? Will you?"

I struggled backward two steps and out of Pete's tenacious grasp. "Patient, calm thyself! Certainly I will talk to Augie and bring up the subject.

But I will be of little use to you or to any of my other patients if my upper arms don't function and my hearing is diminished. Cool your jets, Pete."

"Sorry once more, Doctor Watkins. Ellie would be really ticked off at me if she knew how out of control I have acted today. Have I stepped over the line once too often?"

I rotated my shoulders, snapped my middle finger from behind my thumb and pinged myself on the right temple, and replied with huffy bravado, "All systems still intact, Professor. Now you scoot on home to that long-suffering spouse of yours and let me hustle out of here so that I can change identities from eyeball doc to mayoral consort. I'll call you after I have talked with Augie."

Pete backed out of my office door, his hair flapping and his sweater askew, bowing in an oddly Oriental fashion and expressing fervent gratitude as he brought our lengthy initial conversation to an end.

Walking Across Murryville

Precisely at the hour of six on Tuesday morning I knocked lightly on Augie Dupree's back door. The temperature was 41 degrees, an overnight shower had left the streets dotted with puddles and the bordering vegetation damp, and a bracing wind from the northwest buffeted the sleeves and trouser legs of my spiffy Nike exercise suit, underneath which I wore a no-frills sweat shirt and faded gray cotton warm-up pants. I tugged downward on the woolen ski cap necessary to keep my balding head from becoming transformed into an ice cube, already eagerly anticipating the day in later spring when I could switch to my favorite Moffatt College standard-issue baseball cap, white with orange letters and a black bill. But today I was pleasantly awaiting my routine early morning exercise jaunt with my fascinating new friend, Caesar Augustus Dupree, Captain of Detectives (retired), City of Memphis Police Department.

Augie and his wife, the former Mary Alice Cate, had moved to Murryville in June of 1994. Mary Alice, who was born here, grew up in the same neighborhood with my Julianna and became a lifelong dear friend of the petite babe who blessedly later became my wife and also, of course, Her Honor the Mayor. When Augie decided to take early retirement from the Memphis P. D., Mary Alice was able to accept a long-standing offer to become a principal in our city's system of public schools. As luck would have it, the Baldwin place next to our house was available. Augie and Mary Alice looked it over carefully several times, deemed it suitable to their needs, and made an offer on it that was acceptable to the Baldwin heirs. They spent the summer happily engaged in a whirligig of remodeling the central core of the edifice, rearranging the landscaping, and adding a new screened-in porch to the rear of the house. By the time that Mary Alice took up her duties at Waggoner Elementary School in early August, Augie and I had discovered a mutual interest in ambulatory exercise, made necessary for me because of my love of tacos, pizza, cheeseburgers, and ice cream, and essential to

Augie for two reasons: his desire to retain his lifelong flat belly, and his dedication to rehabilitating himself fully from the injuries that in 1993 nearly ended his life and that later persuaded him to accept the offer of early retirement from police work.

My mind snapped back to the present as the back door noiselessly opened and Augie softly stepped out onto his newly reconstructed deck of treated pine. "Morning, Speck," he spoke in his Southern gentleman's pleasant educated drawl, delivering his habitual greeting to me.

"And the same to you, my friend, on this blustery new day in March. Ready to ramble?"

"Let me lock up, and I'll be right with you," responded my partner in sunrise strolls.

Augie stuck his head back inside the door, presumably to let Mary Alice know he was leaving, and the gesture allowed me time to look carefully at him once again and to reflect on my original positive impression of him that was merely reaffirmed whenever we got together. Augie's physique, demeanor, and measured mannerisms have always seemed to communicate a combination of mental and physical vigor, strong self-discipline, and inner confidence. Six feet tall and a rock-hard 170 pounds, Augie maintained his rigorous conditioning not only through our frequent walks (alas, my only regular formal exercise) but also through daily sessions on his Nordic Track machine, regular bouts of yard work or gardening, and periodic outdoor expeditions involving hiking, backpacking, and camping.

Aside from his trim and muscular appearance, even more a source of envy to me because he is three years my senior, his most striking feature is either his head of hair or his eyes; I have never been able to decide which. His full, thick reddish-brown hair has recently begun to show several strands of silver, and the contrast in color is made even dramatic by his clear gray eyes that fix directly on any person with whom he converses and that shift away only when someone else speaks. During his most recent visit to my office I told him that he can boast of distance vision typical of a man twenty years younger than he, but I did slightly increase the magnification of the reading glasses that he has been using for ten years now. Most of the time, such as during our morning perambulations, he wore no spectacles, and the intensity of his gaze still struck me as remarkable, even after our acquaintanceship of several months. His burnished red, neatly trimmed short moustache is also showing a few hints of silver.

Dressed for exercise in a baggy blue Memphis Tigers sweatshirt, faded Levi jeans, well-worn Reebok running shoes, and a white baseball cap bearing in blue letters the legend "Murryville P. D.," Augie stepped briskly toward me, and I joined him as we descended his wooden back steps and circled his house in the direction of the nearby sidewalk running parallel along the north side of Summit Avenue, our residential street. I noticed that the limp in his right leg was less pronounced than it had been at the end of our most recent walk on the preceding Friday.

"Is your leg continuing to feel stronger, Augie?" I inquired as we passed under the streetlight at the corner. The sky was beginning to lighten faintly in the east, with sunrise still more than a half-hour away.

"Somewhat better, thanks, Speck. I'm still doing my special exercises and hope to get the leg back to normal very soon."

When I remembered that as recently as May of 1993 surgeons had extricated a .45 caliber bullet from the thigh of that leg and that just last month Augie had twisted his right knee while playing handball at the Moffatt College athletic center, I took note once again of Augie's stoic refusal to allow a physical setback to slow him down. According to Mary Alice, Augie had to call upon all of his considerable inner resolve to sustain himself as he recuperated from his bullet wounds, especially the piercing of his right lung. While trying to resolve a hostage crisis in a north Memphis housing project, Augie had jumped in front of an abused wife named Connie Cumberland when her husband Monte had finally gone off his rocker and started blasting away. Augie had taken some of the bullets that were intended for Connie, but Monte was captured before he could fire off any more rounds, and Connie and her two berserk children were spared the ignominy of becoming sad statistics in the modern marital guerrilla wars. Augie spent five days in an intensive care unit but pulled through and eventually decided that perhaps the goddess Fortuna was hinting to him to consider early retirement. When Mary Alice once again talked to him about her leaving the Memphis schools and their returning to Murryville, the Duprees concluded that the Fates indeed were conspiring to direct their destinies to this town some 87 miles northwest of Memphis on the bend in the Churchill River where the Delta meets the foothills of the Ozarks.

Since their relocation, Augie has concentrated on his rehabilitation but in recent months has agreed to consult with the Murryville Police Department on cases for which his extensive experience in investigation and detection could possibly be of some assistance. Because he had helped to close out a baffling case during just the previous weekend, on this damp, murky Tuesday I was the fortunate auditor of the details of a weird crime that Augie's analytical skills and probing intellect had solved.

We had ambled six blocks from our houses, angling toward the river from the northwest, gradually descending a series of low hills, and passing under numerous pin oaks, sugar maples, river birches, and a weeping willow or two, when Augie chuckled and asked me, "Have I told you about Rodger Compton's latest escapade?"

My friend had designated the principal malefactor among the student populace of Moffatt College and persistent thorn in the side of kindly Ogbert Merriwell, Dean of Students.

"What has the infamous Rodger the Dodger been up to now?" was my return query. By this time we were beginning to walk past some of the stores, churches, and offices on the fringe of Murryville's historic downtown shopping district. Across the street sprawled Coulter's Feed and Seed, an interconnected series of ramshackle loading docks, counter rooms, storage bins, and porches that served as a favorite hangout for many of Crowder County's farmers during the slow winter months. We were maintaining our customary pace that would allow us to complete our three-mile trek in approximately 45 minutes.

Augie pointed toward the Anderson place, one of Murryville's older existing houses, the first three rooms of which had been built in 1837. "Looks as if George and Jennie are adding some more space," he pointed out. The current Anderson residents, descendants of the house's first tenants, continually undertook additions and repairs to their two-story white frame antebellum mansion, with its twin massive front columns, four upstairs balconies, and green shutters all the way around. This latest project appeared to involve extending a side porch almost right up to a garden area of thick azalea bushes and flowering pink and white dogwoods. The house and grounds occupied a full half-block and marked the merging of our town's residential district with the downtown area that covered most of the land within the bend of the Churchill River, an area stretching ten blocks east and west and six blocks from the north to the last street on the south before the thirty-acre plot that comprised River Bend Park. I agreed with Augie that the Andersons were building once more, suggested that today we swing by the river and hope to catch a glimpse of the first rays of the sun creeping up over the Delta to the east, and then asked him to tell me more about Compton's latest clash with the law.

"Oh, yes. Well, Buddy called me at seven-fifteen last Saturday evening and asked me if I could stop by the station and help him out with a puzzling crime." Augie had named our town's veteran Chief of Police, the earnest and estimable Elmer Raymond Cotham, better known lifelong by his proverbial Southern nickname. Buddy tried not to impose on Augie's time too often, and the fact that the Chief would call on the retired detective during a Saturday evening revealed that Buddy was truly in need of expert assistance.

Once more Augie picked up the narrative. "I had already showered after helping Mary Alice dump leaves onto our compost pile, so I was happy to come downtown." By coincidence we were just then passing the one-story blonde-brick police headquarters and city jail located at the corner of Main Street and Fourth Avenue. "Buddy and Dean Merriwell were waiting for me in the Chief's office. They were trying to decide what to do with young Rodger, who appeared to be guilty of the crime but against whom they had no clear evidence."

As we passed the police building, Augie told me of the frustrated frowns on the faces of Buddy and Ogbert as they plaintively asked Augie for his help. Augie chuckled at the memory of their varieties of attire. The dapper Buddy had been wearing his starched and pressed blue chief's uniform, even on the weekend; Ogbert appeared in a faded flannel shirt, rumpled dark trousers, and unlaced military boots; and Augie showed up in his all-Levi outfit: jeans, a blue work shirt, and a western jacket.

We crossed Third Avenue and turned south, passing Sanders Jewelers, Dodgen Dry Cleaning, the Hughes Community Theatre, and Hines Mercantile. The last establishment had been open for business, in its present location but in different structures, since 1841, when Alistair Hines had journeyed up the river from the east and had opened the first general store in frontier Murryville. Most of the lifelong residents of our town still bought their clothing, decorative furnishings, and wedding gifts at Hines's, even though the inevitable Wal-Mart had recently opened in a strip center on the northeast side of the town and was siphoning away business, particularly among members of the younger and newer families of our community.

I picked up the story again. "Where was Rodger when you got to the police building? In a holding cell?"

Augie turned his head toward me and smiled faintly. His piercing gray eyes were becoming more perceptible in the increasing early light. "No, Buddy had not charged Compton yet, but he wanted him detained until I could be called in. So I passed Rodger in the public waiting area as I was heading back to Buddy's office. The Dodger was shouting at the patrolman on duty, Mickey McCarty, as each of them tugged on one end of a television remote control device. Rodger, in his Grateful Dead T-shirt and torn jeans, was demanding to watch MTV, while Mickey was insisting on a Lawrence Welk rerun showing on the Nickelodeon Channel. Buddy's office provided a welcome sanctuary from this cross-cultural, clamorous pitched battle. Two other Moffatt students waited on chairs outside Buddy's cubicle."

We reached the corner of Second Avenue and River Street, the crossroads of our small town's legal district. Taking up the entire block enclosed by Second, River, First, and Main is the pale-red-brick, four-story Crowder County Courthouse, with its surrounding lawns, trees, and scattered park benches, on which sit various older men of the town as they hold court and dispense advice, opinions, local history, and county gossip in roughly equal parts. On the southwest corner of River and Second sits Story's Cafe, christened in 1843 by its founder as Story's Dining Establishment for Gentlemen and Ladies. Story's has been providing country breakfasts, ample and tasty plate lunches, and standard meat-and-potatoes supper fare to Murryville's citizenry for 152 years now. For several decades it also has endured as a popular gathering spot for the attorneys whose offices line the nearby streets, as well as for their paralegal assistants, secretaries, and clients, in addition to the various clerks, office workers, and other functionaries who toil in the courthouse. A trip to Story's for coffee or for a meal allows any curious patrons an opportunity to catch up on all of the local news concerning arrests, pleadings, depositions, verdicts, and appeals. Despite the temptation to stop in at Story's for a cup of freshly brewed coffee and an hour of informative chatter, Augie and I kept up our brisk walking, since I faced an office full of eye patients beginning at 8:30 and my friend Dupree had a hot date with a pair of hedge trimmers later in the morning. As we walked east on River Street, then north on First, and next crossed Main, I asked him the nature of Rodger's crime.

"That was the pressing problem facing Buddy and Ogbert," Augie told me. "They were certain that Compton was responsible for the burns on the Southeastern student, but they could discover no proof. And sly Rodger was confessing exactly nothing."

I stopped abruptly and grabbed Augie's left arm. "Did you say 'burns?' On a student from Moffatt's principal rival college?"

Augie obligingly filled me in on the necessary background information. His recapitulation took up most of the walk back home past insurance, dental, and medical offices on the edge of the downtown area, the First United Methodist Church and Trinity Lutheran Cathedral, four blocks of restored antebellum homes, and then our neighborhood made up of a mixture of large two-story houses built between the world wars, one-level bungalows or cottages dating from the Eisenhower era, and a few scattered brick or frame dual-level apartment buildings. "On Saturday afternoon the Southeastern Polecats baseball team came by bus to play the Moffatt Bulldogs in a doubleheader. Rodger and a few of his rowdy companions sat conspicuously in the bleachers during the games and, according to eyewitnesses, yelled incessant insults at the opponents while heaping vituperative language on the umpires for every call adversely affecting the Bulldogs' fortunes. Everyone assumed that Rodger and crew had been sipping the golden brew, but the bad boys of Moffatt had enough sense not to bring any cans or bottles of intoxicants to the baseball field. Ogbert strolled over two or three times and fixed the group with his malevolent glare, so by the sixth inning of the second game matters were under at least tenuous control, as the Dean later reported. And he also said that if the small group of Southeastern fans sitting in the opposite bleachers had managed to stay cool for one more inning, then no fisticuffs would likely have broken out."

Now we were getting to the juicy part. "So Rodger's rabble-rousers started an old-fashioned rumble?' I queried.

"More like two packs of mutts woof-woofing at each other from a distance than a genuine donnybrook," Augie informed me. "But Rodger managed to provoke one Polecat supporter, who happened to be a linebacker on the football squad, into invading the D. M. Z. between the groups and launching a left hook at Rodger's jutting and jeering jaw."

We now had completed two-thirds of our customary route, and I was eager to hear the entire story before we reached our adjacent houses on Summit Avenue. "What did Compton do?" I asked, "question the manhood of the pigskin gladiator?"

"You guessed it, Speck. And he also made a wicked reference to the linebacker's fondness for flirting with female orangutans at his school's neighboring metropolitan zoo. But Ogbert quelled the potential riot before it could escalate, and he evicted both groups from the bleachers, following them to the parking lot and making certain that they drove away. What he did not predict was that Rodger's group would follow the Polecat supporters onto Interstate Forty-Eight, eastward bound."

"So the battle spilled over onto the highway? And some burns resulted? Surely there was not a fiery crash?" I asked in alarm.

"Fortunately no wreck occurred, Speck. But there was a fire of sorts. And therein dwells the mystery that Buddy Cotham asked me to help him solve."

I looked ahead and quickly calculated that we were eight blocks from our destination. A shave, a shower, breakfast, and office hours awaited me, and I asked Augie to cut to the chase.

He congenially obliged. "An appropriate metaphor, my friend, because a chase by automobile is exactly what occurred. Monkey Walton was driving the car with the Moffatt students in it, with Ratface Tilton riding shotgun and Rodger in the backseat by himself. Apparently Monkey owns a souped-up Pontiac Firebird, and he quickly caught and passed the blue Volvo driven by the Polecat boys. But surprise! The Volvo was supercharged, apparently, because it overtook the Firebird and passed it in return. Monkey told Buddy that the Volvo was soon doing eighty for sure. The driver of the Volvo then swerved his car toward the right lane and appeared to be trying to force Monkey and his pals into the nearby ditch."

"Whew," I commented. "This gets serious. Sounds as if a major accident was in the offing."

"Luckily, one did not occur," said Augie, "because once the Southeastern guys knew that they could outrun the Firebird they slowed down. If Monkey sped up, then so did they, as Walton later reported. So the guys in the Volvo simply hugged the left lane, sped up and swerved over if Monkey tried to pass on the right, and began to stick every available hand out a window with the middle digit raised in derisive salute."

"Ah, yes," I nodded. "The traditional International Sign of Good Will. I assume that Rodger and crew were not amused."

"Correct you are, Speck. But the lava truly began to spew from Rodger's volcano when the Southeastern boys slowed down to thirty, lowered the right side windows, and, hmmm. . . . How shall I phrase this next part delicately? Ah, yes. They displayed two full moons over Crowder County, Arkansas, even though the sun had not yet set."

We reached Summit and turned westward toward our respective domiciles. "Great God, Augie," I guffawed, "do you mean that they defenestrated their naked posteriors in broad daylight on Interstate Forty-Eight? What a bizarre sight that must have been."

"Doubtlessly so, my friend," replied Augie. "And at this point the true mystery begins. All that Monkey and Ratface can recall is that Rodger, who was sitting directly behind Monkey the driver, went absolutely bonkers at the sight of what we might call the dual Polecat big-ass hams. First Rodger grabbed an umbrella from the floorboard and tried to jab his taunters in a vulnerable spot, but the Volvo would merely speed up and swerve away. Rat reported that Rodger screamed foul curses for a short time but then grew quiet."

We came to our neighboring homes and took seats on the front steps of Augie's dwelling, with Augie two steps up from me. "Please finish this ribald story, Augie, so that I can embark on my daily rounds of medical mercy," I pleaded.

"Five more minutes and I'll be through," promised my friend the sleuth. "Ten at the most. All right? Well, then, Monkey and Ratface have no idea what happened next. All that they can report is that Rodger told them to slow down and to get as close to the Polecat car as possible. Rat reports that he looked back just as Rodger leaned out the window, and then both Monkey and Rat saw a large ball of fire swallow up the protruding bum of, as it turned out, the Southeastern linebacker. Rodger then fell back into the Firebird and calmly ordered his companions to take the next exit and return to Moffatt."

"Did Compton fire off some sort of blowtorch? Light a flare? What was the source of this ball of fire?" I asked in bafflement.

"Ah, therein lay the mystery," responded Augie. "You have phrased exactly the question that bewildered Buddy and Ogbert. They could find no weapons or projectile devices in the car when they searched it later. But they called Rodger in for questioning when Ogbert received a call from Doctor Ted Jefferson at the Churchill River Medical Center emergency room, informing the Dean that a Southeastern student was then being treated for severe burns on his buttocks and the victim was claiming that Rodger had assaulted him. Soon Buddy became involved, and then the Chief called me."

"I am completely dazed and confused, Augie," I said plaintively. "Did you ever figure out this crazy situation?"

"Yes, Speck, I did, but only by questioning fellow Firebirders Tilton and Walton closely and then by surreptitiously observing Rodger as he continued to argue with Mickey out in the waiting room. Ratface and Monkey told me the same story that they had told Ogbert and Buddy, but I insisted that they ransack their memories for any further details, however seemingly inconsequential. I asked them about any brief glimpses they may have had of Rodger in the back seat or of any unusual noises. Ratface finally remembered that he had glanced back just as Rodger was reaching into his right front jeans pocket, but Rat never saw what Rodger was reaching for because at that moment the Polecat driver honked, swerved his Volvo to the right, and stayed just ahead of the Firebird as the mooners shook their exposed derrieres vigorously. When Rat looked back, Rodger's upper torso was leaning fully out of the left rear window, and the fireball then exploded into view. But then Monkey remembered that he had looked backward to his right just as Rodger flopped back into the car and had seen Rodger toss an object out of the lowered right rear window."

I sat in musing contemplation. "So, to the storehouse of facts you added the pocket incident and the object that went out the window."

"But these two clues were sufficient, my friend, to enable me to form a hypothesis. First I asked Ratface and Monkey if Rodger were a smoker, and they replied in the affirmative. Then I also learned from them that Compton preferred a pocket lighter to matches and that the Dodger uses an old Zippo lighter that his father had flicked for many years before going cold turkey on cigarettes. I walked out of Buddy's office and stood quietly where I could peer around a corner in the hallway and observe Rodger. On three occasions within a span of five minutes he sauntered to the water fountain and vigorously washed out his mouth. At two other intervals he inserted his right index finger into his open mouth, leaned his head back, and rubbed the surfaces of his outer teeth. He then gargled with his saliva and again went to the water fountain, these times in order to expectorate loudly. Once he asked Mickey for some mouthwash and received only a profane and negative response."

As turned out to be the case several times in the upcoming months, I was foggily unenlightened by the same facts that pointed my astute friend toward the plausible solution to a mystery. "All right, Detective Captain Dupree," I said in exasperation. "Lay it all out for me. I know the identity of the criminal, or I guess that I should call him an arsonist this time. But how did Rodger cause the fire ball?"

Augie stood up and assumed the erect posture of a pedagogue behind an imposing lectern. "Let us review the clues, Speck. First, Rodger extricated an unknown object from his jeans pocket. Of course, later I asked him what it was, but he would only smile and refuse to answer. Second is the brief episode of ditching this evidence out the car window. And third are the attempts by Rodger to cleanse his mouth. Add to these the assumption that our culprit always carries his father's ancient Zippo cigarette lighter. Any theories, Doctor Watkins?"

I stared at Augie in perplexity. A wisp of a thought blew past my mind's eye, but I rejected it as too absurd to mention.

"Go ahead, Speck. I can tell that you have a hypothesis. Float it out here on this damp morning air."

Once again my canny friend's acute powers of observation impressed me. Just how he always seemed to know what I was thinking was a secret that he never would share with me. But I was glad that he was rarely sitting beside me at Moffatt College athletic contests when the shapely cheerleaders in their miniskirts executed their saucy twirls. . . . Back to the puzzle at hand.

"Okay, Augie. All that I can conjure up is that Rodger held the object he took out of his right front pocket in his mouth so that he could grab his lighter out of his left pocket while he steadied himself with his other hand. Then he ignited the object—a firecracker or a flare?—and threw it at the Southeastern car, toasting the linebacker's buns. How am I doing, Captain?"

"Very ingeniously, my compatriot; you are correct in several respects. When I interrogated Rodger, I did discover that he habitually kept his hallowed Zippo heavy-duty lighter in his left front pants pocket. And the Dodger did hold something in his mouth. But remember how often and how thoroughly this normally slovenly college sophomore rinsed out his mouth? Would he ordinarily be so fastidious if he had held a mere firecracker or flare in his mouth?"

Thoroughly vexed by now, I found myself reduced to begging in an irritable tone of voice. "Tell me the solution, Augie, so that I may venture forth into an area where I have some expertise, today's ophthalmic conflicts and skirmishes."

"Sorry, Speck; I apologize for perversely baiting you. The solution that you have presented is a cogent one in every respect save one: the mysterious contents of Rodger's mouth just prior to the appearance of the flames. You assume that he must have pulled an object from his jeans pocket—correct—and then placed that object into his mouth. No. Actually, Rodger placed the object's CONTENTS into his dental orifice. You see, he pulled a small can of lighter fluid from his jeans pocket and squirted as much fluid into his mouth as he could hold; leaned as far out the window as he was able to stretch, risking serious injury or even death in his state of outrage; and forcibly spat the fluid toward the beckoning Polecat behind, simultaneously flicking the lighter and igniting a large fireball in the air above the passing pavement of Interstate Forty-Eight. Unfortunately for the Southeastern linebacker, the resultant fireball exploded directly next to his hirsute hindquarters, and the painful burns resulted."

I stared at Augie in consternation. "How did you ever think of lighter fluid? Who has ever heard of such bizarre behavior?"

Now that he had flummoxed me again with his inductive abilities, Augie grew more modest. "I admit to prior knowledge, Speck, but any decent detective stores up as much information as his mind can reasonably hold. When I was in the Navy, one of my mates in basic training would perform similar tricks with lighter fluid and any cigarette lighter that was handy. Rico Harrison was this fellow's name, and he particularly enjoyed emitting a fire storm at an unsuspecting spider crawling up the wall of our barracks. Of course, this dragon-breathed sailor would always leave soot on surfaces wherever he performed. Once Rico attempted to impress a blind date with his unusual talent, and the young woman indignantly ordered Rico to take her back to her apartment immediately. All of us in the barracks laid heavy odds that Kid Rico went without a good night kiss on that memorable evening."

Shaking my head in admiration of his skills as a detective, I said, "Augie, I can now understand how you solved the crime, although a mere mortal such as I would have given up fifteen minutes after I first learned of the case. But how in the world did you ever trick Compton into confessing?"

My friend chuckled softly. "I asked Buddy to send some patrolmen to scour the south roadside of the Interstate within the approximate area of the appearance of the fireball, and surely enough Patrolman Bill McManis returned with an empty and dented can of Zippo brand lighter fluid. When I showed this can to Rodger and then puffed out my cheeks, miming his presumed actions in the car, he exploded into convulsions of laughter and confessed. He also admitted to me that ordinarily he did not carry a can of lighter fluid around with him but that earlier in the day he had been showing some wide-eyed freshmen in the basement of Martini Hall his talents with lighter and pyrotechnics, much to the eternal regret of several cockroaches."

"What will Buddy and Ogbert do now?" I wondered.

"They are trying to decide. Charge Rodger with felonious lunar firebranding? With arse arson? With ass-ault by use of a combustible weapon? Apparently no one at the police building knows how to handle young Rodger the Torcher and Scorcher."

When I got my guffawing under control, I warmly shook Augie's hand and thanked him for another memorable walk for exercise and enlightenment. And then I remembered young Professor Prefont and his predicament.

"One final question, Augie, and a total change of the subject. Have you read much Faulkner?"

Augie raised his eyebrows and replied, "New topic indeed. Do you refer to William Faulkner, from Oxford, Mississippi? I admit to having dabbled in some of the man's fiction, and it is among the most challenging literature that I have ever read. I especially enjoyed his detective stories in that collection . . . let's see, the name of it is something about chess . . . yes, *Knight's Gambit*. And years ago I read his murder mystery, *Intruder in the Dust*. But I'm certainly no authority on his stories or novels. Why do you ask?"

I briefly explained about Pete and about my own perhaps intemperate suggestion that the young man could benefit from the assistance of an ace detective. Augie greeted my request with typical generosity.

"I don't think that I deserve the status of 'ace,' but sure, I'll talk to the lad. I've been meaning to tackle some serious fiction during my retirement years. This might turn out to be fun, even if we can't come up with any answers to those questions. And there is another reason that my delving into American literature would be appropriate." The detective lowered his chin and fell silent.

"Yes, Augie?" I queried. "What are you leading into with that remark?"

With a single quick shake of his head Augie said, "Oh, never mind, Speck. I promise to explain later. You need to go now, and I want to see Mary Alice before she takes off for school."

We agreed to gather in Augie's den on the next Friday evening, assuming that Pete could come. And then I hurried off to a waiting breakfast of Julianna's buttery blueberry pancakes followed by a hasty trip to the office and a day of eyeballs on parade.

Our Ratiocinist Revealed

On Friday evening, March 24, three couples gathered for a convivial evening of dinner and conversation in the Dupree home. I had attempted to set up this initial meeting between Augie and Pete on the previous Friday, but the Prefonts already had social plans for Saint Patrick's Day, an especially meaningful holiday for the former Elvira Maureen McKenna, and in addition Julianna was facing a budget crisis with the Public Works Department that kept her occupied until late at night on the 17th. Mary Alice and Augie insisted that on the next Friday we all come to their place for dinner, and when Augie announced that the entree would be his incomparable Cajun catfish, no one objected too strenuously. In addition to his recognized skills as sleuth, raconteur, and yard man, Augie knows how to prepare scrumptious seafood dishes as originally concocted by his south Louisiana relatives. Until I had feasted on Augie's blackened catfish extraordinaire, I thought that the fried catfish fillets at Story's Cafe were the tastiest fish delicacies available in our area; but they groveled at the bottom of the pond compared to Augie's secretly spiced treats.

Five congenial diners, my wife being noticeably absent, had sipped mint juleps, nibbled on fried cheese sticks, and savored a spicy shrimp gumbo, when Julianna knocked lightly on the back door and then hurried through the kitchen and into the connecting dining room. "Oh, Mary Alice, Augie, I'm so sorry to be late. Those Neanderthals at the Planning Commission meeting never would shut up, even when it was plain to anyone with a functioning stomach that civilized people should be eating dinner. I'm glad that you didn't wait for me." Wearing a jacket-skirt combination of black and white checks along with a lacy beige silk blouse, Julianna hugged both Mr. and Mrs. Dupree, delicately hoisted her lonely mint julep from the side table, and slid into the dining room chair next to mine, with nary a strand of her poodle-cut dark gray hair out of place. "And Archie, these must be the Prefonts," she exclaimed, tasting the julep held in her left hand while she stretched her right toward first Ellie and then Pete. My wife the adroit politician can shake hands with two people while simultaneously juggling drink, food, kissable babies, or the latest election results.

I gallantly furnished the unnecessary introductions and reminded Her Honor that Ellie is the soccer coach and Pete the English professor. I have become quite adept at always behaving in public with my wife as if we are on the campaign trail and I am her amiable go-for boy. Julianna filled us in on one more political tidbit while she underwent the psychological transformation from imperious mayor to gracious dinner guest.

"Professor, since you teach English courses, you might enjoy hearing this unusual use of the language that just occurred tonight in the Commission meeting. Kingsford Smockley, one of our local real estate tycoons, was orating endlessly, talking as usual mostly to himself, about a proposed ordinance to allow more billboards along the new highway bypass, when he proposed a motion." Julianna pressed her chin into her clavicle and lowered her voice from her natural soprano into a credible imitation of a booming baritone: "'I move that we make this ordinance radioactive to January first of this year.'" Back to her natural voice. "Silence ensued, no one seconded the motion, and I asked Smockley to repeat it. He complied and made the same mistake again. What do you call this, uhh. . . ."

"A malapropism, Mayor Watkins," replied Pete from his seat across the table from Julianna.

"Yes, thank you. Anyway, he repeated his malapropism. And then he looked around the table at all of us as if we were dunces. I tried to suppress my giggle but couldn't, and soon everyone except Kingsford was chortling loudly. In order to keep the meeting from descending into total chaos, I asked for a second to the motion, got one from Bosley Hoggard, and then called for the vote. The motion passed unanimously, and Kingsford smiled smugly. He still must not realize that we just voted to inject Uranium two-thirty-eight into his ordinance."

"I'll see if I can figure out a way to use that story in class, Mayor. Thanks for telling me," replied Pete as he drained his julep glass and dipped the sole remaining cheese stick in parmesan-flavored tomato sauce before gobbling the appetizer, in the act earning a stare of reproval from his wife.

While my missus was regaling us with a dispatch from the political front, Augie and Mary Alice had served the main catfish dish, complete with dirty rice, starkly onion-flavored hush puppies, and tangy coleslaw. For the next several minutes the primary sounds were those of cutlery against china, exclamations of delight at the taste of the subtly spicy food, and unembarrassed requests for seconds, with at least one humble petition—*mea culpa*—for thirds on catfish and slaw. When we were all able to shake off our postprandial torpor induced by collective overindulgence, the guests cleared the table, overriding the objections of our hosts, and made quick work of cleaning up the dinner dishes and storing the leftovers.

Mary Alice, typically elegant in appearance with her short, thick raven-black hair framing an oval face graced with glowing amber eyes, a dimpled chin, and a perpetually gracious smile, supervised the kitchen patrol and speedily ushered us all into the paneled den for exquisitely tart key lime pie and steaming chicory coffee. A silver tray replete with brandies and liqueurs drew several visitors, myself included, as I am a sucker for Bailey's Irish Cream or Kahlua, whichever is available. Julianna, Mary Alice, and Ellie gathered on a sofa beneath the picture window, and the two older women politely quizzed young Mrs. Prefont about her family in Stow, Ohio (Irish on her father's side, German on her mother's), and her prospects for next fall's soccer squad. Pete sat in an armchair near Augie and me and smiled proudly at his strikingly attractive wife, who reminded me of paintings of Teutonic goddesses of legend—six feet tall, creamy complexion, long, brightly blonde hair bound tightly into a flowing pony tail, and vivid sky-blue eyes. I admit that I cast my aging peepers toward Ellie myself once or twice, taking special notice of the tanned and shapely lower legs that demurely appeared below the hem of her long flower-print skirt. But soon I fixed my attention on the energetic conversation developing between Pete and Augie as they chatted from either side of me.

"So, Professor, my friend the doctor here tells me that you teach courses in American literature, and one this semester in Faulkner; is that right?"

"Yes, I do, Captain Dupree. Earlier I was looking over your collection of books in this room and noticed that you and your wife appear to be fans of crime fiction, legal thrillers, espionage novels, and police procedurals." Pete gestured toward the shelves lining two of the room's walls. "Here are several novels by some of my favorite contemporary authors . . . let's see, James Lee Burke, Ridley Pearson, Jonathan Kellerman, Sue Grafton, Robert B. Parker, Tony Hillerman, Grif Stockley, Patricia Cornwell, John Grisham, Scott Turow, Frederick Forsyth, Ken Follett, and Ed McBain. And you must like traditional who-dun-its and tough-guy fiction also, because you have several books each by Agatha Christie, Rex Stout, Sir Arthur Conan Doyle, Dashiell Hammett, Raymond Chandler, and Ross Macdonald."

From her seat on the sofa Mary Alice spoke up. "Pardon me, Professor. I couldn't help overhearing your listing of some of Augie's best-liked writers—and they are among my favorites, also. Ask Augie about how he always seems to be able to figure out the endings to the thrillers and espionage novels when he is about halfway through a book, and also about the times that he has picked out early the guilty criminal from the cast of suspects being interrogated by, say, Hercule Poirot in an Agatha Christie mystery or by Nero Wolfe in that series by Rex Stout."

In a gesture of modesty Augie lowered his head and slowly shook it from side to side. "Now, dear," he said with calm forcefulness, "our guests don't want to hear about my annoying reading habits."

"On the contrary," I piped up. "Your keen ability to solve puzzles and mysteries is the principal reason for our arranging this evening together, Mister Detective, sir."

Pete nodded vigorously in agreement and resumed his inspection of the Duprees' abundantly stocked shelves. "As for William Faulkner, you have *Intruder in the Dust, The Collected Stories, Knight's Gambit,* and *The Sound and the Fury*. Captain Dupree, I am curious if you have ever read *Sanctuary*, which is Faulkner's principal novel involving crime and the Memphis underworld."

"Let's become Augie and Pete; all right with you, my young friend?"

"Fine with me, Captain . . . uhh, Augie. I'll be glad to go by first names, if you will not judge me to be an impertinent whippersnapper."

I felt compelled to intervene. "Augie is old enough to be your dear papa, Pete, but humor him by using his first name. Since he is now retired, he needs to associate on an equal footing with younger, more energetic people such as yourself so that he doesn't soon find himself pleading to the admissions committee for acceptance at Nunn's Nursing Home."

Augie ignored my tasteless jibe, leaned back in his chair, crossed his ankles, and spoke directly to Pete: "I know of *Sanctuary,* Pete, but I have never tackled it. A friend in Memphis gave me the secondhand paperback copies of Faulkner that you can see on my shelves, but I've read only *Intruder,* the stories in *Knight's Gambit*—both books many years ago—and a few other short stories. Let's see, I remember "A Rose for Emily," "Red Leaves," and a couple of the other Indian stories.

"So you have not read *The Sound and the Fury*?" Pete asked.

Augie lowered his head slightly and smiled ruefully. "I am embarrassed to admit that I started reading that book at one time, quickly got lost, developed a severe headache, and quit. I promised myself that I would return to it some day, but I never have."

Pete spread his arms widely and chuckled. "Well, Augie, you just may get your chance. If I can talk you into reading *Sanctuary*, then perhaps *The Sound and the Fury* will be the next one we undertake—if you haven't gotten sick of my questions by then."

Our detective host gestured toward me as he continued to address Pete. "Speck mentioned that you possibly could use the help of someone who has worked in the criminal justice field. Just what do you have in mind?"

Pete stood, clasped his hands behind his back, and began pacing from his chair toward the other side of the room, where our wives sat, and then back to his home base. Ellie looked at him with an uneasy expression and spoke.

"Pete, do you really think that you should fall into your typical thinking trot right here? Remember that we are guests."

The young professor stopped, straightened his back, and looked around at all of us with alarm on his guileless countenance. "Oh, sorry; I guess I forgot where I was. . . ."

Mary Alice quickly intervened. "Now you just walk around our house all that you please, Pete. Make yourself at home here. Augie and Speck walk about three miles several mornings a week, and I've been known to pace in my office at school when I'm talking to a misbehaving child or to a teacher with a curriculum problem."

Julianna chimed in. "Don't you run all over a soccer field in your work, Coach Prefont? No need to blow your whistle at restless Pete here."

Ellie broke into a rainbow smile and relented. "I can see that I am outnumbered. I was just afraid that Pete would retreat into a mental fog, as he always does at home when he walks and talks and walks some more. And sometimes in class when he walks he forgets where he is. Pete, tell these nice people about the time in American lit survey class when you started talking about a World Cup soccer game, tossed a paper wad into the air, and head-hit it almost into the open mouth of that sleeping student on the third row."

Pete plopped heavily into his armchair and responded, "You just told them, Ellie. I'll remain stationary, dinner companions, if you will all unite behind me now in persuading Augie to read *Sanctuary* and then see if he can answer my questions about the Memphis lawyer, the beating up of Clarence Snopes, and some of the strange actions taking place at the book's climactic trial. I could really use the services of a literary detective, sir—I mean, Augie. How about it?"

Julianna came to Pete's assistance. "Could you use a motion from the floor, Professor, preferably a non-radioactive one?"

Ellie joined in. "How about if I say 'Pretty please with sugar on it'?"

It was my turn. "Misery, company, and all of that, Augie. I'll read the book along with you, and perhaps we three can all work together—that is, if Pete agrees."

The lanky pedagogue bounced to his feet and clapped his hands loudly. "A capital idea, Doctor. If three of us put our heads together, then maybe we can figure out some solutions."

Augie calmly met the gaze of each speaker in turn, smiling mysteriously, nodding, and uttering nary a syllable. While we males were haltingly moving toward our literary accord, Mary Alice had been quietly moving three dining room chairs into a semicircle facing the upholstered furniture in which Augie, Pete, and I rested. Our wives perched themselves on the straight chairs, and Mary Alice leaned forward to address her husband.

"Go ahead, Augie. Tell everyone what you and I were talking about earlier while we were fixing dinner. Don't you think that now is the time?"

"Eh, wot!" I exclaimed, "another wrinkle in this complex web?"

Augie rose from his armchair, pivoted to his left, and extended his right hand to his young male guest, who gripped the proffered hand with alacrity. In a sincere tone Augie spoke: "I apologize for forcing you into the posture of a supplicant, Pete. Of course I will read *Sanctuary*—and will start it later tonight, as a matter of fact. Yesterday at West's House of Books I picked up a copy of what Charlie West says is the latest version of the novel; is this the same edition that you use in your class?" Our host extricated the volume in question from a stack of books on the table beside his chair.

Pete pawed at the presented paperback. "Yes, that's it: the Vintage

International edition of 1993, with the corrected text. Perfect, sir. I am delighted that you will help me in this endeavor. And you are most cordially invited to join us, Doctor Speck."

I pushed myself up from my soft armchair, admittedly with more difficulty than that experienced by Pete or Augie when they had earlier stood. "We have an agreement and a new literary alliance, then; here's my hand, gentlemen." I vigorously clasped hands with my partners, and then curiosity (or pernicious nosiness) once more achieved the better of me. "But what was the meaning of Mary Alice's reference to the topic that you and she were discussing earlier tonight, Augie?"

Our gracious host asked the four guests to be seated again, and then he and Mary Alice poured more savory coffee and filled up several liqueur glasses, including mine, of course. When Captain Dupree was once more settled in his armchair, he inclined his head in my direction and asked, "Do you remember, Speck, on our walk that Tuesday morning my mentioning another reason that Pete's proposal was attractive to me?"

I placed my jaw in my upturned palm and replied, "Yes, now that you bring it up, Augie, I certainly do. Is this the key to the persistent intrigue?"

Augie leaned to his right, opened the single drawer in his chairside table, and lifted out what appeared to be an old ledger book of some sort. The volume featured a binding of faded green cloth, showed spots of mildew in several places on its cover, and was scotch-taped in four places along its spine where threads had begun to unravel. "The key, as you figuratively phrase it, my medical friend, lies in these venerable pages," responded our evening's interlocutor as he settled his reading glasses on his nose.

We six dinner companions hunched forward into a tighter circle. Augie turned to his left and held out the volume. "Perhaps you will be kind enough, Pete, to read to us the words on the title page."

Pete blinked once, looked inquisitively around at the rest of us, and replied, "Certainly, sir. Let's have the book. Now let me see. . . . The words are handwritten:

The History of the Dupin Family

Wait a minute." Pete stared at the title page again. "I assumed that this would be your family history, Mr. Dupree, er, uhh, Augie, but the name is . . . hold on—"

While Ellie, Julianna, and I swiveled our heads at one another in complete bewilderment, Augie and Mary Alice exchanged confident smiles, and Pete continued to speak, his tone growing more intense: "Why do you have this particular family history, Augie? Are you related to this family named Dupin? Hey . . . how DO you spell your last name, anyway?"

Augie nodded at Mary Alice before turning toward Pete. "Dear, I knew that this sharp young professor would catch on just as soon as he saw the name 'Dupin,' which is, Pete, the authentic cognomen of my ancestral family in France. In America, my name is Caesar Augustus Dupree. But within my extended French family, including its American branches, my actual name is Cesar Auguste Dupin the Fifth."

Pete's mouth dropped open in abject astonishment. "Do you mean to say that you have the same name as. . . ? Are you kidding me? Is this some kind of a hoax? The Dupin I know about is a fictional character. Are you just named after him, or what?"

The room erupted into a cacophony of questions, interruptions, and exclamations as the unenlightened trio in our dinner group pleaded for elucidation. Augie raised both of his arms and asked us to cease and desist so that he could proceed with his explanation.

"Display your erudition, Pete," our host commanded. "Pray remind your wife and the Watkinses of the identity of this mysterious man named Dupin, specifically C. Auguste Dupin."

"I had better know who Dupin is, if my doctorate in American literature means anything. C. Auguste Dupin is. . . ."

"Wait!" I brusquely interjected. "Could you possibly be referring to the detective in the stories by Edgar Allan Poe? One of the few times I stayed awake during my American lit class at Moffatt College occurred when we talked about that wonderful story in which the letter is stolen and. . . ."

"Sure; that's right." Ellie widened her stunning blue eyes and then raised her right arm, pointing her index finger at me, then Augie, and then Pete. "You mean 'The Purloined Letter.' And the man who solves the crime by using his superior intellect is named . . . Dupin, yeah. In fact all of the other characters in the story, if I remember correctly, are known only by titles or by the first letter in a name. Are 'T' or 'G' or maybe 'B' or 'D' in there somewhere?"

Pete and Augie exchanged knowing nods, and then the professor spoke. "My wife the coach remembers the story well, doesn't she? Honey, 'G' and 'D' are the capital letters referring to people's names. But let's get back to this business, Augie, about your family name."

Julianna ended what was for her an uncharacteristically lengthy silence. "I vaguely remember that story from my high school English class, but doesn't the same detective play a major role in that mystery story about the gruesome killings in Paris? Let's see, some type of escaped ape—no, an orangutan turns out to be the killer."

The tone of Pete's voice became clearly magnanimous. "Ah, Mayor Watkins, you have correctly placed Dupin in Poe's story 'The Murders in the Rue Morgue.' All of you earn 'A's' for using your memories keenly under pressure. But once more I ask, Augie. . . ."

Our amiable host turned his palms upward. "The time for revelation is at hand, my friends. As this ledger book will prove to you, I am the direct descendant of the younger brother of Cesar Auguste Dupin, the famous ratiocinist. By the way, Poe never calls him a detective, although C. Auguste

Dupin is universally acknowledged to be the first genius detective appearing in the world's literature and is recognized as the prototype for such literary descendants as Sherlock Holmes, Hercule Poirot, and Nero Wolfe. The original C. Auguste Dupin is my great-great-great uncle, although I usually refer to him simply as my ancestor."

"Objection, your honor!" shouted Pete in a convincing imitation of an attorney's courtroom voice. "Dupin is a creation of Poe's incomparable imagination. He is a FICTIONAL character. Augie, somehow you must be mistaken."

"Ah, my new friend," responded our host, "I must point out that you are only one of millions of people who long have been victims of a misconception. Edgar Allan Poe was a master at borrowing people and events from real life and transforming them into components of his stories and poems. My honored ancestor actually solved the true crimes that Poe made immortal in the two stories named earlier by Ellie and Pete, with worthy assists from Julianna and Speck. And there is also a third crime investigated by my ancestor that Poe wrote about, 'The Mystery of Marie Roget.' These are only a few of the many complicated crimes that my ancestral uncle Dupin solved during his illustrious career as an investigator in Paris."

Pete stared at Augie, the befuddlement obvious in his drooping jaw and his tremulous tone of voice. "If Dupin really existed, then how did Poe. . . ."

Augie finished Pete's question. ". . . garner the credit for the creation of the detective himself as well as for the crimes forming the main plots of the stories?"

Mary Alice laughed softly behind her reversed hand. "If you were one of the third grade students at Waggoner, Pete, I would tell you to close your mouth before an insect flies in." Ellie and Julianna immediately joined their hostess in discreetly giggling at the gaping professor.

I spoke in stentorian haughtiness. "Ladies, you sound like sorority princesses checking out the newest campus hunks. Remember your professional positions of authority, and be so good as to behave accordingly!"

Julianna instantly hurled a small pillow at my unprotected pate, while Ellie turned to address her bewildered husband. "Let's all examine this old ledger book, sweetheart, and then concern ourselves later with the question of Poe and his sources. I'll bet that this family history is full of surprises."

Pete stared intently at each of us, fixing his gaze for the longest time on Augie, who merely smiled graciously in response. Shaking his thick hair vigorously and then moving the vibration down his altitudinous body like a grizzly bear shaking off the water from a bath in a river, Pete stretched out his arms, interlaced his fingers, sharply cracked four knuckles, and announced, "Okay, I'll play along. Let's start looking at the ledger. My mind is a clean slate. Fill it with information, Captain Dupree, honored sir."

Standing quickly and clapping her hands once, Mary Alice took charge of the proceedings. "I'll clear the plates and cups away. Speck, Pete, please bring those chairs over here next to the couch. Ellie, would you mind shifting that stack of magazines to the other end of the coffee table? Thanks. Now, move in more closely, Pete, and the rest of you. Sit where you can see the pages of the ledger book while Augie explains about his ancestry."

The five of us formed a tight semicircle, with Augie in the middle of the couch, Ellie to his left and Julianna his right, and Pete and I on the outer edges, ensconced in straight-backed chairs. When Mary Alice returned from the kitchen, she sat in another dining room chair on the opposite side of the coffee table. Augie opened the venerable volume to the first leaf after the title page, and then he spoke.

"You may remember that in 'Rue Morgue,' the first of the stories featuring my uncle, Poe states that Dupin is—and I am quoting from memory here—'of an excellent—indeed of an illustrious family.' These first several pages of the ledger list my Dupin predecessors, but we are interested in the family beginning . . . here, on page six. You see the name printed here:

Cesar Auguste Dupin

and then just below it:

Phillipe David Dupin

Phillipe David is the name of my great-great-grandfather. He is the younger brother of the detective made immortal by Poe."

I peered at the spidery, faded lettering on the yellowing page. "Augie, I don't see any dates of birth for these two men, but . . ." I turned to the next page. ". . . birth dates appear for members of later generations."

"An astute observation, friend Speck," replied Augie. "You see, my grandfather wrote all of these entries in the ledger columns, and he began with the first Dupins for whom there were documented records. He started this ledger book after he had immigrated to America. Working from a list he had brought with him, he entered the names back through many generations, but only with his own father was he certain of an actual year of birth. See here:

Cesar Auguste Dupin II b. 1847

Ellie leaned to her right and flipped back to the previous page. "So Phillipe David named his son after his older brother the famous detective—er, I mean ratiocinist?"

"Correct, Coach Ellie. Apparently Phillipe was very proud of his brother and the man's exploits. Uncle Auguste's ingenious solution to the Rue Morgue double homicide made him a man to be admired by the Parisian police, as Poe tells us in the introduction to 'Marie Roget.' And my ancestor uncle's later restoration of the anonymous female aristocrat's valuable pilfered epistle only increased his public notoriety and his stature in Phillipe's hero-worshipping eyes. So Phillipe honored his childless sibling by naming his own first-born child 'Cesar Auguste Dupin the Second.' And thus was initiated a direct line of male children with this name, reaching all the way to me—I am the Fifth—and to our son Gus, who is the Sixth.

Julianna quickly raised her head and fixed her eyes on Augie. "So Gus has your same name? I never knew that before. By the way, is he still in law school at Emory"

Augie met my wife's stare. "The answers are 'Yes' and 'Yes.' Let me flip over to here—" On the final page with writing on it appeared these names:

>Valerie Janine Dupin b. 1970
>Valerie Janine Dupree

>Cesar Auguste Dupin VI b. 1973
>Caesar Augustus Dupree

I knew that Valerie was a resident physician in internal medicine at the medical center in Little Rock, but this was the first time that I had seen her last name printed as "Dupin." I piped up: "But Augie, . . . what's the story on the change in the last name?"

Pete leaned in. "My question exactly. Who changed the spelling and the pronunciation? Your grandfather, or somebody else? And why?"

Augie reassumed his pedagogical pose, with his erect spine pushed completely flat against the supporting vertical cushion of the couch and his arms, with elbows locked, pressing diagonally into his knees. "For the answer to that essential query, my companions in genealogical research, let us turn back a few pages. . . . Ah, here we are, returning to C. A. D. the Second. See here, this worthy gentleman was born in 1847. Also, my grandfather later added this biographical sketch about his father: 'Joined Parisian Police Force, 1867. Promoted to Detective, 1881. Chief of Detectives, 1891-1907. Died in Paris, 1915.' Now look to the next page. Here are listed the children of C. A. D. the Second, and the final name is. . . ."

Pete read aloud with emphasis, "'Cesar Auguste Dupin the Third, born 1885.' And he was the youngest of his generation. Let's see, one, two, three, four girls preceded him. He would be—ummm—your grandfather?"

Augie nodded. "Right, Pete. And note the next information that Grandpapa entered about himself."

All eyes dropped back to these lines in the ledger book:

> Sailed to America, 1905. American name
> changed to Dupree, Port of New Orleans,
> June 1905.

Augie leaned back on the sofa. "From here on I can amplify on this sketchy written information, since I knew my grandpapa well. He lived until 1975, always within New Orleans or near the city, after he had immigrated to this country, and he told me many stories about family history."

Drawing a deep breath, our host continued his narrative. "In 1905 it seems that my grandfather decided America offered more opportunities then did France for an adventurous young man, so he saved his money and bought passage on a steamer sailing from Le Havre. He knew only a few words of English, and when his ship docked at New Orleans and he made it to the front of the line at the Immigration counter, a man he later learned to be a political appointee of the Teddy Roosevelt administration asked for his papers and his name.

"When Grandpapa pronounced our family name and pointed to it on the papers, the official, who proclaimed himself to be the cousin of the congressman representing Plaquemines Parish—an area along the Gulf Coast southeast of New Orleans—well, this formidable bureaucrat apparently became somewhat peevish. Grandpapa could understand only a few words that the perspiring official was spewing out, but my grandfather reconstructed the gist of the intemperate salvo later on by talking to a bilingual immigrant who stood in line two places behind him. My grandfather's imitation of the man's words went like this: 'Dew-paaa, you say? Whut kind of a piss-poor faincy pants name is tha-yut? How in hell duh yuh axe-pect enny bawdy ovuh hyar in Ah-muhr-uh-kuh to pro-nounce this? I know lots of Dew-preees down yonder in Plaquemines. Good Ah-muhr-uh-kin name, too. Yore name is gonna be Dew-preee frum now on.'

"The beefy bureaucrat crossed out 'Dupin' and wrote in 'Dupree' on my grandfather's official immigration papers. Grandpapa didn't really understand what had happened until other government officials whom he consulted later that day all referred to him as 'Mister Dupree.' So he decided to live with the situation and use 'Dupree' as the family's American name while retaining 'Dupin' as the ancestral cognomen. All of us descendants have continued this tradition."

Pete hopped excitedly to his feet, received a cold stare from Ellie, and gingerly perched once more on his chair. "That's quite a story, sir. And you say it was your grandfather who started writing in this ledger book?"

"Yes," Augie answered, but that came later. First let me fill you in on a few more details. My grandfather soon found work as a waiter in the French Quarter, and after he became fluent in English he followed the family tradition by joining the New Orleans Police Department. In 1910 he married Janine Cordon, an American of French descent, and they eventually had four children, including my father. See here in the ledger:

> Cesar Auguste Dupin IV b. 1915
> Caesar Augustus Dupree IV

As you can tell, Grandpapa began entering both the French and the American versions of the names of new members of the family. He kept this ledger book on a shelf in an abandoned commissary at the small family farm on the northwest edge of town. He and my grandmother had moved out there in 1930, after Grandpapa had been promoted to detective. I spent many happy summers on the family acreage when I was a boy. By the way, Grandpapa had a distinguished career with the N. O. P. D.; his specialty lay in solving complicated homicides.

He retired in 1950 and happily fished out of a one-man boat in the southern Louisiana bayous until he passed on."

I found myself constantly looking back and forth between Augie and the family book of history. "Now that leaves your father and then you, Augie. Please bring us up to date."

"I'll be happy to," Augie assented, "if I am not sending all of you, my gracious guests, into a collective coma with all of this egocentric prattle about my family."

The four of us exclaimed and uttered enough sincere assurances of our curiosity about the Dupin-Dupree genealogy that Augie agreed to continue.

"I'll try to be brief, my tolerant friends. My grandfather was known in New Orleans as Caesar Dupree, and my father came to be called Caesar Junior, or simply Junior, when he joined the police force in 1933 as a patrolman right after his graduation from high school. Dad enlisted in the Navy in December of 1941, two days after Pearl Harbor, and when he came back from the Pacific Theater in 1944 he returned to the N. O. P. D. He and Mom had married in 1938, and I was born in 1940. Here is the entry for me:

>	Cesar Auguste Dupin V b. 1940
>	Caesar Augustus Dupree V

And now we are up to date."

With a rueful smile directed at her husband, Mary Alice spoke up. "I was afraid that you would require a little prompting when you yourself entered the family picture, dear. Let's see. . . . Oh, yes. The most influential event of your childhood was the move to Memphis, right?"

"Yes, as usual you are right on target, my dear," replied our host, as he returned his wife's subtle smile. "Dad had decided that he needed more than a high school education, so he began taking courses in criminal justice at L. S. U., the

New Orleans branch. In 1951 representatives of the Memphis P. D. came through town on a recruiting trip, and Dad and Mom decided to move us up the Mississippi River because of better professional opportunities. Dad joined the Memphis force in 1952 and became a detective three years later. From the age of twelve on, I grew up in Memphis. By the way, Dad dropped the 'Junior' and went by 'Caesar Dupree' while he lived and worked in Memphis.

"It's clear that he moved to Memphis at least in part so that he could establish his own identity apart from the fame garnered by my grandfather, who became a specialist in solving crimes that baffled everybody else on the New Orleans force. Anyway, Dad developed his own reputation in Memphis as an investigator who could almost always close cases that stumped his colleagues; robberies and kidnappings were the crimes that best suited his talents. My father retired from the Memphis P. D. in 1980 as one of several assistant chiefs, and he and Mom are happily continuing to live in their longtime home off Walnut Grove Boulevard in the Galloway Park area. Mary Alice and I visit over there as often as we can."

Ellie stretched her arms above her head—ahh, what a tantalizing sight to these aging eyes—and spoke. "Now fill us in on yourself, Mister Dupree, or should I say 'Dupin?' You continued the family tradition of becoming a detective, right?"

Mary Alice leaned forward from her chair, placed her hand on Ellie's arm, and politely intervened. "If you don't mind, I'll talk about Augie, because he never has been a man who toots his own trumpet. My husband graduated from East High in Memphis and then went to Memphis State. He majored in accounting, with a minor in political science, and graduated in . . . sixty-two, right, dear?"

Augie merely nodded in affirmation.

"Then he was in the Navy for three years, working in Naval Intelligence and serving a tour of duty in Vietnam, where he made use of his knowledge of French. He came back to Memphis and joined the FBI. I met Augie in 1965 when

I was working on my master's in education at Memphis State. We married in sixty-seven, and then for four years, I think it was, the FBI sent us all over—to Missoula, Montana; Bridgeport, Connecticut; Roanoke, Virginia; and Tampa, Florida. Nice weather at that last stop, but the place was not home. We both grew tired of the relocating, so we settled back in Memphis, where Augie became a detective on the Memphis force and I taught first and second grades. Later I was promoted to principal. I think you know the rest—how Augie became well known for solving crimes that no one else could figure out. . . ."

Augie fidgeted in his seat on the couch. "Now, dear. No one wants to hear about that boring police stuff. We have bombarded our kind guests with way too much information about the Duprees and the Dupins."

Pete could sit still no longer and was instantly on his feet. "On the contrary, Augie. I could listen all night, but I'm assuming that I'll have further opportunities to learn about some of these famous cases. Now . . . how do we proceed from here, Monsieur Detective Dupin? Are you ready to probe into *Sanctuary*?"

I interjected, "Give Augie and me time to read the novel, Pete, and we three can meet at my house in, say . . . about two weeks." I riffled pages hastily in my handy-dandy pocket calendar. "How about Saturday afternoon, April the eighth? Okay with you fellows? Maybe at that time we can get off to a healthy start toward a solution to Pete's first case."

Augie arose and chuckled. "First case, you say, Speck? Do you think that there will be more than one?"

I had no chance to respond as we guests warmly thanked Mary Alice and Augie, shook hands all around, and walked out into the cool and pleasantly damp March late evening. But my inadvertent reference to "first case" turned out to be more prophetic than I could ever have predicted, since Augie, Pete, and I wound up intently examining six complex puzzles in four novels written by the brilliant authorial deity of Jefferson, Yoknapatawpha County, Mississippi. Quite frequently during the next several months Augustus Dupree, veteran detective, was called upon to assume the identity of C. Auguste Dupin V, master literary sleuth.

Chapter Two

The Case of the Furtive Memphis Lawyer in *Sanctuary*

Bullish Back-Porch Boogie

"Have you two gentlemen had a chance to finish reading *Sanctuary*? Are you prepared to be peppered with questions?"

Young Professor Prefont's eagerness caused Augie Dupree and yours truly to exchange indulgent smiles as the two of us sat side by side on the wooden swing suspended by chains from the ceiling of my back porch. We three rookie literary sleuths were enjoying a cool breeze on a sunny April early Saturday afternoon, with the ghostly blossoms on the nearby Bradford pear trees starting to fade just as the pink and white flowers on the adjacent dogwoods were beginning to burst into bloom. Pete leaned forward from a wicker rocking chair situated five feet across the porch from us and next to my wooden railing. His lap was overflowing with overturned opened books and scholarly journals from the Moffatt library, legal pads, scraps of yellow and white loose notebook paper, and two copies of *Sanctuary*. Poor Pete kept attempting to create some semblance of order out of this printed chaos while simultaneously he juggled his glass of iced tea precariously on his left knee. Even if Augie and I had wanted now to back out of our agreement to tackle Faulkner, Pete's enthusiasm was so obvious that we would not have dared to demur. Besides, we both were quite curious about where this adventure in literary detective work would lead us.

Augie gestured toward Pete's pile of miscellaneous material. "I assume that you have brought with you some critical studies on Faulkner, Professor. Friends who have been brave enough to read some of the man's most famous novels have told me that I might need some guidance from scholars to help me through the thickets of Mississippi Southern-fried prose. But I found *Sanctuary* not to be overly difficult to follow. Certainly it is no supermarket Gothic romance or a mere page turner best suited for reading at the beach, but I think that I was able to figure out most of what was happening. How about you, Speck?"

I responded to my cue. "Agreed, Augie. The book demands total concentration, but I believe that I picked up on the main elements of the plot. However, I did find myself having to fill in some gaps and make some guesses in places along the way, particularly during the trial scenes near the end of the book."

Augie had been studying me intently while I jabbered. Although earlier in the day he had raked the leftover leaves from his lawn, he appeared now to be well rested and alert. As usual, he was dressed in immaculate good taste, this time in a light-blue Levi work shirt, pressed dark-blue Duckhead casual trousers, and polished black work boots. Many years ago I had hired a local professional landscaping service to take care of my shrubbery and lawn, using the excuse that Julianna and I were too busy with our careers to pay any attention to yard chores. Actually, we both detested working with shears and mowers. Augie's bushes, trees, and grass all looked much greener and more bounteous than did mine, a testament to the positive results of meticulous expertise and attention. "To hell with winning 'Yard of the Month' anyway," I thought in finality.

Augie interrupted the rhythms of our synchronized swinging, planted both feet on the interlocking boards of my porch, steadied himself, and leaned back into a hearty laugh. "Speck, I know that you are mentally comparing our yards again. The sweep of your gaze, from your property over to mine and back again, has given you away. Let's get back to Faulkner. What do you say?"

"Well damn you double, neighbor. There you go again, reading the invisible printouts of my dim brain. Remind me never to think of Sharon Stone or Julia Roberts when both you and my wife are in the vicinity, or you may blurt out some revelations about my brain waves that could damage my long and happy marriage." My tone was not quite as jocular as I intended to make it.

Pete seemed to pick up on the incipient tension between Augie and me. "Captain Dupree, it sounds as if you are ready to assume the identity of your ancestor C. Auguste Dupin and to listen to my questions now. Doctor Watkins, I am still working on making sense of the trial scene myself. But first let me affirm that you"—Pete pointed a grasped legal pad in my direction—"have hit upon a central issue in *Sanctuary*. Doctor Speck, you mentioned filling in gaps and making guesses. You are exactly right. One of the principal challenges resulting from a reading of *Sanctuary* is that of discovering all of the pieces of the narrative puzzle and then figuratively fitting them together so that they make sense. *Sanctuary* is similar to a traditional detective novel in that the readers of the book must attempt to participate in the solution to a mystery, or to several interlocking mysteries. The difference, however, is that Faulkner rarely supplies us with all of the facts that we need in order for us to be able to draw plausible conclusions."

Augie intervened at this point. "Pete, I noticed this very tendency in *Sanctuary* and couldn't help but compare this book to the detective novels I have read by Doyle, Christie, Hammett, or Chandler. Some of the plots in these books are torturously complicated, but most, if not all, of the crucial facts eventually emerge to each mystery or crime. The same is not true for *Sanctuary*, right?"

Pete sat up straight in his wicker rocker, grabbed at a legal pad and a book that were both headed for a crash landing on the boards, balanced the debris of his trade on his legs, lap, and chair, and pronounced, "Correct-o-mundo, sir. Pardon the bad Fonzie imitation, but I want to applaud your insight. We have to employ deduction and supposition galore in trying to make sense of this book. Listen to what one critic says about this issue. Let's see . . . I'll find this quotation. . . ."

The professor shuffled frantically through his landfill of printed matter, sputtering volubly while snatching at scraps of paper, until he suddenly shot his lengthy right arm skyward: "Aha. Here it is." He read from a ragged piece of notebook paper in his left hand. "This statement comes from an essay by a Japanese critic, Tamotsu Nishiyama, who writes, 'unless we solve the mystery caused by implication, omission, or concealment, we can never hope to understand the whole proceedings of the story, still less interpret the meaning of the work. We have to use speculation or inference by the help of some hints, which become meaningful only when connected with later occurrences.'"

Augie and I both listened closely; I was the first to respond. "So we are looking for whatever hints we can find, Pete?"

"A more accurate term might be 'clues,'" stated Augie, "since we want to think of this experiment in literary sleuthing as being analogous to the investigation of a crime."

"Right, right," yelped Pete, as paper began to fly into the air from several spots on his body and chair. A book crashed to the floor on its spine and flopped open. "Remember, you are investigating a crime, or several crimes; the only difference is that they appear in a novel rather than in real life. Let me read to you another pertinent quotation from a critic. This one recently appeared in a major journal, *Mississippi Quarterly*, and the critic is a gentleman named Andrew J. Wilson: 'In *Sanctuary*, Faulkner reveals only by persistently veiling a part of what he uncovers. That is, he rarely offers the reader a thorough illustration of any person or event. Rather, he provides glimpses, parts of the whole. He offers data as the typical eye sees, or '"detects"': sporadically, collecting mere bits of information about people, objects, events, all of which are seemingly chosen willy-nilly. Only occasionally does the typical human eye, in a typical moment, zoom in and thoroughly imbibe a person, thing, act in its entirety. Likewise, seldom does Faulkner wholly scrutinize a person, thing, act in *Sanctuary*. Even upon finishing the book the reader is without every parcel of the whole.'"

As the professor read from his notes, Augie fixed his clear gray eyes first on Pete, then on me, and then back on Pete. "All right, gentlemen, let us proceed," said the Captain of Detectives. "As I understand the situation, Speck and I will be searching in *Sanctuary* for clues that will help to solve some of the puzzles in the book, the ones that most perplex you, Pete. Perhaps I can apply some of my experiences as an investigator to this situation. Anyway, I'll try to think as would my ancestor uncle."

At this point Augie reached behind a nearby deck table and pulled out a baseball cap that I had never seen before. He must have hidden it when earlier I had gone into the house to take a telephone call from the medical exchange. The cap was navy blue and had embroidered on it, in bright gold letters, the word "DETECTIVE," underneath which appeared in smaller letters and also in gold, "Memphis P. D."

Augie explained, "I don't own a deerstalker, a bowler, or a brown fedora, so I'd better don this special cap that was given to me by colleagues in Memphis when I was promoted. Let's see if it helps me to approximate the intellectual powers of C. A. Dupin the First. You may fire when ready, Pete."

Comfortably seated on the rhythmically swaying swing, accompanied only by our paperback copies of *Sanctuary*, Augie and I watched in amusement as Pete sent books, journals, and a blizzard of loose paper into turbulent motion surrounding him while he prepared to stand. "I can sit still no longer, gentlemen. Do you mind if I walk around? I can think so much more clearly while on my feet." Pete extricated himself from beneath his mountain of paper refuse and stretched to his full seventy-seven inches. Despite the cool fifty-three degree afternoon, he was wearing khaki Eddie Bauer shorts, white socks, and battered Nike Pegasus running shoes. His T-shirt for the day was black and celebrated, in print and picture, front and back, the success of the Rolling Stones's Steel Wheels Tour of 1989. Several times during the ensuing conversation he removed and then put back on his bright purple Adidas soccer warm-up jacket. I felt almost overdressed in my dark-blue dress slacks, red-and-white striped Hathaway shirt, and tea-colored J. Crew sweater, but I had made rounds at the hospital earlier in the day and had been too lazy on this Saturday to change clothes, except to doff my pseudo-regimental tie with the wide crimson and black stripes.

Pete assumed his pedagogical pose, hands alternately clasped behind his back and waving in the air while he leaned forward, strode across the porch and back, and addressed Augie and me in stentorian tones. My next-door neighbor and I contentedly assumed the identities of surrogate students during Pete's mini-lecture.

"Doctor Speck, sir, you remember that I first mentioned *Sanctuary's*

Memphis lawyer to you in your office last month, and that casual reference led to our delightful catfish dinner and then to this meeting today. I have not been able to decide just what role in the novel's events this shadowy character plays, but I have a hunch that he is more important then he may first appear to be. The initial reference to the Jewish lawyer from Memphis appears, strangely enough, in the bitter racist diatribe by Senator Clarence Snopes; this scene is on pages two-sixty-five and two-sixty-six of the novel."

Augie and I quickly opened our copies of *Sanctuary* and flipped to the pages designated by Pete. Captain Dupree donned his reading glasses, and I adjusted my bifocals.

"If it is okay with you guys, I want to set up the problem a little further before we look at this passage," said our pacing professorial pal.

Augie and I both grunted monosyllabically in assent, so Pete resumed his informal lecture. "The next reference to this character comes soon afterward in the book, on pages two-eighty-one, two-eighty-two, and two-ninety, when the lawyer shows up in the courtroom at the trial in Jefferson of a small-time criminal named Lee Goodwin, who is falsely charged with the murder of a mentally retarded farmhand named Tommy. Scholars and critics who have written on *Sanctuary* have usually assumed—an example of their filling in of a Faulknerian gap—that this lawyer is an agent of the Memphis gangster Popeye and that the lawyer has collaborated with Eustace Graham, the devious district attorney from Yoknapatawpha County, to stage-manage Temple Drake's perjured testimony that incites the local vigilantes to lynch Goodwin. As you remember, Temple is the Ole Miss coed who is perversely raped by Popeye and then kidnapped by him from Goodwin's hideout and taken to Memphis, where she is kept locked up in Miss Reba's brothel."

Augie held up his right hand and interrupted the peripatetic pedagogue. "Could you furnish us with a couple of examples of what these critics have to say about the lawyer?"

Pete pivoted toward his pile of books, journals, and notes. "Sure, Augie—I mean, Detective Dupin, heh, heh. Let's look here—no—okay, here's an example from a book by a scholar named Robert Parker at the University of Illinois: 'the Memphis lawyer who presumably works for Popeye.' Note the use of the word 'presumably.' Oh, and let me read this sentence from the noted critic Leslie Fiedler: 'And lurking in the background is the predictable shyster mouthpiece, "the Jew lawyer from Memphis,"' who apparently orchestrates the final courtroom scene.' Again, friends, a key word: 'apparently.'"

I intervened at this juncture. "These comments make sense, Pete. As I was reading *Sanctuary*, I assumed that the Memphis lawyer was present at the trial to make certain that Temple did not name Popeye as the murderer of Tommy, which of course he is. But now that you point out the problem, I don't remember any direct links between Popeye, the lawyer, or even Graham, the district attorney."

Augie was sitting with his head bowed, his eyes fixed on some pages in the book. He then spoke: "Speck, certain passages in the novel imply a connection between Graham and the Memphis lawyer. Look on page two-eighty-one. On the second day of the trial Horace Benbow, the defense attorney, enters the courtroom and sees Goodwin, the defendant, at one end of the long table facing the judge's bench. I'm quoting here: 'At the other end of the table sat a man picking his teeth.' This turns out to be the Jewish lawyer, who is sitting at the end of the table where Graham, the prosecutor, logically will also sit; proximity clearly suggests complicity. And on page two-ninety, this linkage is also suggested by the seating arrangements: 'the long table where the prisoner and the woman with the child and Horace and the District Attorney and the Memphis lawyer sat. . . .' The prisoner is Lee Goodwin, and the woman is Ruby Lamar, Goodwin's common-law wife. But most significantly, the Memphis lawyer and Graham appear to be sitting side by side."

Pete had been staring fixedly at the designated pages. "Very good, Augie—

or more accurately, Auguste. I had not noticed this clue before. Possibly Parker, Fiedler, and other critics had seen it and used the seating arrangements as part of the reasoning behind their assumptions that Graham and the Memphis lawyer are in cahoots. Now, guys, let me point out that William Faulkner himself, in 1950, supported this interpretation with his presentation of some remarks by Temple Drake in the novel *Requiem for a Nun*, the sequel to *Sanctuary*."

Rummage time again, as Pete dived into the print dump and emerged, grinning triumphantly, with a hardbound copy of *Requiem*. "Pages one-twenty-eight and one-twenty-nine of this edition, gentlemen. In reply to the Mississippi Governor's leading question about her earlier testimony at Goodwin's trial, the now older Temple, here using the third person, says the following about herself. Quoting here, 'and so produced by his'—that is, Popeye's—'lawyer in the Jefferson courtroom so that she could swear away the life of the man who was accused of it'; end of quotation. I think that the key word here is 'produced' and that it has a double meaning. In *Sanctuary* Popeye must have instructed the Memphis lawyer to make certain that Temple duly appears in court since, as Faulkner later has Temple say in *Requiem*, quoting again, 'the murderer'—Popeye—'kidnapped her and carried her to Memphis, to hold her until he would need his alibi.'" At this point Pete picked up a piece of yellow lined paper from the porch floor. "Let me paraphrase this note I have written to myself. Okay, here goes. But Faulkner, perhaps influenced by his years as a reluctant Hollywood screenwriter, also suggests here that the Memphis lawyer helped to 'produce' an imagined scenario, in this case Temple's blatant and lethal lies on the witness stand."

Pete stared inquisitively at Augie and me in our places on the swing, and I was the first to respond. "I am convinced of the existence of a conspiracy among Popeye, Graham, and the Jewish lawyer. How about you, Augie, or rather Monsieur Dupin?"

The Captain continued to stare at pages in his copy of *Sanctuary*. "These passages from *Requiem for a Nun* are quite persuasive, friends, but I think that I can hazard a guess at what rankles Pete and causes him to slap his head in frustration, as he is doing at this exact moment."

Pete was standing with his back toward the swing, and as he spun around he first looked with eyes widened at Augie and then with an expression of exasperation toward me. I responded immediately.

"Don't worry, Pete. I have disclosed no confidential information to Augie. You have whanged yourself on the forehead three times already this afternoon, and it takes no cerebral detective to deduce that the head banging is a nervous habit of yours."

Pete fell heavily backward into an empty deck chair, moving his open right hand in a blur toward his head and stopping its motion an inch away from his protruding eyebrow. "Doctor Watkins, I have cut down on the frequency of my assaults on myself, and my vision has definitely stabilized. But occasionally I forget, as this afternoon's relapses indicate. Ellie tells me that I am doing better, and if I can ever figure out these Faulkner puzzles I should be able to cease my head walloping altogether."

I returned the conversation to the topic at hand. "Our becapped Detective Dupin here"—I gestured to my swing mate with a sweep of my left arm—"earlier stated that he knows what is still bothering you, Pete. So tell us, or should I say tell me, Augie, since I seem to be coming in at my customary third place in the detection derby."

Augie looked at Pete, who nodded vigorously to the retired policeman as an inducement to proceed. "You will notice, Speck, that the evidence cited by Pete appears not in *Sanctuary* but in the novel's sequel," said Augustus Dupree of the family Dupin.

Pete now intervened: "Despite Temple's disclosures in *Requiem,* there appears to be no direct connection in *Sanctuary* itself between the Memphis lawyer and Popeye or Temple, or at least no definitive connections that any published scholars or I have been yet able to find."

Augie took his turn. "And the additional puzzle remains as to why Senator Clarence Snopes, with a black eye and a damaged nose and mouth—I'm looking now, fellows, back at pages two-sixty-five and two-sixty-six, and quoting—'Two days before it opened'—meaning the trial, of course—so stridently and maliciously denounces, in Clarence's words, '"a Memphis jew lawyer."' Listen to Clarence fulminate: '"But the lowest, cheapest thing on this earth aint a nigger: it's a jew.... And the lowest kind of jew is a jew lawyer. And the lowest kind of jew lawyer is a Memphis jew lawyer."' Good gracious, with what abominable vehemence this politician spews forth his venom."

Pete responded to Augie's dramatic reading of the text. "I truly do not understand why Snopes is so furious here. He seems to be denouncing the same lawyer who later appears in the courtroom, but what is the connection?" Pete paused and picked up two books from the porch floor. "Here, let me read from the renowned critic Cleanth Brooks of Yale, whose pioneering analyses of Faulkner's works still rank as some of the most lucid and comprehensive ever written, in my opinion. Quoting Professor Brooks: 'What happened to Clarence? Who gave him the beating?' And another helpful critic, John Pilkington of the University of Mississippi located in Faulkner's own town of Oxford, asks a similar question: 'Why did Clarence Snopes turn up in Jefferson with a black eye before the trial?'"

For several minutes I had been switching my attention back and forth between Augie and Pete and was beginning to feel like a tennis spectator at Wimbledon. "Well, Pete, does either critic answer his own questions?" I asked.

Pete shook his floppy mop of hair in dismay. "As you might expect, Speck, the answer is, 'No.' Brooks and Pilkington both conclude that Faulkner has not provided enough facts about this matter and related elements of the plot." The professor read first from an opened book in his right hand and then from another in his left. "As Brooks says, 'There is simply not enough evidence presented in the novel to allow any clear answers to the questions.' According to Pilkington, the reader is then left with, and I quote, 'no more than theories, conjectures, or guesses.'"

All three of us fell silent as we individually contemplated the challenge before us. Augie spoke first. "Gentlemen, the issue before us is clear. Speck, you and I will search in *Sanctuary* for any clues that might explain the connections among Popeye, Temple, the Memphis lawyer, Eustace Graham, and Snopes—that is, if any such clues exist. Perhaps we could better call what we are looking for—what does the critic Wilson write about, uh . . . 'mere bits of information'? Is that his phrase?"

Pete responded with gratitude. "Right you are again, Monsieur Dupin, in both your discernment of the challenge before you and the correct terminology, although you could also use the suggestion of Nishiyama." Yanking a ragged piece of paper from his pile, Pete continued. "Here are his words: 'some hints which become meaningful only when connected with later occurrences.'"

"Clues, bits of information, hints: time to start digging," I cheerfully pronounced. "Of course, we may find nothing."

Augie glanced at me, a sly smile on his lips. "I am optimistic that we can turn up a possible theory at least, neighbor. Shall we give ourselves a time limit? How about if we meet again in say—two weeks? Is that enough time, Speck?"

I stood and stretched my arms and legs to the limits allowed by my spreading stubbiness. "You decide, Auguste; you are the chief detective, and I serve merely as your sidekick and sounding board."

Pete and I both agreed with Augie that two weeks should be a sufficient time for our first investigation, and I said in conclusion, "Then a fortnight it will be, friends, and let us convene once again here on this porch."

"Thank you, gentlemen, thank you," spoke Pete with sincerity. "Happy hunting to you both. Would you like to borrow any of this material? I have several helpful books of criticism here—and my notes, although they are probably indecipherable to anyone except for Ellie, me, and a CIA cryptographer. Sometimes I can't even comprehend my own scrawlings, but my astute wife usually can."

Eager to undertake the task at hand, Augie gently interrupted the meandering professor. "Pete, I would appreciate borrowing your copy of Brooks's book, and Parker's, and those articles by Nishiyama and Wilson. Does any critic construct a chronology of the events in *Sanctuary*?"

As Augie was speaking, Pete was energetically stacking books and articles. "Brooks has the most complete and accurate analysis of the sequence of events in *Sanctuary*. Here: I've marked the relevant sections in his book. Edmond Volpe also has a useful chronology in his excellent guide to Faulkner's fiction." Rummage, rummage. "And here is my tattered copy of Volpe. Anything else I can lend to you?"

Augie strode to Pete's side, with warm thanks accepted the printed material, and assured our young friend, "My most humble assistant"—a wink in my direction—"and I will reconvene with you in two weeks. Be kind to your abused skull until then."

Tapping the Stein and the Spine

Saturday afternoon, April 22, brought a steady spring shower that blanketed Crowder County and most of northeastern Arkansas in a persistent slate-colored mist. The farmers out in the Delta or up in the hills were happy because they needed this type of soaking rain for their spring plantings, and I was pleased because the steady precipitation drumming softly on my roof greatly assisted me in my enjoyment of a weekend post-luncheon snooze. Captain Augie Dupree, alias C. Auguste Dupin V, was decidedly unhappy, even to the point of barely disguised grumpiness, with the timing of the rain, for on Saturday morning he had taken a risk and had spread several pounds of weed killer on his emerging Zoysia. At 4:30, as he and I sat in my enclosed sunroom and watched the moisture descend, I did not have to match his skills as a reader of minds or moods to be able to discern his attitude toward the day's climatological conditions. But Augie was too polite to gripe about weather over which he had no control or a yard man's gamble that he had lost, so he ignored my smirks of satisfaction concerning the rain and asked if I knew where Pete could be.

I shrugged in ignorance. "He said that he would come over just as soon as he finished refereeing the select-league soccer game between Murryville's under-seventeen team and the squad from Batesville. The rivalry is a heated one, as you know, so Pete may be worn out both mentally and physically when he gets here." Pete has kept his hand—I should more accurately say his feet—in soccer by serving as a licensed official at games, by sometimes working out with the Moffatt College men's team in the autumn, and by helping Ellie with the women's team, if she asks him for special assistance in teaching a player, for example, how more effectively to use her head in passing or shooting the ball. Athlete Pete had told me all of this information four days ago when by chance I had seen him with a coed running along the edge of the campus, exchanging a ball back and forth between their upper foreheads.

"Would you like to have a Heineken or a Lowenbrau, Augie?" I asked my guest. Julianna was busy in the adjoining kitchen, preparing ingredients for the lasagna dinner that the couples Dupree, Prefont, and Watkins would be voraciously consuming later in the evening.

"Thanks, Speck, but I'll wait for Pete. He should be pleased to hear what solutions you and I have come up with."

My reply was sincerely self-effacing. "What YOU have come up with, Mister Detective by heritage and intellect, not I. My role has been limited to that of listener and sycophant."

Augie laughed and added, "Don't forget the title of research assistant, Doctor."

"I will concede that point, my friend. But you could have telephoned Phil Luther as easily as I."

"It's better that physician talked directly to physician. . . . Aha, here arrives young Pete the referee."

Pete knocked on the glass panel of the door leading into the sunroom from the back porch. I hastily admitted him and looked with some asperity at his aqueous appearance. In a phrase, he was soaked from head to foot, from plastered mop of sandy hair to saturated black Reeboks.

"Speck, Augie, I'm so sorry to be running late, but the game went into overtime, and then we had to settle it with penalty kicks. Batesville pulled out the victory, three p. k.'s to two, by the way. I didn't even stop to change clothes except for my game shoes because I didn't want to delay our discussions any longer."

I had managed to wrench a welcoming smile onto my face and to drape a large beach towel over a cushioned wicker chair in the far corner of the sunroom. Pete still wore his all-black referee's uniform—shirt, shorts, and long stockings, and his whistle dangled on a cord in front of his heaving chest.

Julianna called out a welcome from the kitchen and told Pete that he could stay wet, dry off, or do whatever he wanted, but that perhaps Ellie would prefer that Pete change clothes before dinner. "We will be dining at about seven, and it's five now, so you have plenty of time to shift into dry clothes and escort your wife back over here later."

"Thanks, Mayor," responded Pete. "I have really been curious about what these two detecting dudes have come up with ever since Augie called me on Wednesday to confirm, tantalizingly I might add, that we have a reason to meet on Saturday—today."

Julianna dried her hands on her apron and turned back toward the refrigerator. "You three Sherlock Hemlocks go ahead and blab while I check on the status of the pasta."

I gestured toward the prepared chair. "Perch on the towel, Pete, and Augie will inform you of his findings. We won't make you wait any longer."

"Should I take notes, Monsieur Dupin?" queried our soaked friend Pete from his post in the corner.

"You may if you wish, Pete, but I have prepared an outline of my conclusions. Speck has gone over it with me, and we agree about the central argument. After we three converse, I will give you a photocopy of the outline. You did bring along your copy of *Sanctuary*, I see."

"Do you mean that you have found a connection?" Pete was having a hard time controlling his intellectual hunger for the solution that had long evaded him.

Augie nodded, reached down beside his chair, and spoke while in motion. "Here, let me put on my detective cap for inspiration. There, now. Yes, I think that we have found a connection, Professor. Two sentences appearing in different chapters of the novel combine to form a major clue, the application of which can fill in a major gap for us. Look first at the end of Chapter Twenty-Eight, on page two-ninety."

Augie paused and carefully placed his reading glasses on his nose and over his upper ears. "Just after Temple has completed her false testimony and left the courtroom, Faulkner describes our enigmatic Memphis lawyer in this way: 'The Memphis lawyer was sitting on his spine, gazing dreamily out the window.' Now turn back to an earlier scene in the novel, in Chapter Twenty-Four, when Popeye takes Temple to the roadhouse outside of Memphis called the Grotto. On page two-thirty-five Faulkner mentions four men who apparently are henchmen of Popeye, and for one of them the author uses this significant description: 'The fourth man sat on his spine, smoking, his coat buttoned across his chest.' My conclusion? This menacing character, only briefly but tellingly described, is also the Memphis lawyer."

Water dripping off his nose and from his chin onto his referee's black shirt with its white collar, Pete stared with a gaping mouth toward Augie. He snapped his head in my direction and blurted, "I'll be damned. Do you mean that—wait, could these two men be the same guy? If they are, or I mean he is, then. . . . Hold on, I have to think. . . ."

"No need to, Pete," I said with genuine bonhomie. "Augie in his identity as C. Auguste the Fifth has already worked through this problem for you."

Augie glanced at me and said, "Not completely, Speck, not yet. I'm still ransacking the novel and trying to piece together all of the possible ramifications of my hypothesis. But I do feel confident about my preliminary findings. Shall I proceed?"

Pete hopped to his feet. "Hell yes, Augie. This is really exciting. Oh, excuse me, Mayor Watkins, for that slip of the tongue."

Julianna leaned her head through the framed open space over the kitchen sink, where she was washing lettuce, and spoke to us in the adjoining sunroom. "Never mind, Pete. 'Hell' is a word in ordinary use at Town Hall, or perhaps I should say that Town Hall is hell—hmmm, 'Town Hell': I like that name. Most of the members of the Town Council can speak only in words of one syllable, anyway, so I'm accustomed to such language."

Augie cordially resumed his explanation. "Once we know the identity of this character who sits on his spine, the meaning of the events in *Sanctuary* becomes clearer in two ways. First, direct evidence in *Sanctuary*—and not only in the novel's sequel—demonstrates the lawyer's complicity in the abduction of Temple from the nightclub on—let me check my notes here—on Monday, June seventeenth, 1929, and her subsequent appearance at Goodwin's trial on Friday, June twenty-first. Undoubtedly acting on Popeye's orders, the lawyer takes Temple into hiding where he coaches her in the lies that she later tells to the jury."

Augie looked up and spoke directly to Pete. "Professor, I have made extensive use of the chronology in Brooks's book and have found it to be very useful. Thanks for lending it to me."

Pete had resumed his seat in the white wicker chair but was now teeteringly poised on the precise edge of its seat cushion decorated with a vivid array of red, yellow, and pink flowers. "Monsieur Dupin, it is I who should thank you profusely. Now, did you mention a second way in which the events in the book make more sense?"

I chose to interrupt the proceedings. "Gentlemen, anyone for a stein of beer? Lowenbrau, Heineken, Michelob, Miller Lite, or root?"

Pete preferred Lowenbrau, Augie asked for Michelob, and I stoically settled for a diet A&W root beer, since I knew that later in the evening I would likely gorge myself on my bride's succulent lasagna, tossed Italian salad, and steaming garlic bread, and I wanted to save as much storage space as possible in my capacious g. i. system. With refreshments in hand and at lips, we resumed the confab, with Augie taking the lead.

"Professor, the second solution pertains to the puzzling behavior of Clarence Snopes at the barber shop in Jefferson on Tuesday, June eighteenth. Snopes is fulminating at the man whom he calls the 'jew lawyer' on this day because the lawyer himself, now understood to be a tough, even brutal man with extensive gangland connections, administers the beating to the obnoxious pie-faced Senator. At the barber shop—let's look back at page two-sixty-six—Snopes is careful not to mention the lawyer by name and to keep his invective in the abstract. However, the listening barber grows weary of Snopes's mewlings and challenges the veracity of the Senator's story by confronting Snopes with a direct question. I'm quoting here, "'What was you trying to sell to that car when it run over you?'" At this point Snopes, obviously afraid of giving away too much information best kept private and thereby eliciting a second pummeling by the Memphis lawyer, quickly dodges with the reply, "'Have a cigar.'"'

Pete continued to stare at Murryville's resident descendant of the illustrious C. Auguste Dupin I. "By God, I think you've figured it out, Captain," Pete shouted as he jumped straight up from his chair, waving his ceramic German stein of Lowenbrau at Augie, flipping his copy of *Sanctuary* from his lap to the floor where it landed with a resounding "blap," and barely avoiding a collision between his frazzled pile of hair and my sunroom's rotating ceiling fan. "This explanation makes sense. But are you basing your hypothesis, as you earlier phrased it, only on the two appearances of the word 'spine?' Couldn't these be coincidental?"

Augie and I exchanged wise smiles. "Exactly our first reaction, Pete, when Augie noticed the two references to the spine," I replied. "But then we began to examine the issue more extensively, and we soon rejected the possibility of a coincidence."

Our ratiocinist chimed in here. "Speck and I both searched carefully through *Sanctuary*, Pete, looking for other uses of the word 'spine.' Neither of us found any, and we have concluded that Faulkner's exclusive and vivid descriptions of a man sitting on his spine in only these two scenes constitute what some of your favorite scholars might call a major clue."

My turn now. "We did discover that Faulkner includes several references to the human back, but all of these appear in descriptions of identifiable characters. Here is a representative sample of these references." I pulled a slip of paper out of the back pages of my copy of *Sanctuary* and passed it to Pete. THE

LIST:

    Tommy the murder victim

        "His back still shook with secret glee." page 48

    Popeye

        ". . . watching Popeye's back." page 74

    Temple Drake

        "She . . . leaned her back against it." page 88

    Lee Goodwin

        "Popeye . . . looked at Goodwin's back." page 97

    Horace Benbow, defense lawyer (speaking)

        'I'll know whether or not I have any backbone when you tell me what the other way is.'" page 131

After Pete had read the list to himself, I addressed a remark to the professor: "Here's my favorite—on page two-oh-nine. Miss Reba, the rotund Memphis madam, is talking about Senator Clarence Snopes and how the Senator, while he was visiting her house of ill repute, "'sat around the dining-room blowing his head off and feeling the girls' behinds. . . .'" I looked up from my copy of the novel and said, "Please excuse that ribald quotation. I just couldn't resist reading it. Now look at the list, Pete. That final reference to 'backbone,' the one spoken by Benbow, although expressed as a metaphor comes the closest to a synonym for 'spine' of any that I found in the novel. In my searches I did come upon one other similar description of a man sitting angled low in a chair. It appears on page fifty-one, reflects a thought process of Temple's mind, and refers to, I quote here, 'her father sitting on the porch at home, his feet on the rail, watching a Negro mow the lawn.'"

At this juncture Augie took over the exposition. "Don't assume, Pete, that we stopped here. Like you, we desired further proof. So we decided to examine more closely the question of this posture of 'sitting on the spine.' Luckily, we have direct contact with a man who possesses expert knowledge about the human musculoskeletal system." Augie arose and turned in my direction. "Doctor, Doctor, Mister M. D., Sir Archibald Fulmer Watkins of the Crowder County Royal Academy of Physicians, puh-leeze pro-ceeed." Apparently feeling the effects of his one stein of Michelob, the Captain declaimed his oratory of introduction with a dramatic bow and a sweeping flourish of his right arm.

The sounds of clamorous clapping, cheers, whistles, and the stamping of feet cascaded from the kitchen. "Huzzah, huzzah. Encore, Sir Alec Guinness, Sean Connery, Monty Python, or whoever ye may be." My dainty wife, accustomed to public histrionics, led the ovation from the culinary quarters. Accompanying Her Honor were Mary Alice and Ellie, who, unbeknownst to us three absorbed rookie scholars, had entered the Watkins domicile, with proper etiquette, through the front door. They had both arrived early in order to offer kitchen assistance to the Mayor.

"Don't let us stop the show, guys. Just pretend that we're not here. . . . OH NO! Pete, you're sopping wet. Didn't you even go home to change after the game?" Ellie had strolled into the sunroom and was staring aghast at her befuddled spouse, who could only pivot his head from Augie to me to Ellie and utter, "Uhh, well, I mean, you know, you never know, you know, I mean, er, uhhh. . . ."

Augie saved the tattered remnants of Pete's dignity and perhaps averted a Prefontian marital spat by stepping forward and proclaiming, "Ladies, how delightful that you have arrived. Perhaps Speck will take your requests for libations, and then, if you are willing, you can assist us in the next phase of our investigation. It's time for a hypothetical demonstration. How about lending a hand, or I should say a back, or perhaps—hmmm, a backside, to our endeavors?"

Mary Alice, Ellie, and the trailing Julianna exchanged glances, clearly communicating to each other their unanimous decision that their husbands had gone collectively loco, and then Mrs. Dupree spoke for the group: "We will participate—correct, girls?"—nods from her female cohorts—"as long as our, as you put it, 'backsides,' play only an appropriately discreet role in the proceedings."

I jumped into the fray. "Certainly, ladies. This is 2318 Summit Avenue, the Watkins manse, not the Follies Brassiere or the Va-Va-Voom Boom-Boom Room. Take chairs in here, fair ladies, if you please. Now, drinks, anyone? Oh, I see that Julianna has already furnished you with beverages. So, let's continue."

Augie had resumed his seat and was organizing his notes. "We were talking about the spine, friends. Speck, tell us about your research."

"A simple quizzing of a colleague would be a more accurate way to phrase what I did, Augie," was my reply. I continued: "Our chief detective, Captain Dupree here, and I both wondered about this key phrase 'sitting on his spine.' Therefore, I called Phil Luther, Murryville's orthopedic surgeon and my longtime friend, and asked him under what conditions a person would sit on his or her spine. Here is what Phil told me." I read aloud from my notepad. "'Sitting on the spine is not a natural position for a person. Someone who sits on the spine does so for one of two reasons: because of deformity or by choice, and if by choice then usually for the sake of appearance.'"

Pete flailed his arms outward, in the process almost decapitating a nearby lamp with his left paw. "'The sake of appearance?'" he yelped, unable to keep the excitement out of his voice. "So these two guys—oops, I mean this one guy, the lawyer—he is sitting this way to show off or to send some sort of message?"

"You are getting the idea, Pete. Let's have a demonstration—no, not you, Pete," Augie spoke to the eager young teacher. "I want to witness your reaction. Mary Alice, Ellie, would either of you volunteer?" Her Royal Shiftiness, the Mayor, had already slipped silently into the kitchen.

Mary Alice arose and walked toward Julianna's safe haven. "I yield to Ellie, my more youthful soul sister, Augie dear. She is the athlete and coach, and at my age I might fall out of the chair and injure my. . . . Oh, never mind. I'll see if I can help Julianna with the dinner preparation."

Ellie was graciously willing. "I assume that you want me to sit on my spine, Mister Dupree, or should I say 'Dupin?' Okay, here goes." Ellie stood to her full height, lowered herself backward into her white cushioned wicker chair, and propelled her legs forward, sliding her back and neck downward and raising her knees. Her posture visibly defined the word "slouch." She was wearing her Moffatt College shiny orange-and-white synthetic athletic pants and matching zippered jacket, so she didn't have to worry about retaining a ladylike pose. For a fleeting moment I imagined the lovely display of pulchritudinous flesh that would have been visible if she had been wearing shorts and a tank top—but reluctantly I wrenched my naughty thoughts back to the present moment.

Augie resumed the questioning. "Pete, what attitude is your wife communicating to you as she sits that way on her spine instead of on her—uhh, instead of in a more normal position?"

Pete placed his right index finger beside his mouth and stared at Ellie. "One of haughtiness, arrogance, superiority. By her body language, she is expressing the attitude of 'Screw you, everybody; I'm in charge here and can sit any damned way that I choose.'"

Maintaining her slouching position, Ellie rotated her head from right to left and back to the right, all the while moaning in exasperation. "Peee—TUR! Wouldn't a phrase such as 'To heck with you' be more polite than what you just said?"

Pete stared at Ellie in bewilderment. "I thought that I made a good choice, sweetheart. My first reaction was to say, 'F-uh, er, uh, you.' Uhh, I guess I'd better shut up."

Augie chuckled as I guffawed. "Pete's response was authentic and very helpful, Ellie, as has been your demonstration," pronounced our chief sleuth. "Let's review what Doctor Luther told Speck; remember the words 'deformity' or 'by choice?' Obviously you, Miss Ellie, are certainly not deformed and indeed are formed quite beautifully."

"Understatement of the millennium," methought with chagrin.

"Why, thank you, Captain Butluh, suh," Ellie pronounced to Augie in a saucy imitation of Scarlett O'Hara herself, complete with a graceful flip of the right wrist. Straightening herself in her chair and reverting to her regular voice, she concluded, "I sat that way by choice, and I assume that the character in the book does also—at two different times, right?"

Augie asked me to continue with the explanation. "In neither the nightclub scene nor the one in the courtroom," I said," is there any evidence that the man 'sitting on his spine' is deformed. Indeed, in the Grotto the man 'with the buttoned coat'—I'm referring to page two-forty—moves about the roadhouse smoothly and stealthily, helping to lift Temple and whisk her out of the building. And later, in the courtroom scene, the lawyer sits wordlessly but with a kind of—shall we say—leonine watchfulness. I'm quoting here: 'he gazed lazily out a window above the ranked heads, picking his teeth'—on page two-eighty-two. In each instance the lawyer certainly exudes arrogance, to use one of your observations, Pete, and a menacing arrogance at that. Augie and I agree that the lawyer chooses deliberately to sit on his spine at the Grotto as well as in the courtroom as a way of expressing both his command of each situation and his contempt for first the shallow, vapid Temple and later the fully controlled participants—Goodwin, Benbow, Temple—in the trial."

Pete plopped backward into his chair, slapped his hands on his knees, and stated emphatically, "You have convinced me, Monsieur Dupin and companion detective Watkins. Since we can now conclude that the lawyer is definitely an agent of Popeye and a tough guy, it makes sense that he would be the man who beats up Clarence and that Clarence would later be afraid of him. But wait—how does Snopes get mixed up in all of this criminal activity? Where is my book. . . ?" Pete looked wildly at the area around his chair and then with widened eyes at Ellie.

"Relax, young man," said Augie with a soft laugh. "Speck and I are working on the question now of unstated but implied connections in the novel, but first allow me to present a third reason that we believe the phrase 'sitting on his spine' is a major clue."

"More beer, anyone?" I inquired with as much pub-like cheeriness as I could muster. "Ladies, another libation of some sort?" I shouted to the kitchen crew. For the next few minutes I busily procured and served steins of cold beer to Pete, Augie, and my wife the pol, passion-fruit wine coolers to Ellie and Mary Alice, and a genuine, non-diet, full-strength Beer of the Root for yours truly. Hey, a man's gotta drink what a man's gotta drink so he can live a little and go for the gusto. Gee whiz, that's not nearly as memorable a mixed metaphor as my two all-time favorites: "The hand that has rocked the cradle has kicked the bucket," and "We are about to open Pandora's can of worms." Seriously now, folks. . . .

Please forgive your demented narrator for that sidetrack into wisecrack land. As the aroma of lasagna spiced heavily with parmesan cheese and oregano began to waft tantalizingly into the sunroom, Augie said to Pete and me, "Fellows, we have just a few more minutes before Julianna and her assistant kitchen wenches"—yelps of protest came from the next room—"treat us to an Italian banquet. I'll make this summary brief. Pete, do you remember two weeks ago when we first began talking about *Sanctuary* and you talked to Speck and me about Faulkner's authorial technique of withholding vital information from his readers?"

"Definitely, Augie. Faulkner does this in all of his novels, especially the major ones such as the book we are now studying, *The Sound and the Fury, As I Lay Dying, Light in August, The Bear, Absalom, Absalom!*—hell, all of his books, I guess, although I haven't had the time yet to read all nineteen of his novels or his more than one hundred short stories. Faulkner rarely presents all of the information needed to draw a necessary conclusion, apparently preferring instead to create suspense by weaving in fact after pertinent fact until the full truth—perhaps—is finally revealed. At least, that explanation is the one that I use in my introductory lecture in the Faulkner course."

"Very helpful, Pete," responded our retired policeman and fledgling literary investigator. "It seems to me that Faulkner uses this technique in *Sanctuary*, for example, as a way of revealing the full horror of the rape of Temple Drake, beginning with the scene in the corncrib—page one-oh-two, gentlemen, where Temple screams '"Something is happening to me!"' This gradual revelation of the truth continues with Temple's references to her bleeding—look on page one-thirty-seven and then on two-thirty-one—and concludes at the trial with Eustace Graham's display of—turn to two-eighty-three, guys—'a corn cob' which 'appeared to have been dipped in dark brownish paint.'"

"Correct you are again, Monsieur Detective. Are you about to tell me that Faulkner also uses this technique of withheld meaning in disclosing to us the identity of the Memphis lawyer?" Pete asked with hope clearly implied in his tone.

"I believe so, Pete, and Speck, my loyal sounding board, agrees. Let me outline the sequence of Faulkner's revelation of the Jewish lawyer. The man first appears at the Grotto in Chapter Twenty-Four, but at this place in the narrative we readers have no way of knowing his true identity. The next reference is Snopes's vitriolic eruption against the 'jew lawyer' at the conclusion of Chapter Twenty-Six. At the end of the next chapter Horace enters the courtroom on the second day of the trial and spots the lawyer. Look on page two-eighty-one. 'At the other end of the table sat a man picking his teeth. His skull was capped closely by tight-curled black hair thinning upon a bald spot. He had a long, pale nose. He wore a tan palm beach suit; upon the table near him lay a smart leather brief-case and a straw hat with a red-and-tan band, and he gazed lazily out a window above the ranked heads, picking his teeth.' Significantly, Benbow is dismayed to see the man but is not surprised. He even surmises the man's professional and ethnic identity: '"It's a lawyer," he said. "A Jew lawyer from Memphis."' Also, Horace deduces that Temple must be present, 'produced' as she indeed has been, by the lawyer who earlier in the week had abducted her from the Grotto.

"At the end of the final courtroom scene, Chapter Twenty-Eight, Faulkner provides a significant fact, this time the key description of the Memphis lawyer 'sitting on his spine, gazing dreamily out the window.' Slouched cockily in his chair, controlling the proceedings without having to speak or take any overt action, the lawyer provides a vivid representation of the omniscient evil that runs through the entire novel."

"All right, all right, Augie, yes sir; this is truly helpful." Pete was once again pacing around the room, this time with a wide grin on his face and a glint in his eye.

C. A. Dupin V gently thrust his upraised right palm toward Pete. "There's one more appearance by the lawyer, Professor—and an important one. Near the end of the novel Faulkner finally confirms that the lawyer is an agent of Popeye. Moreover, in this scene the lawyer actually speaks, for the first time since the scene taking place in the nightclub, when we could not yet know who he is. In Chapter Thirty-One, as Popeye languishes in a jail cell in Alabama, unwilling to extricate himself from a death sentence, the Memphis lawyer appears 'unbidden' but fails to convince Popeye to try to beat the charge. Popeye even threatens the lawyer, saying '"I told you once, I've got enough on you,"' likely a reference to the lawyer's participation in the abduction of Temple, his complicity in the murder of Red, and his role in coaching Temple to commit perjury."

The conversation ceased as Augie and I mulled over the inductions he had just completed based on the appearances of the phrases "sat on his spine" or "sitting on his spine"; Pete continued to scribble furiously on a legal pad that he had earlier borrowed from Julianna. The professor finished writing and looked up, meeting Augie's steady gaze.

"Oh Captain, my Captain, master detective sir, I am so grateful to you. Now I will be able to explain this puzzle to my Faulkner students and to overturn my reputation of being a dumb ass," gushed young Pete.

"Hold on, my youthful and impetuous friend," cautioned Augie. "I am still attempting to use our identification of the Memphis lawyer as a means of drawing connections among some of the other seemingly disparate events and outcomes in the novel. Give me another week or two for contemplation and for conversations with Speck, and then we three can meet again for a final gabfest on this challenging topic."

Julianna and her volunteer helpers marched briskly into the sunroom. "Dinner is served, gentlemen. Stifle the literary blather for now and come feed your flaccid faces," proclaimed my sweetheart the Mayor.

"By fortunate coincidence we are at a natural stopping point, my dear," I responded. "And the dictates of our stomachs take precedence over our intellectual hungers any old time. Shall we accompany these debutantes to the banquet, my fellow Faulkner aficionados?" No dissenting votes were voiced, and the sumptuous Italian feast commenced.

Ballads at the Old Cafe

Twelve days slipped by more swiftly than I thought possible, and on Thursday, May 4, at 11:30 a. m. I telephoned Augie and asked him to meet me for lunch at Story's Cafe. After a busy morning in the operating room at Churchill River Medical Center with a complicated cataract operation followed by a laser procedure on a glaucoma patient, I was finishing some dictation in the office in preparation for a pleasant noontime repast and an afternoon away from ophthalmology. Following our most recent discussion with Pete at the lasagna foodfest, Augie and I had met several times in his den or in one of our backyards for further joint forays into the intricacies of *Sanctuary*. We needed to tie up a few details, and then we planned to visit with Pete again—hence our lunch at Story's.

I checked with May Ellen about my call schedule and my pending hospital consultations, found out that the afternoon looked unencumbered, hustled out of the office to my car before I could be paged, and motored sedately down to the river district and to a parking place one block away from my destination. As I opened the plate-glass door and entered Story's Cafe, a wave of clashing sounds washed over me: chatter, laughter, ice clinking in glasses, cutlery clanging against chinaware, food orders shouted by waitresses in the direction of the bustling kitchen, and a country-and-western tune emanating raucously from the ancient jukebox in the corner; the whining refrain of the song seemed to be, "I knew I'd reached the bottom when I woke up on top of you."

The interior air of the venerable cafe smelled of fried meats, sizzling onions, and bacon grease. Traditional Southern country cuisine has always been the staple of Story's menus. Mo McAinsh, the harried owner and current proprietor of Murryville's most popular dining establishment, waved from behind the long counter at the front of the narrow dining room that featured booths with red plastic seats along both walls and haphazardly arranged wooden tables in every other available space. While filling a glass of water from a spigot beneath the counter, Mo pointed to my standard table next to the back wall. Ten years ago Mo had purchased Story's from the descendants of the Cafe's founder, Pfeiffer Knickerbocker Story, and had retained the business's loyal clientele while also attracting substantial numbers of Murryville's growing population of yuppies. Augie was already ensconced at the back table, reading the menu as he arranged legal pads, pens, and his copy of *Sanctuary* to his right side on our table. His reading spectacles sat firmly on his nose.

"Hail fellow, well met," I clichéd shamelessly as I slid into my chair. "Ready for some food and book talk?"

"Glad you could get away from the office so readily, Speck. I fertilized our flower beds all morning and have worked up a ferocious appetite. Do you still recommend the chicken-fried steak?"

"Most definitely, Monsieur Dupin, since we are unlikely to find chateaubriand or pheasant under glass on Story's menu. I am definitely ordering my favorite foods today."

We delivered our orders to Lucille the frazzled waitress: chicken-fried steak, mashed potatoes, black-eyed peas, turnip greens, and iced tea. After Lucille returned within five minutes juggling our plates, we gratefully assaulted our farmers' fare, conversing amiably while we chowed down. Augie filled me in on his latest call for assistance from the local police force.

"This one turned out to be a no-brainer, Speck. Just as I arrived at headquarters to try to help Buddy Cotham, the case was solved by Stew Tyler, our town's fire chief; he certainly didn't need me."

I wiped a smear of white cream gravy from the left side of my mouth. "Was this the arson case that everybody was talking about earlier in the week, Augie?"

"That's right, Speck. Mary Alice was pretty upset when the fire department called and told her that Waggoner School was on fire. Fortunately, the firefighters got there quickly, and they confined the damage to a storage closet and to the waiting room of Mary Alice's office." Augie carefully chewed on a piece of steak and then helped himself to a forkful of greens.

"I heard that the arsonists spray-painted graffiti on your wife's walls. Did they sign their names? Is this how you caught them?" I asked.

Augie laughed softly. "No, but they might as well have. When I showed up at the station, Stew Tyler had just gotten a phone call from George Workman over at Brown's Drugstore. It seems that our brilliant criminals had taken photos of themselves setting the fires and then had taken the rolls of film to Brown's for developing. When the photo lab called George, next George called Stew, the fire chief got in touch with Buddy, and Buddy and I picked up the kids—two boys, eleven and twelve—who had lit the matches."

I munched on a hot buttered roll and laughed around my mouthful. "Mary Alice must be relieved to have the case closed," I said.

"Yes, she is," replied Augie. "But she is also embarrassed, because the two kids attend Waggoner, and here is what they wrote on her office wall." Augie wrote some words on a napkin and then handed the napkin to me. I read the following:

kis my but

up yur asss ladie

Shaking my head in dismay, I concluded, "Neither boy seems to be a threat to win a Nobel Prize for Literature any time soon. At least now they will enjoy some leisure time in the reformatory, during which they can work on their language skills."

As Augie and I were trying to decide whether to sin boldly by ordering pecan pie for dessert, we heard a loud whoop breaking through the standard Story's clamor. "Augie! Speck! How delightful to find you guys in here. And do I spy with my little eye a certain novel by Mister William Faulkner, late of Oxford, Mizz-sippi?"

Pete hovered over our table like a condor that had arrested its dive toward the Pacific in mid-swoop. "Please join us, Professor. We have finished the main course, but we are about to indulge in dessert, and you can catch up with us," I said cordially.

With fervent expressions of gratitude Pete plopped into a vacant chair, ordered from Lucille a B. L. T. and a glass of milk, and looked eagerly at Augie. "Have you unearthed any other gems, Investigator Dupin? I have been very busy trying to make sense with my students of *The Bear* and have selfishly left *Sanctuary* to you and to the good Doctor Watkins here. Any news?"

Augie waved a hand over the awaiting legal pads and novel before replying, "As a matter of fact, Professor, Speck and I were planning to spend an hour or two this afternoon jawing about our findings. Are you free for the next couple of hours so that we can finish up this project?"

"YES, *ja, ja wohl, oui, si*—you betcha," spieled Pete with a wide sweep of the left arm. A neighboring lunch patron ducked backward in alarm, thereby saving herself from a jolt to the jaw. "I'm free until a blasted committee meeting at three-thirty—AARGH! What a waste of time: when in doubt, form a committee. Oh, well. Lay your info on me. Once again, I'm truly indebted to you for your help."

Augie and I ordered pecan pie and coffee, and we relished our consumption of the sticky, gooey, crunchy treat as Pete wolfed down his sandwich. Then it was time to resume our conversation about Faulkner's most famous crime novel. Augie consulted his top legal pad. "In review, gentlemen: we have the exclusive two uses of the phrase 'sitting' or 'sat on his spine'; the orthopedic research about deformity or choice; and the textual evidence concerning the gradual revelation of truth after the initial withholding by Faulkner of vital information. Now, Pete, I feel confident in telling you that Speck and I have found a fourth reason supporting the validity of our thesis that the man sitting on his spine in the Grotto is the Memphis lawyer who later beats up Clarence Snopes. The fourth and final reason may be summarized in this way: we think that we can fill in several gaps in Faulkner's narrative by plugging in our insight about the lawyer. Once we assume that the lawyer is the same man who directs Temple's abduction from the Grotto, we can reconstruct a plausible explanation of his role in the events leading up to the trial and to Temple's perjury."

Pete listened intently as he finished his B. L. T. and sipped his milk. "I don't have a legal pad with me, Captain Dupree. Should I use my napkin?"

Augie held up his notes so that Pete could see them. "Again, there is no need, Professor. Here is an outline, and I plan to write out this information in detail later. For now, let me take the liberty of lecturing to you, and you can look on with Speck at his copy of *Sanctuary*. Doctor Watkins," Augie stated in a pompous tone with an exaggerated British accent, "pray to interrupt me if you wish to disagree or to elaborate upon a point."

"To the hunt, my good Holmes—err, I mean Monsieur Dupin," was my reply.

Placing his blue "Detective" cap on his head and resuming his soft Southern speech pattern, Augie became Cesar Auguste Dupin V, leaned forward in his chair, and began consulting his notes. "Gentlemen, this scenario begins with Clarence Snopes; Horace Benbow, the defense attorney; and Eustace Graham, the local district attorney. As you remember, Snopes finds the missing Temple at Miss Reba's brothel in Memphis, and Snopes sells the information of Temple's whereabouts to Horace: '"She's in a Memphis 'ho'-house,"' to quote Clarence. The day after Horace travels to Miss Reba's in order to talk to Temple, Narcissa Benbow Sartoris betrays her brother Horace by telling Eustace Graham, '"Three nights ago that Snopes, the one in the legislature, telephoned out home, trying to find him."' By the word '"him"' she means her brother Horace here. Quoting again, '"The next day he"'—Horace again—'"went to Memphis. I dont know what for. You'll have to find that out for yourself."' I'm looking at page two-sixty-four here, friends. Graham, who—I'm quoting now from the preceding page—'had let it be known that he would announce for Congress on the record of his convictions,' end of quotation, senses large political advantages for himself in the case of Tommy's murder and is determined to get Goodwin convicted by any means at his disposal. As Narcissa leaves his office, he reveals his elation at her news. Look at two-sixty-four again: 'He closed the door and struck a clumsy clog-step, snapping his fingers. . . .'"

Augie looked up from his legal pad. "With us so far, Pete?"

"Oh, yes, Monsieur Detective. Please proceed."

"Where was I? Oh yes. Armed with two significant items of information—'Snopes' and 'Memphis'—Graham must have chosen the more specific and closer of the clues and contacted Clarence Snopes. We know that Snopes has already sold to Horace—on Sunday, June second, according to the Brooks chronology—the information of Temple's incarceration in Miss Reba's. On June fourth, before Narcissa goes to see Graham, Horace meets Snopes on a Jefferson street, and the Senator says that he is—look on two-sixty-one—'"Going down to Jackson for a couple of days on a little business."' Now that Snopes has soaked some money out of Horace, he appears to be on his way to visit Judge Drake, Temple's father, in order to pry a similar payment out of him. We know that Snopes wheedles one hundred dollars each from Horace and Judge Drake, because two weeks later, bandaged from his beating, Snopes bombastically proclaims to the listeners in the barber shop—read with me from two-sixty-six: '"When a jew lawyer can hold up an American, a white man, and not give him but ten dollars for something that two Americans, Americans, southron gentlemen; a judge living in the capital of the State of Mississippi and a lawyer that's going to be as big a man as his pa some day, and a judge too; when they give him ten times as much for the same thing than the lowlife jew, we need a law."'"

Augie paused, looked over his reading glasses at Pete and me, observed no obvious confusion or disagreement, and proceeded. "Evidently Snopes has been trying to parcel out tidbits of information to various interested people in such a way that he can extort as much money as possible. When he first sells to Horace the crucial fact about Temple's location at Miss Reba's hot-pillow joint, Snopes tells Benbow that if the information doesn't interest defense attorney Benbow, then, quoting here from two-oh-six, "'I'll dicker with the other party'"—meaning the prosecution side of the case, headed by Graham. Therefore, when Graham, alerted by Narcissa, presumably contacts him, Snopes likely smells the aroma of more cash and discloses Temple's whereabouts in Memphis in exchange for Graham's promise of a payment. Snopes earlier says to Horace, quoting here, "'I'll trust you,'" and he probably would also trust Graham, out of necessity as well as greed."

Pete emitted a snort and a loud guffaw. Augie and I looked at one another and then at the professor. "Was I unintentionally amusing, Herr Prefont?" queried Augie.

Pete vigorously shook his head of copious hair and spoke with conviction in his tone: "No, no, Augie. When you read Snopes's use of the word 'dicker,' I couldn't help but remember an incident that happened at a recent meeting of the campus concert committee. When I told the group that the popular alternative rock group the Free Love Virgins was willing to come to Moffatt and that the band's female agent was asking for five thousand dollars for the appearance, one of my colleagues, Gene Follett, said, 'Don't take the woman's first offer. Try to reason with her. And if that doesn't work, then . . . Dicker!'"

After I finished chuckling, I asked my tablemates, "Is it politically correct to laugh at such a story? Am I revealing myself to be a male porcine sexist?"

Pete was reassuring. "This conversation will never be reported at Town Hall, the hospital, or the Moffatt campus. As one of my dewy-eyed freshmen once said, we will all be incommunicable about it."

"Back to the business at hand," Augie said. The standard lunch crowd had devoured Mo McAinsh's tasty victuals and had departed, and only a few customers dawdled in booths or at tables dispersed around the cafe. Most of us malingerers were enjoying pie, coffee, and conversation, although our table doubtlessly could boast the only discussion devoted to literary analysis. "Speck," requested Augie, "why don't you take over here and tell Pete what you noticed about Faulkner's narrative structure in Chapter Twenty-Six?"

"Thanks, Augie, I will." At this point I consulted my pocket notepad. "It seems to me, Pete, that Faulkner strongly suggests a causal connection between Narcissa's disclosure to Graham and the later beating of Snopes—with Graham and the Jewish lawyer as necessary links in the chain of events—by placing Snopes's diatribe against the, quoting here from two-sixty-six, '"durn, stinking, lowlife jew,"' end of quotation, immediately after the passage in which Narcissa tells Graham the information he needs in order to find a friendly witness."

I continued to read from my notes and to talk directly to Pete. "Once Graham learns from Snopes that Temple, who was nearby when Tommy was killed, is at Miss Reba's and that she is under the control and protection of a gangster—earlier Popeye had, quoting Miss Reba here, '"held the match to the back,"' end of quotation, of Snopes's neck as Snopes peered through a keyhole at Temple—Graham must consult sources in Memphis, find out Popeye's name, and learn the name of the lawyer who works for him. Presumably Graham refrains from contacting Temple directly, because Miss Reba never mentions to Horace that anyone other than Horace and Snopes—along with Popeye and Red, Temple's lover—has come looking for Temple. How about if you take over here, Monsieur Dupin?"

"Delighted to, Doctor," responded Augie. "I appreciate your insights about the placement of the Narcissa-Graham scene just before the one with Snopes after he has been beaten. There must be a direct link between these two occurrences, as you have shown. All right, here we go. Okay, Pete?"

"Dukes of detective-dom, I am all ears—and hair, elbows, feet also, as Ellie would say. The novel is making better sense all of the time. Do you have more pearls to cast before this humble swine?"

"Certainly, Professor Oink-Oink," replied Augie, with a friendly wink at Pete. "We will take this scenario all the way to the trial scene and then regress again to Snopes in his appearance at the barber shop. Now, where were we? Oh yes. Graham must contact and then strike a bargain with the Jewish lawyer, arranging to have Temple testify that Goodwin is guilty and thus accomplishing two goals: Popeye's nefarious one of avoiding implication in the murder that he actually has committed; and Graham's own political one of gaining a conviction in a highly publicized case. We know that Snopes expects to be paid by the Jewish lawyer. At the barber shop Snopes says—look on page two-sixty-six—'"when a jew lawyer can hold up an American, a white man, and not give him but ten dollars. . . ."' So Snopes had reason to expect payment directly from the lawyer and not from Graham. The district attorney may have pawned Snopes off on the Jewish lawyer as part of their agreement, or Snopes may have sensed another victim—the lawyer—and tried to pry loose some funds. Whichever the case, Snopes gets only ten dollars, not his desired one hundred."

As Augie was talking, Pete had been staring at the detective, then back at me, and then at the copy of *Sanctuary* that he and I were sharing. Now the professor intervened: "So we can assume that Graham and the Memphis lawyer have struck a bargain and that all they have to do at this point is to wait until the trial opens—when would that be?"

I checked my notepad again. "On Thursday, June twentieth."

"But Temple gets abducted first, right?" said Pete.

I looked at Augie, he nodded politely, and with the aid of my notes I assumed the leadership role. "Temple attempts to escape from Miss Reba's on the evening of Monday, June seventeenth, first bribing Minnie the housekeeper so that she, Temple, can telephone Red, and then later sneaking out the door. However, Popeye's henchmen are staking out Miss Reba's, and Popeye picks up Temple in his car and drives her to the Grotto. Popeye has already placed four men at the nightclub, including the Memphis lawyer."

I continued my spiel. "After Temple has talked alone to Red, the lawyer and an accomplice lift Temple and carry her from the building. The lawyer, who earlier is described as sitting on his spine with his coat buttoned across his chest, is obviously in charge, as he reveals in his command to Temple. Look on page two-forty: '"Yell," the man with the buttoned coat said. "Just try it once."' In the waiting car the 'man in the buttoned coat took the wheel.' The Memphis lawyer must then drive Temple to a prearranged hideout somewhere in the north Mississippi countryside between Memphis and Jefferson, where Graham joins the lawyer in coaching Temple about what lies to tell at Goodwin's trial. Remember that at the trial the Memphis lawyer sits next to Graham, clearly signaling that they are in cahoots."

I nodded to Augie. "Will you take over here? You are the investigator who figured out what is revealed by Temple's strange behavior on the witness stand."

Augie inclined his head toward me and said, "Certainly, Speck. Let's look at Temple's responses to Graham's questions—pages two-eighty-five through two-eighty-eight. We can safely assume that her testimony has been rehearsed. Graham carefully leads Temple through a damning series of false revelations, constantly drawing her back from her dazed state by catching her gaze, 'holding her eyes,' and eliciting 'her parrotlike answers.' If she attempts to deviate from the script, Graham recurringly interrupts her and directs her back to her prearranged lies."

Looking up from the book, Augie said, "Friends, let's arrange a little dramatic reading at this point. Speck, you portray Graham, and Pete, you take the role of Temple. Read this passage"—he pointed to his copy of *Sanctuary*—"from page two-eighty-seven."

I sat straight up in my chair, raised my eyebrows at Pete, and asked, "Ready, Temple?"

"Yes, go ahead, Mister D. A.," replied my fellow amateur thespian in a squeaky soprano Southern drawl.

Squaring my shoulders and lowering my voice in a feeble attempt to sound like F. Lee Bailey at the O. J. Simpson trial, I commenced my reading, with Pete (as Temple) responding to my questions and commands.

"Was anyone else there?"

"Tommy was. He said—"

"Was he inside the crib or outside?"

"He was outside by the door. He was watching. He said he wouldn't let—"

"Just a minute. Did you ask him not to let anyone in?"

"Yes."

"And he locked the door on the outside?"

"Yes."

"But Goodwin came in."

"Yes."

"Did he have anything in his hand?"

"He had the pistol."

"Did Tommy try to stop him?"

"Yes. He said he—"

"Wait. What did he do to Tommy?"

At this point in the reading Augie held up his right hand, palm outward, and read the one sentence of exposition in the passage: "She gazed at him." Then the detective-director nodded at me, and I delivered Graham's final line, followed by Pete's reading of Temple's concluding words:

"He had the pistol in his hand. What did he do then?"

"He shot him."

For several moments our repertory company of traveling dramatis personae was silent, each man lost in his own thoughts. Then Pete, still staring at my copy of *Sanctuary*, said, "When Graham says to Temple, '"Just a minute"' and

"'Wait,'" obviously he is directing her to stick to their rehearsed false testimony."

"Agreed, Professor," intoned Augie. "And between Monday night and Friday morning Graham and the Jewish lawyer had ample time to create this blatant prevarication and force Temple to memorize it."

Again the three of us fell quiet as we thought of Temple's perjury and its horrific result, the vigilante-style mutilation and burning alive by the Jefferson mob of the not-guilty Lee Goodwin, a despicable act that Benbow attempts to prevent but cannot. Pete was the first to break the silence. "Augie, did you earlier mention that you wanted to return to discussing Snopes again?"

"Yes, Pete," replied Augie. "Then I think that we will be finished with this exercise in literary detective work and we can spend our days in more mundane pursuits: teaching and committee work for you, Professor; saving Murryville's vision and dabbling in politics for you, Doctor Watkins; and in my case, the busting of the sod."

Shifting aside his notes on the trial, Augie picked up another legal pad, the top page of which was headed by the word "Snopes," and said to Pete and me, "Let's turn to the barber shop scene again, gentlemen. Pages two-sixty-five and two-sixty-six. Remember that our entire investigation began with Pete's questions about Snopes's nasty comments concerning the Jewish lawyer."

Looking at his tablemates, C. A. Dupin V assessed correctly that we had all found the designated page, and he resumed his explanation. "On Tuesday, June eighteenth, the day after Temple has been taken by the lawyer and his sidekicks into involuntary hiding—I'm quoting now—"Snopes emerged from the dentist's office and stood at the curb, spitting." Later at the barber shop he claims that he "'got hit by a car in Jackson.'" However, rather than giving the details of the accident and cursing the ineptitude of the driver of the car, Snopes launches into his vituperative denunciation of a "'jew lawyer'" and discloses that the lawyer, with ten dollars; Benbow, with one hundred; and Judge Drake, also with one hundred, are the sources of his funds, not a "'bastard'" driver in Jackson. Snopes obviously is lying about being hit by a car. He mentions Jackson, which is more than one hundred miles to the south of Jefferson, rather than Memphis, as the site of his alleged accident, although he stupidly goes on to say, '"And the lowest kind of lawyer is a Memphis jew lawyer."'"

Pete snorted with contempt. "It seems to me, fellows, that Snopes's inane attempt to explain his battered appearance and to save face with the good old boys at the barber shop succeeds only in proving that he has been beaten up by the lawyer himself."

"Indubitably, Professor," I expostulated. "The brute who carries Temple out of the Grotto and who later appears arrogantly 'sitting on his spine' again at the trial would doubtlessly make short work out of the rotund and unctuous Snopes."

Wiping his hands on his smudged long white apron, Mo McAinsh strolled toward our table. "Anything I can get for you guys? Has all of this palaver worked up some thirsts?"

"How about cold drinks, guys?" I asked cheerfully. "I could use a Diet Coke, Mo."

Augie and Pete ordered a Sprite and a Coke respectively, and when Mo brought our beverages Augie asked our host, "Have we overstayed our welcome, Mister Tavern Keeper? Should we vacate this choice table at your roadside inn?"

"Hell, stay around the clock if you want to, Augie. Having classy guys like you three in my place is good for the public image of Story's. You can help to bring in the carriage trade and keep the riff-raff out. Enjoy your co-colas."

Augie smiled as Mo headed for the kitchen. "I should have known better than to ask. Now, let's see; where were we. . . ."

"Let's look at the chronology again, Augie," I replied.

"Right, Speck. Here Cleanth Brooks helps us again. The beating of Snopes probably occurs in Memphis sometime during the day on Monday, June seventeenth, since Snopes seeks assistance from a dentist in Jefferson on Tuesday the eighteenth and at the time he already has a black eye and a bandaged nose. With the trial due to open on Thursday, the Memphis lawyer could feel safe in spurning Snopes's requests for a promised hundred dollars and in pounding him into humiliating submission. Likely the lawyer beats up Snopes out of contempt, tossing to him an insulting ten per cent of the agreed payment. But there is probably another reason for the beating, don't you think, Pete?"

Our young friend bounced up and began to pace among the tables at the rear of the cafe, apparently elated now to be a participant in and not mostly an auditor of this literary investigation. "Sure, Detective Dupin. The Memphis lawyer also appears to be furnishing Snopes with a warning to keep his mouth shut or to suffer even more painful consequences. After all, look what poor Red receives when Popeye gets upset with him: a bullet hole in the forehead," Pete proclaimed.

"An astute deduction, Pete," replied Augie. "And look at page two-sixty-six again. In his diatribe at the barber shop Clarence allows his mouth to run too much before the barber challenges the obviously preposterous story: '"What was you trying to sell to that car when it run over you?"' Snopes realizes that he has exhibited diarrhea of the mouth, and before he reveals any more dangerous information he quickly sidesteps with the words, '"Have a cigar."'"

"One more point here, Pete, and then we can close up literary shop for the afternoon," I interjected. "If I may, Monsieur Dupin?"

"Most definitely, Doctor, since you noticed this bit of evidence before I did. Let me stress again, Pete, that our solution to this puzzle in *Sanctuary* has been a dual activity, not a one-man show. Actually, I should say that it has been a three-way collaborative enterprise, since you raised the question in the first place and then have filled in some necessary info for us at places along the way."

"Thank you, Captain, and Pete and I will certainly not quibble with your overly generous attributions of credit," I said. "But let me finish here, before Mo does grow weary of us and bounce us out into the street. Pete, here is what finally convinces me that the lawyer has himself beaten up Snopes at least in part as a warning—'dire threat' might be a more accurate term—to stay out of the way after Monday, June seventeenth. The evidence is the eventual conspicuous absence of Snopes. The novel contains no reference to any appearance by Snopes at the trial. He disappears from the book after his oration in the barber shop, not again contacting Benbow, Graham, the Memphis lawyer, or, presumably, anyone else.

"As you know, Pete," I continued, "Snopes is the state senator from Yoknapatawpha County, and Goodwin's trial has aroused intense interest throughout northern Mississippi. Also, he has played a devious but crucial role in the case itself, and for such a gossipy self-adulator as Snopes to pass up a chance at seeking political gain from the publicity surrounding the trial suggests strongly that he has been ordered to stay away and to keep his chronically blabbing mouth clamped tightly shut."

Cesar Auguste Dupin V finished the argument. "And that command has been underscored with a few well-placed blows from the fists of the Jewish lawyer from Memphis."

"Yes, yes, yes," Pete shouted, leaning like a grizzly bear over the table to hug first Augie and then me. "Gentlemen, I can't thank you enough. Now I must hurry off to my dreaded committee meeting, but you will send me that outline, right, Captain? I can't wait to tell my Faulkner class all about this solution. Goodness knows that we need some relief from *The Bear* before we start *The Sound and the Fury*. Say...."

I looked at Augie, and his countenance displayed the same look of panic that was on mine. "Let's wait a while before we tackle another of these mind-stretching volumes, Pete. After a respite, perhaps C. Auguste Dupin, ratiocinist, and his faithful, self-effacing companion will be ready to dive again into Faulkner," I entreated.

Agreeing unanimously with this premise, and gathering all of our pads, books, and pens, we three sleuths walked to the cash register at the front of Story's, where Pete leaped past Augie and me and had paid for our food and drinks before we could stop him. As we were saying our goodbyes at the door, Pete was agreeably surprised to encounter his close friend Maxwell Talley, Ph.D. in psychology, the youthful and recently appointed director of the undergraduate counseling service at Moffatt College. Copious brown curls drooping across his creased forehead, Dr. Talley presented the picture of dejection.

"Hey, Max, old buddy, why the downcast look, and what are you doing at Story's at—a glance at his watch—"two-fifteen?" was Pete's inquisitive statement.

"Hi, Pete. I need to fall into a booth here, swig down a large, icy Doctor Pepper, and feel sorry for myself," Talley said mournfully in reply.

Pete graciously performed the introductions, and Max cheered up slightly. "I'll summarize quickly my experience of an hour ago, and perhaps then you will understand why I'm pouting. I just had my professional self-image damaged, if not shattered."

"What? Do you mean as a head shrinker?" yelped Pete.

"Yeah, you could say that," replied Talley. "Remember Deanne Cogburn, the young mother who recently enrolled as a special student at Moffatt?"

I jumped into the conversation. "Doctor Talley, Captain Dupree and I both know the former Deanne Forbush and admire her for holding up so courageously after the death of her husband in the Persian Gulf War."

"All right, Doctor Watkins," replied Max, "so you must also know that she recently married Tybalt Cogburn, the widower and prominent planter who owns that huge spread along the Churchill east of town."

"Yes, Doctor Talley," said Augie, "and we also know that Ty has been wonderful to Deanne's two children, although he has grandchildren who are older than those young Forbush boys."

"All true, gentlemen, but lately at school Deanne has appeared, to her teachers and fellow students alike, to be depressed—seriously depressed. So hotshot counselor that I am, I decided that I should drop in on her and—Voila!—I would magically solve all of her problems."

"So you went out to Cogburn Farms, Max?" asked Pete.

"Right, and Deanne was not very glad to see me. After some small talk, I assured young Mrs. Cogburn that I was a crackerjack counselor and that she should tell me what was making her so sad. She refused to discuss the matter, and foolishly I pressed the issue. Finally, she mashed her cigarette into the ash tray, looked me straight in the eye, and asked, 'Doctor Talley, do you know my husband?' I assured her that I did, and she leaned back on the couch, 'Look at him, look at me, and enough said. He is seventy-eight, and I'm thirty-one. I am very grateful to him and do care for him in an affectionate way, but. . . .' Her voice trailed off. Dolt that I am, I continued to press. 'Please, Mrs. Cogburn, spell out your problem,' I insisted, trying to put into practice some of the theories that I recently learned in graduate school. 'You will feel better if we both can define the troublesome issue clearly.' 'Okay,' Deanne snapped back. 'I'll put it this way, Doctor Know-It-All Shrink. Have you ever tried to put a marshmallow into a piggy bank?'"

Chapter Three

The Case of Ms. Quentin's Second-Story Job in *The Sound and the Fury*

Campus Shaft

"OH MY GAWD! I can't believe this! Gee Whiz! OOOO-WEEE!"

These mildly furious sounds of dismay ricocheted off the undecorated beige walls, the perforated ceiling panels, and the dark red tile floors of the wide hallway separating rows of classrooms and offices on the third level of Shoemaker Humanities Hall at Moffatt College. At 9:00 a.m. on Friday, May 19, the last class day of the spring semester, C. Augustus Dupree, apprentice literary detective, and yours truly, junior apprentice assistant sleuth, gazed in bewilderment at each other as we attempted in vain to discover a passageway into the faculty office of our new friend, Dr. Peter Prefont, whose hyperactive larynx was the source of the enigmatic shouts that echoed along the lengthy corridor, out a propped-open double window, and across the lush lawns, verdant flower beds, and spraying fountains of the park-like Moffatt campus. In frustration I waved first my left arm toward the interior of the building, and then my right in the direction of the window, and addressed my companion.

"Augie, how do we get into Pete's office? When he telephoned me last week and invited me to visit his Faulkner class, he said to meet him on the third floor of Shoemaker Hall. This index card taped to the wall proclaims the presence of the office of"—here I read aloud—"'Peter E. Prefont, Assistant Professor of English,' but all that I can see are the sliding doors to this freight elevator." With a loud "blap!" I slapped my open palm on the facing of the metal door, and then I pivoted to my left. "And here is the door to a classroom, but golly dang it all, I see no office anywhere along this hallway."

Augie carefully surveyed our location and agreed with me. "Speck, I have been sitting in on Pete's Faulkner class for two weeks now, but this is the first time that I have tried to find his office. The class meets on the first floor, and customarily I attend the class and then make myself scarce, since Pete is always busy afterward talking with students about reading assignments and papers."

"WHOA! How did he ever come up with this topic? GEEZ!"

Pete's bellows again surrounded us, and our dual consternation grew. The words seemed to emanate from the elevator shaft, but I still couldn't believe that Pete, even as junior in rank as he was, would be assigned a clanking, ponderously slow freight elevator as his on-campus headquarters. Five minutes earlier Augie and I had pushed the available button and summoned the elevator from below. Just as we had expected, the compartment was empty. Quite dusty, but empty.

Even though a literature class was in session in the adjacent classroom—we could hear the muffled sounds of a discussion through the closed door into the hallway—Augie and I had just about decided to interrupt the scholarly proceedings by knocking and entering when the two metal sliding doors to the freight elevator creaked, banged, and separated, revealing the grinning presence of the evasive Professor Prefont his own self.

"Doctor Watkins and Captain Dupree, I presume. Gentlemen, a hearty good morning to you, and welcome to my inner sanctum."

Holding his right index finger on the "open-door" button of the control panel, Pete made a half-turn to his left and flapped his left arm in the direction of the elevator compartment's opposite side, which turned out to be two separating metal doors matching the ones facing the hallway. Pete pushed another button, and the interior elevator doors parted, revealing a tiny room with one casement window high within the opposite wall and a solitary door to the left that apparently led into the neighboring classroom.

"Come in, if you please. *Entrez vous*, silver plate. See where the Prefont phantom hides out between classes, fellas. I'm really glad that you could rearrange your office schedule and be able to come here today, Doctor Speck."

Rotating our heads so that we could orient ourselves to these bizarre surroundings, Augie and I walked gingerly on the balls of our feet from the hallway through the freight elevator and into Pete's hideout. From the high ceiling one long fluorescent tube provided ample illumination. A battered gray-metal desk sat shoved against the wall featuring the solitary small window. Next to the desk squatted a portable table holding a Macintosh IIsi personal computer, color monitor, and laser printer. The ancient desk was littered with books, journals, several piles of student essays, and a forlorn, scarred black rotary telephone. Completing Pete's sparse furnishings and homey touches were a faded blue cushioned chair resting on rollers and missing the right arm rest, two metal folding chairs, a black-and-white Umbro soccer ball on the floor, and two pictures on the west wall: a framed photograph of the poet William Carlos Williams (identified by an attached typed card), and a reproduction of William Faulkner's map of the author's own Yoknapatawpha County. The air was heavy with the commingling odors of floor wax, bathroom disinfectant, and recently sprayed pesticide.

"Did you guys have any trouble finding me?" Pete asked, following us into his very private quarters. "Augie, you have been coming to my class, and Speck, you went to school here at Moffatt, so I thought that you both would be able to make your ways to my Spartan cell."

Impetuous as always, I was the first to respond. "Pete, how in heaven's name did you wind up being housed—or is the trendy term 'officed?'—behind an elevator shaft? Did you alienate your departmental chairman and get sentenced to solitary confinement?"

"No, Speck, no. Actually, I chose to set up shop here, at least for this my first year. On your way in, did you observe the renovations underway down on the first and second floors?"

Augie and I both nodded in confirmation, and Pete continued.

"Our department is really pinched for office space right now, and rather than invading a senior colleague's treasured solitude by doubling up with him—or her—for the year, as some of my peers have done, I was happy to move into this hidden room which formerly served as a custodial storage area. If a class is in session out here"—Pete feigned a tap on the office's only door, a wood-framed one featuring a heavy brass knob—"I enter or exit through the elevator. For temporary digs, these quarters are just fine. If I'm working on class preparations, grading, or research, I stand little chance of being disturbed here. Now, sit down, friends, and thank you for coming."

Augie and I each hesitantly chose a metal folding chair, and Pete resumed speaking, this time from a perch on the only bare corner of his waste dump of a desk.

"As you know, this is a special day. We wind up class sessions at Moffatt today, and my Faulkner students are supposed to appear at ten o'clock armed with any lingering questions about *The Sound and the Fury*. Augie, or Monsieur Dupin, I am honored that you have attended class for the past two weeks. I feel pretty good about how the young Faulkner fans have made some sense out of this complex and difficult book."

Augie leaned back in his metal chair and smiled graciously. "Your explanations during the first three class meetings were especially helpful to me, Pete. The Benjy section became much more comprehensible when you put on the blackboard your chart specifying the sixteen different levels of time in the first part of the novel."

Unable to sit quietly even for a moment, I interrupted at this point. "Augie took careful notes and then last weekend explained the Benjy section to me, Pete. With your chart, I could make pretty good sense of what happens in the novel on that Saturday of Easter weekend, when Benjy, the mentally retarded Compson brother, is looked after by Luster, grandson of Dilsey, the Compsons' housekeeper."

"April seventh, 1928," Pete pointed out.

"Yes, thanks," I responded. "And also the days of Damuddy's death, Caddy's wedding, Benjy's castration. . . . Well, these events certainly have become clearer to me. I'm still struggling with the Quentin section, but again your charting of the events of June second, 1910, and of the principal memories and obsessions of Quentin Compson provides vital assistance to my befuddled brain."

Augie placed his right hand on my shoulder. "When we can find another free evening, Speck, I will catch you up to date on my notes from the latest class sessions during which Pete led his students and me through an analysis of the Jason section and the final one, sometimes called the Dilsey section, although it is not an interior monologue as are the three preceding it."

I let out a low whistle of appreciation. "Most impressive, Captain Dupree. You are now talking the talk as well as walking the walk—'interior monologue,' if you please. Whoo, whoo. Hubbah, hubbah!" I leaned to my left, puckered my lips, and repeatedly brushed the knuckles of my right hand against my shirt collar in abject admiration of my friend's newly acquired literary knowledge. Augie's response was typically self-effacing.

"Calm down, neighbor, or chill out, as Pete's students might say. Rest assured that I remain a humble retired policeman and no literary scholar, rookie or otherwise." Augie turned so that he faced Pete directly. "And, Professor, as a former professional snooper, I am certainly curious about the stimulus for those shouts of disbelief that Speck and I heard as we stood in the hallway and tried to find out where you were hiding."

Pete abruptly stood, spread his arms widely, and dropped his jaw in embarrassment. "Gentlemen! Do you mean that you could hear my yelps of dismay? If I was audible to you, then I must also have been disturbing my senior colleague Carter Modlin, who is, harumph, as we speak, teaching an American lit class next door."

The flimsy connecting door opened, and a leonine head graced with bounteous wavy silver hair poked through. "Right you are, Professor Prefont. Apparently you are still not acquainted with the volume of your very own personal vocal cords."

Dr. Modlin, with carefully trimmed silver moustache a-quiver, leaned into Pete's office, left hand on the knob and his right one placed halfway up the door frame. "We've talked before, Pete, about the noise level. . . ."

"Sorry, sorry, Carter," sputtered Pete. "I'll try to put a muffler on my mug. I certainly did not intend to interrupt your class."

Tastefully attired in a blue blazer with metallic gold buttons, a red-on-white pinstriped shirt, a tie of vivid red and blue amoeba-like shapes, tan slacks, and polished cordovan loafers, Modlin smiled graciously and nodded toward Augie and me. "I apologize for barging into your colloquy in here, Pete. I'm just now finishing up an analysis of Poe's 'The Cask of Amontillado' with my students, so please excuse me." As Modlin backed out of the doorway and began to pull the door toward himself, Pete threw out his right arm and leaped at his colleague. Modlin instinctively hopped back in alarm, releasing the door.

"Carter, you would be amazed to learn of the connection between Mister Edgar Allan Poe and"—Pete's arm flailed in the general direction of Augie—"my distinguished visitor here. Stop in after class, and I'll explain my cryptic reference."

Shaking his head and clucking indulgently, Modlin established eye contact first with me and then with Augie. "Gentlemen, I look forward to conversing with you in a short few minutes. Not for the first time has my youthful department mate baffled me with his words." The senior professor quietly withdrew and closed the door, and we remaining three squatters in Pete's cubicle could clearly hear Modlin through the thin wall as he walked toward his lectern, speaking while he strode, "Pardon the interlude, people. Please note on page fifteen-twenty-two the passage in which the chained Fortunato desperately suggests that Montresor's incarceration of him behind the nearly completed stone wall may possibly be an elaborate practical joke...."

Modlin's voice trailed off as a student asked a question, and Pete, eyes alight and fixed in a demonic gaze, whispered to Augie and me, "Does either of you remember Poe's authorial comments on the concept he called 'perverseness?'" Poe defined the term as, and I'm paraphrasing here, committing a vile or silly action solely because it is wrong to do so. Well, the imp of the perverse has just bitten me. I simply cannot resist this impulse."

I glanced at Augie and then stared intently at Pete. "What do you intend to do, Professor? Did you use the word 'perverse,' or did you say 'pervert?'"

As I sputtered my inane interrogatories, Augie leaned back in his metal chair, folded his arms across the chest area of his unbuttoned beige cardigan sweater, and informed me, "Speck, methinks that yon pedagogue plans a pernicious prank on his professorial pal."

Baring his teeth wolfishly, Pete placed his inverted left index finger vertically across his parted lips, tiptoed to the closed door, and hissed to us, "Listen. . . ."

Augie and I cocked our ears in the direction of Modlin's classroom as we heard the veteran teacher read from Poe's "Cask" story the taunts of the horrendously malicious Montresor, ending with this line: ""Yes," I said, "let us be gone."" We then bounced in alarm up from our chairs as Pete pounded the thin connecting door with both fists and shrieked the final anguished words of the chained, entombed, and hopelessly doomed Fortunato: ""FOR THE LOVE OF GOD, MONTRESOR!""

For the count of two beats, utter silence filled the office and the adjacent classroom, and then whoops of laughter, shouts of "All right! Neat trick! Nifty surprise, Doctor Modlin," and a loud groan emanating from near the door filled the auditory vacuum. We three eavesdroppers, one of our number the merry perpetrator himself, then heard a shout of "Class dismissed," and we inhaled collectively as Carter Modlin loomed menacingly in the doorway, his visage evoking images of Mount Vesuvius prior to eruption.

Pete stood in the middle of the cramped office, facing Modlin. Augie and I warily observed as young Pete meekly raised his right hand, palm outward, formed a "V" with his index and middle fingers, and, with head respectfully lowered and eyebrows raised, squeaked, "Peace, brother. Let the sun shine in."

Carter snorted like a champion stallion at the state fair, threw up both arms in resignation, and proclaimed, "Oh hell, Pete. You've pulled another successful prank at my expense. You know that I can't stay irritated at you for long. Doctor Watkins, hello. And this must be Captain Dupree, of whom Pete has so often spoken during the past couple of months."

Congenial handshakes followed, and, nosy soul that I am, I inquired about the meaning of Modlin's words "another successful prank." Carter lowered himself carefully into Pete's one-armed chair and exhaled expansively. "We older dudes in the English Department sometimes find Pistola Pete exasperating, but actually we are glad that he lurks among us," Carter said. "Peter provides us with a youthful exuberance that serves to moderate our middle-aged stodginess. Why, only last week he sneaked into my classroom some ten minutes before I was to begin teaching *The Scarlet Letter* and wrote two statements on the blackboard, much to the malicious delight of my students."

Carter yanked a legal pad from the trash pile on Pete's desk, scribbled hastily on the top piece of paper, and held up the results for Augie and me to read:

Hester Prynne was a woman of sin.
She got her "A" the easy way.

Famous Misspellings
Hester Prynne has committed the sin of
adultery for which she is PUBICLY
condemned.

Carter continued: "And then Pete pulled a similar trick on our colleague Dottie Campbell by writing this question and answer on the board in Dottie's classroom just prior to a session of her course in Southern literature." Carter displayed a second piece of paper:

Famous Misspellings, the Sequel

What literary award did Harper Lee win for To Kill a Mockingbird?

The Pullet Surprise

Carter then raised his right arm and pointed his index finger directly at Pete's nose. "But the day that he most seriously disrupted my class—until moments ago, of course—AHEM!"

Pete wedged his hirsute head beneath his left arm pit as Carter continued his recitation. "That day has to be this past Monday, when he threw open my classroom door in the midst of my session on Poe's "The Raven" and shouted out this question: 'What two great American poets married their young teenaged cousins?' Answers, Doctor or Captain?"

Augie glanced at me, shrugged, and replied, "Well, Poe, of course. But I am stumped on the other one. Speck?"

"I have no clue, neighbor. Pete, is there really such a poet?"

Our host hopped up from his precarious perch on the corner of his desk, began dancing energetically to an imagined rock-and-roll beat in the office's restricted space, threw his head back, thrust out both arms, and began moving his fingers rapidly in a funky simulation of a piano player in full-tilt action. When he quickly turned around and bounced his posterior on the invisible keyboard, Augie and I shouted in unison, "Jerry Lee Lewis!" Augie guffawed, I shouted, "Aww, wow; what a trick question," and Carter chortled clamorously.

"It's gratifying to be in the presence of some new butts for Pete's jokes, if you will pardon my figure of speech, gentlemen. But now you may possibly understand why some of us teachers at dear old Moffatt College behave in a cautious manner around unsaintly Peter here."

Augie glanced at his wristwatch and spoke to Pete. "It's almost time for Faulkner class, Professor Pete. But could you take a moment and explain those brash, echoing shouts, about which we inquired several minutes ago, back before you ruined Doctor Modlin's day once more? I am still insatiably curious."

Obligingly, Pete approached his desk, shoved aside some books stacked haphazardly in the semblance of a pile, and pointed to an unearthed student essay. "Monsieur Dupin, please read the title of this classification paper that I received yesterday from a student in my freshman writing course."

Augie leaned over the desk, read silently, emitted a deep, booming "Haw, haw, haw," shook his head gleefully, and announced to Carter and me the title in question:

> Who Put the "Art" in "Fart?": The
> Taxonomy of Human Flatulence

Chortles, snorts, guffaws, and snuffles cascaded around the small office. "Now I can understand your vocal reactions, Pete," sniffed Augie. "But what about the contents of the essay?"

Pete shook his head resignedly. "I almost couldn't force myself to read past the title page, Augie. The introductory question in the title is too cutesy keen, but admittedly this student does use punctuation correctly in his title. However, the presence of the colon signifies an attempt to imitate stuffy academic title structure, and I have warned my students to avoid colons in titles. How about 'taxonomy?' Does anybody want to disagree with my presumption that this writer owns a well-thumbed thesaurus?"

Augie intervened. "We heard subsequent shouts from you, Pete. Were they elicited by this paper, or by another one perhaps?"

"Oh, this one, Captain, definitely this artsy-fartsy one. Here, let me find the thesis sentence...." Pete flipped over the title page and read from the end of the first paragraph. "'Despite the enormous variations in the expellers of intestinal gas and in the gases themselves expelled, the vast majority of eructations of the posterior'—thesaurus again—'can be classified into four groups, each one distinguished by a clearly identifiable sound: the toot poot, the tallyho poot, the fizz fuzz, and the rattler.'"

More spasms of laughter enveloped the room, and wheezily I inquired of Pete, "What grade did this paper earn, Professor? That structure sounds plausible to me."

Pete tossed the paper back into the maelstrom on his desk and replied, "I agree that the categories are logical and clearly defined. Probably the paper will earn an 'A' or 'A-,' if the grammar and mechanics are correct. But I probably should design my assignments to include more restrictions. . . ."

"Oh hell, Pete, kick back and enjoy this student's ingenuity," admonished Modlin. "This is the most highly entertained I have been by a basic composition paper in twenty years. Now, may I shift the subject, fellows? Earlier did I hear Pete call you 'Dupin' rather than 'Dupree,' Captain?"

We three nascent Faulkner sleuths looked at one another, and I took the bait. "Let's amble on downstairs to Pete's Faulkner class. Walk along with us, Carter, and I'll explain en route the puzzle of the nomenclature. You see, Augie's original family name in France is actually 'Dupin,' and when his ancestor arrived in New Orleans in 1905. . . ."

Augie fell into line behind Carter and me as we walked through the classroom and into the hallway, and Pete, juggling legal pads, ball-point pens, two copies of *The Sound and the Fury*, note cards, and several books of Faulkner criticism, became our short academic train's very own too-loose caboose.

Blackboard Jumble

Thirty minutes later, in classroom 112 of Shoemaker Hall, Professor Prefont worked rapidly to field inquiries, resolve problems, and ease students' anxieties as the final Faulkner class of the semester ran short of time. "Okay, folks," Pete intoned, "please remember that the third examination of the term is scheduled for next Tuesday afternoon at two and that the exam will cover ONLY *Spotted Horses, Old Man, The Bear,* and *The Sound and the Fury*, and not all of the other Faulkner novels that we have studied during this term. This exam is not a comprehensive final."

Augie and I sat along the west wall of the classroom, our chairs located just below a line of colorful posters advertising a series of past "Faulkner and Yoknapatawpha Conferences" held on the campus of the University of Mississippi in Oxford. We could look above us and view a portrait of a young, brown-haired William Faulkner attired in a shabby tweed sport coat, holding a burning cigarette, and staring intently forward in a coldly arrogant manner. Another poster showed a distant view of the town of Oxford squatting supremely on its hill, crowned with swirling clouds in a painting style reminiscent of El Greco's. Also affixed to the wall were two precise depictions of the Lafayette County Courthouse and its surrounding edifices on the historic Oxford town square, one perspective looking northward toward the Confederate statue facing forever southward, and the other approaching the square from the opposite direction.

From our adjacent seats placed a few feet to the west of the desks of the youthful undergraduates in Pete's class, we could defer to our professor's suzerainty while also allowing sociologically correct space to Moffatt's emissaries to Generation X. Our proximity to the students, however, also on this day allowed us to overhear certain muttered comments not audible to the standing and more distant Professor Prefont. Just as Pete wound up his reminder about the third exam, a shaggy young man on the front row leaned toward the student on his right and responded, "Yeah, right. ONLY those four novels. He might as well have said, 'Define the universe and provide four examples.'"

Augie and I were exchanging amused smiles when Pete's voice boomed in our direction. "Robby, do you have a question? You seemed to be talking to Davey there."

The trapped student, Robert Brockhagen, threw back his head in startled response. "No, Doctor Prefont. I was just asking Big Dee here about when we would be getting together to study for your exam."

Pete's skeptical demeanor revealed his intuitive grasp of student Robby's more likely subject of close conversation, and then the professor slowly grinned. "Mister Brockhagen, I thought that perhaps you and Davey Titus were conjuring up another definition similar to the one that you shared with this class last week when I asked for a definition of the term 'oxymoron.' Remember your collaborative answer? 'A pimple cream for dumb people?'"

Both Mister B. and Mister T. nodded and laughed self-consciously. Then Titus, attired in khaki shorts, tattered Nikes (sans socks), a Murryville Mules baseball cap with the bill in the back, and a T-shirt featuring the words "With Schizophrenia You Are Never Alone—Moffatt Psych Club," raised his hand, was acknowledged by Pete, and changed the subject. "I have a question about *The Sound and the Fury*, Doctor Prefont. May I ask it now?"

"Please proceed, Davey," replied Pete. "Twenty minutes remain before the end of the class period. Ask away."

Davey opened his Vintage International Edition of *The Sound and the Fury* to a page near the end of the novel. "On Wednesday we talked about Quentin's—I mean the female Quentin here—about her theft of Jason Compson's hoard of money, some of which rightfully belongs to her."

Pete waved his left hand at Titus. "Right, Davey. Where are you in the book?"

"Oh yeah, sorry," responded the student. "Page two-seventy-six—no, two-seventy-seven. Jason is trying to find out how his bedroom window got broken."

Pete stared at his copy of *The Sound and the Fury*. "Yes, Davey; I have the passage now." Augie and I had also opened our copies of the novel, as had all of the students in the classroom except two. One of the malingerers slouched backward in his chair, with eyes closed, mouth widely agape, and intermittent snoring sounds spasmodically escaping his nasal passages. The other stared intently at a garishly striped yellow-and-black copy of *Cliff's Notes* in her lap.

Titus resumed his interrogatory. "When does Quentin break into her Uncle Jason's room and steal the money? How does she get away with the crime, if we can call what she does a crime? After all, she rightfully takes back the money that her mother has been sending to her, as well as cash earned and saved by Jason the total jerk."

Muffy Spiffington III, the coed who was reading *Cliff's Notes*, quickly looked up and said quite loudly, "It says right here that Jason not only steals money from Quentin but also that he criticizes her constantly, refuses to spend much money on clothes or makeup for her, threatens her with bodily harm, and calls her a 'bitch' several times." Muffy bleated shrilly, "Jason is a complete P I G, SWINE, I mean, like, gag me to the max. Barf all over him, puh-leeze."

Pete waved his long right arm in Muffy's direction. "*Cliff's* strikes again. Right you are, Muffy, although perhaps a bit too graphic. Go ahead, Davey."

"That's all, Doctor Prefont, except to ask if possibly Jason could be in the house when Quentin breaks into his room."

Pete bobbed his head as he looked first at the novel and then at Davey. "We know that Jason discovers the broken window on Sunday morning, April eighth, 1928—Easter of that year. So Quentin must have broken in the night before. Yes —let's see . . . go back to . . . page seventy-four."

Pages ruffled around the classroom. Augie and I flipped in our books back to the first section of the novel, the interior monologue familiarly known as the "Benjy section."

Pete resumed. "Here Benjy narrates how he and Luster watch Quentin climb out of her window, descend the adjacent pear tree, and move away across the lawn. So this must be her getaway. But as to the question of exactly when the break-in occurs on that Saturday evening—uhh, well, I don't know that there are enough facts in the book to let us determine that answer. Does anyone else have any thoughts here?"

Thirty pairs of eyes looked up from books and stared directly into the ocular orbs of Professor Pete. Their collective gaze communicated clearly the following thought: "Don't ask US. YOU are the teacher. You are PAID to know the answers to such questions."

As Pete gradually discerned from the visages of the students the consensus of their thoughts, he became even more flustered. "Uhh, I can look into this question. Tell you what, folks. Since this is the final day of class, and I can't give you a worthwhile answer, Davey, then all of you may assume that I will not ask this question on the upcoming exam."

Thirty heads nodded in unison, thirty pairs of hands closed copies of *The Sound and the Fury*, and thirty spines nestled comfortably backward into desk-chairs. However, Titus voiced one final petition. "Captain Dupree, what do you think? Doctor Prefont has told us how you solved the crime puzzles in *Sanctuary*. How about this one? It does involve a type of crime, right? In Memphis did you ever investigate burglaries?"

Augie nodded once, in recognition of the recognition. "Mister Titus, I can't answer your questions now, except to acknowledge that I did spend some time working in the Burglary Division of the Memphis Police Department and that, because of your queries to Professor Prefont"—Augie inclined his head to the right and in the direction of our presiding pedagogue—"I am becoming intrigued by this caper carried out by niece Quentin. Tell you what, young man." Augie leaned forward in his desk-chair. "Since I am blissfully retired and have nothing to do, with all day in which to do it—ahem—I will see if I can piece together some clues and reconstruct this break-in."

Davey smiled hugely, leaned to his right, stretched forward, and swung his raised right arm at Augie. "All right, Cap. Give me a high-five on that one. Thanks, man."

His instincts still keen, Augie quickly countered and was able to meet Titus's onrushing paw with his own right palm, and the resounding "Craaackkk" echoed throughout the room. The snoring student scholar, Cranford Slater, jumped out of his chair, snorted loudly, shouted "What the hell?," and with eyes flaring widely, thrashed and pumped both arms furiously. Two nearby members of Moffatt's basketball squads, Free-shot Phyllis Turner and Hoops Garrison, managed to subdue the Slate Man before he broke his own wrist or somebody else's jaw.

Pete quickly restored order to the tumult. "Captain Dupree, on behalf of the class I thank you for your willingness to help us again with a Faulknerian puzzle. But before you tackle this project, let me look in the Faulkner scholarship in order to determine if someone else has solved the problem and written an article or book chapter about it. Students, if you are interested in the solution, whether it comes from the existing scholarship or from the detective work of Captain Dupree. . . ."

Augie interrupted with a raised arm and an out-turned palm. "Professor, I can't promise results, as you know."

Pete bowed in Augie's direction. "Whatever you or I turn up, Captain, I will pass along to any student who will leave me a summertime postal or e-mail address. Fair enough?"

Murmurs of assent, the scribblings of pens, and the zippings of backpacks formed the mingled responses. Just as Robby Brockhagen was elevating his gluteus maximus in anticipation of Pete's dismissal of the students from their academic Alcatraz, a soft soprano voice overrode the myriad ritual shufflings of a class period's termination. "Doctor Prefont, I have one more question about the novel. Do we have time?"

Pete glanced at his watch. "Five minutes remain, Miriam. Will that be long enough?"

"Oh, yes sir," replied the coed, a diminutive brunette attired in pressed Guess jeans, a powder-blue T-shirt featuring gold trimming and a depiction of a mountain scene framed by the words "Yellowstone National Park," and double-sized spectacles with gold-flecked frames. "Perhaps Captain Dupree can tackle this problem while he is investigating Davey's question, because mine also seems to call for police or detective skills, and we didn't talk about it in class."

Pete spread his arms in a gesture of magnanimity. "Same promise, kiddos, with this question. Not to be on the exam. Go ahead, Miriam."

"Thanks, Doctor Prefont. My question comes out of Section Two of the novel, the Quentin section—Quentin the brother of Caddy, Jason, and Benjy, of course—not Quentin, the female who is named after her uncle." Miriam then looked inquisitively at Augie.

"Certainly, young woman," Augie replied, after looking at Pete and receiving an acquiescent nod from our class's peerless leader. "I'll give your question a try, again after Professor Prefont ransacks the existing Faulkner scholarship, although once more I can not promise results. Of course, I will employ my trusty partner here, the inimitable Doctor Watkins, as often as his busy schedule permits."

"Tallyho, Monsieur Dupin. Sure, I'll help, when I can. Oooops—sorry, Pete. I retract my initial figure of speech. Inside joke, students." I pivoted in my desk-chair toward the back of the classroom. "Miriam?"

"Thanks, Doctor Watkins. Quickly, here is my question. Where is Quentin when he commits suicide? When I first read Section Two, I assumed that he must kill himself somewhere near Harvard, where he attends college, or at least in Cambridge. But as I was looking back over *The Sound and the Fury* for the exam. . . ." Boos, hisses, and muttered admonishments such as "Bookworm," "Weenie," "Study jock," and "You organized nerd!" bombarded the unfortunately conscientious Miriam.

Pete quickly intervened. "Calm down, rabble-rousers. Ms. Littlejohn has the floor."

"Thanks, Doctor Prefont," responded a defiant Miriam, "but I pay no attention to dunderheads and vacuum brains who become instantly jealous in the presence of an authentic genius."

Catcalls and imprecations erupted, but Pete trumpeted, "ENOUGH! Hold thy tongues, miscreants. Insult each other on your own free time. Please finish up, Miriam."

"Well, that's about it, except to say that on my SUBSEQUENT readings"—at this point Ms. Littlejohn arose halfway from her desk-chair and arrogantly surveyed the hostile and tight-lipped faces of her peers—"of Section Two, Quentin appears to be out in the countryside somewhere when he finds the bridge over the Charles River from which apparently he later jumps. Does it actually matter where he is when he takes his own life?"

Listening intently to the coed, Augie finished his taking of notes, leaned back, and nodded graciously. "All right, Miriam. Once Doctor Watkins and I hear from Doctor Prefont, we will tackle this question as well."

"Captain Dupree, thank you very much," Pete added. "After class I will start making a list of books and articles in the Faulkner criticism that we will need to look into. And now, loyal students. . . ."

As Pete swung his attention rightward away from Augie and me and toward the waiting Moffatt undergrads, he jumped backward in surprise because most of the students were already in the act of hurriedly bustling past him on their ways to the exit doors. One macho male, Gregory "Bulldog" Gregg, had remained in the back of the classroom, raised a window, and pushed out a screen. With bare feet forward while he carried shoes and socks in his right hand, Bulldog stopped in the act of hopping from the window sill to the ground and shouted, "Yo, Pete. I am V. K. Ratliff, and you are the spotted horse's AAAASSSSs s s s." Gregg dropped toward the thick grass below just as Pete whizzed an eraser past his vanishing ear, and Faulkner class circa 1995 at Moffatt College, USA, came to its merciful end.

Take Me Out to the Mules' Game

During a heavily humid late evening on June 21, 1995, Principal Mary Alice Dupree, Mayor Julianna Watkins, and their errand-boy husbands were enjoying a relaxing visit to Barnett Stadium, baseball home field of the Class A Murryville Mules, a rookie-league farm team of the Saint Louis Cardinals. The summer air contained a faintly acrid aroma of essence of paper mill, compliments of the principal industry of Bleaksborough, twenty miles to the northwest on the Churchill River. Fortunately for us fans, the dominant scent in the ball park was that of hot buttered popcorn, the culinary staple of the Barnett concession stands. Contentedly enthroned on stadium seats along the third-base line, sipping Budweiser from paper cups, and munching on hot dogs or roasted peanuts, we four spectators speculated on which young ballplayers might eventually ascend the professional ladder to the parent club.

My wife Her Honor delicately extricated a smear of mustard from the corner of her mouth by using a wadded paper napkin. "Are any former Mules in Saint Louis this season?" she queried.

I waved my sloshing cup of Bud in distant tribute to the venerable Missouri city on the banks of Old Man River. "First in booze, first in shoes, and last in the National League. Saint Louis, what a town!"

Augie frowned and responded, "In the cellar this season only, Speck. And the Cards will soon be on their way to another pennant, I predict."

Mary Alice pointed with her half-eaten frankfurter bun to a row of seats about thirty feet to our right and behind the area in which we couples were double dating. "Isn't that Pete over there?" asked Madame Dupree. "I thought that he and Ellie were in Ohio."

Julianna answered, "I had lunch with Ellie in late May, after Moffatt's commencement day, and she did say that they would be gone for a couple of weeks. Now it appears that the Prefonts have found their way back to

Arkansas."

I joined in the conversation. "See there, he's spotted us and is headed this way, coming over from what my younger colleagues call the beer-drinking bleachers, where the original party animals all herd together. . . . Here he is now. Hello, Pete, and welcome back."

Youthful Doctor Prefont bounced down three concrete steps that were spotted with the remains of old chewing gum and plopped into the seat on my right. "Duprees! Watkinses! Baseball! Beer! Munchies! Tonight I am living right. It doesn't get any better than this! Well, howdy, and are you folks enjoying the game?"

Julianna replied, "Mostly we are visiting with each other and indulging in a change of pace from the daily grind, Pete. At least Speck and I are, since the Town Council can't annoy me out here, and your loyal ocular doc had to check his white coat, ophthalmoscope, and God complex at the ticket booth on the way into the ballpark."

"Hyar now," I retorted. "I become a fleshly Jehovah only on weekday mornings at eleven, please remember. Hey, Peter, are you back at work yet?"

"Not in the classroom, Doctor Speck, but I am doing some research on William Carlos Williams and"—here he leaned forward and gestured to Augie—"also on those lingering questions about *The Sound and the Fury*. Captain, have you had time to look at those photocopies of scholarship about niece Quentin and about her uncle Quentin, the ones that I sent to you in late May? As I told you over the phone, I found some helpful stuff on the female Quentin. But as far as I could tell, no published critic has attempted to reconstruct her burglary. Have you two tackled the problem yet?"

Augie and I exchanged cocky smiles. "Yes, Professor," replied Detective Dupree, "I believe that my trusty sidekick here and I are ready to talk with you about Quentin la femme. The other problem, the one centering on the death of the male Quentin, we are still investigating."

With my pudgy left arm I swatted Augie good-naturedly on his right shoulder, leaning behind the Mayor in order to be able to reach him. "What Augie really should say, Pete, is that we have not yet done diddly squat on Quentin of the masculine gender-rino. But we are prepared to lay some hea—vy news on you about Mizz Q. of the feminine persuasion."

"That is music to my earlobes, friends," boomed out Pete. "Shall we talk here? Or would you prefer to watch the game?"

At that instant Julianna launched herself straight up from the seat on my left, screamed "I GOT IT!," and with her bare left hand snatched an arcing foul ball out of the damp June air. Gleefully she held the ball aloft and displayed her prize to the nearby Mules' fans in the crowd. Cheers swirled and washed in waves around her. "Good hands, Mayor!" "Way to spear that tater, Watkins!" "Sign her to a no-cut contract, Mules!" "You would do anything for publicity, Mayor Dub-ya!" Julianna beamed, sparkled, and glowed. With her chin elevated imperially and her eyes held steady, she slowly surveyed her nearest seat mates. "I coulda been a star," she intoned, "if the scouts had only seen me in my prime."

Pete shook my wife's proffered right hand and stated, "My question has been answered, genial companions. Tonight this game takes precedence. Shall we set a later time for a *Sound and Fury* session? How about at my apartment?"

"Okay with me, Pete," I replied. "Augie?" A nod from the Captain confirmed the choice of place. I continued, "Will Ellie mind our invading her domestic tranquillity?"

Pete responded, "She is in Dallas at a soccer clinic this week, Speck, so I will bring home some pizza from Bruno's Italian Eatery and a couple of six packs of beer. Is this Friday okay?"

Augie and I enthusiastically agreed with the plan, Julianna and Mary Alice quickly decided to drive to Batesville on Friday in order to investigate a new outlet mall, and we all leaned back in our seats just as Scooter Harkey, the ace Mules shortstop, leaped upward and with outstretched glove caught a wicked, slicing line drive, landed on second base to double off a runner errantly headed to third, and quickly ran down and tagged a startled base runner from first, thus completing that rarest of fielding gems, an unassisted triple play.

When the resulting roar from the Mules' fans subsided, Julianna folded her arms across her chest and uttered contemptuously, "Just leave it to a jock male chauvinist pig to supersede MY great fielding play. HARRUMPH!"

As a nineteenth-century cynic is said to have remarked, "Politics ain't beanbag," but politics is, at its core, always a game of one-upmanship. Amen, and that's the old ball game for tonight, sports fans.

Mysteries of One Kind or Another

On Friday, June 23, I bade a cheerful farewell at the office to my final patient of the day, telephoned the medical exchange and asked to be reached via my pocket pager, drove my reliable Ford Explorer to Summit Avenue where Augie awaited me near the curb in front of his house, and arrived thirsty and hungry at Pete's pad three blocks from the Moffatt campus at precisely 7 p.m.

Ravenously eager to begin to have, as salesclerks universally chirp, a nice weekend, I startled Pete with my greeting as he answered my loud knock on the front door of his apartment. "Let the bachelor bash begin! Bring on the dancing girls! Huzzah, huzzah! PAR—TEEEEE!"

Wearing a faded red Adidas soccer T-shirt, khaki Duckhead shorts, and scruffy Reebok running shoes, Pete elevated his eyebrows and smiled in bemusement. He ignored fraternity-boy-on-the-loose and directed his commentary to the dignified Captain Dupree. "Let his wife and master skip town, and Doctor Spock—er, I mean Speck—immediately transmogrifies himself into a menace to sobriety, virginity, and tranquillity. Hose this dangerous maniac down, Mister Policeman, please."

Dressed casually but impeccably in a deep purple J. Crew pullover short-sleeved shirt and tan Docker slacks, Augie followed me into Pete's place. Carrying two copies of *The Sound and the Fury*, several legal pads, a package of note cards, and his blue "Detective" baseball cap, our ratiocinist surveyed his surroundings, set his cargo of miscellany on a handy coffee table, and responded. "Just give him a few cold beers, Professor, and he will change back into a drooling, harmless old booze hound. He is all blow and no show, but he's also a cutesy-pie, or so all of his blue-haired female patients think."

"Cease and desist, ye scoffing minions," I sniffed in retort. "You are merely jealous of my dynamic charisma. And where IS that pizza, Pete?" As I talked I tossed my Carolina-blue sport coat and unknotted pale pink tie onto a nearby chair. Pete's place smelled as spicily enticing as a bayside cafe in Naples.

Ushering us through the living room-den-library of his square four-room (plus bath) apartment, Pete seated Augie and me at his small dining table, served us tantalizing slices of Bruno's sausage-and-anchovy pizza, graced the banquet with cold bottles of Corona and Dos Equis, and informed us, between bites of chewy pizza and swigs of golden brew, that he had been conducting further research into commentary by critics about Faulkner's female character Quentin, daughter of Caddy Compson. Moreover, he had also been looking into the subject of William Faulkner and the author's personal fondness for detective and mystery narratives.

"Augie," Pete began, "I remember seeing on your den shelf copies of Faulkner's collection of detective stories, *Knight's Gambit*, and of his murder mystery, *Intruder in the Dust*."

"Right, Pete," was Augie's reply. "Until you and Speck snared me into our current wild-haired scheme, those were the only Faulkner books that I had read, cover to cover, anyway."

"I assume that you read them because of their inclusion in a category we could term 'mystery fiction?'" queried Pete.

"Correct again, Professor," came back Augie. I grunted my agreement through a rapidly masticating mouth brimming over with spicy pizza.

From his seat on a nearby kitchen stool, Pete slid out of a pile of scholarly debris on the table a thick, stapled stack of photocopied papers, which he waved in our general direction. "This article tells us that William Faulkner himself was quite a fan of works of mystery fiction. In his personal library he owned copies of detective stories or novels written by . . . Ta Dah! . . . the great Edgar Allan Poe himself, Wilkie Collins, Dashiell Hammett—with whom Faulkner was acquainted, by the way—Rex Stout, Ellery Queen, Agatha Christie, Dorothy Sayers, Georges Simenon, and John Dickson Carr. The renowned Faulkner scholar Joseph Blotner, in his definitive study of the life of the author"—at this point Pete, from a lower step of his stool, picked up and waved a thick beige book with the title *Faulkner: A Biography* on its maroon spine—"tells about Faulkner's work in 1944 on the screenplay for Raymond Chandler's major private-eye novel *The Big Sleep*. By the way, the resulting classic film of the same name became very successful with its stars Humphrey Bogart and Lauren Bacall."

Pete took a swig of Corona, exhaled contentedly, and continued. "And here are some other references in Blotner's biography that seem to me to lend legitimacy to our tentative investigations into mysteries, crimes, and sundry misdemeanors in Mister Faulkner's fiction."

With his left hand Pete whisked a single sheet of notebook paper from his stack and snapped it with his right middle finger. "Take heed of this list," he spoke in an imperative tone.

Augie and I continued to chew Bruno's finest culinary treat, gulp beer, burp, and sigh with satisfaction, silent expressions of homage to the creators of pizza and beer evident in our beatific demeanors.

Pete rambled onward. "When Faulkner was growing up in Oxford, and I quote, 'The members of the Faulkner family had enjoyed and exchanged mystery stories.' And here's more. In later years while in residence at Rowan Oak, Faulkner 'took Jill'—his daughter—quoting here, 'occasionally to mystery films at the early evening show on Saturdays.' Even later, when Jill was grown, I quote, 'He might take in a matinee at the Lyric'—a movie theatre just off the square in Oxford—quoting again, 'if a Western or a mystery was playing.' And, during a trip to Massachusetts in 1951, Faulkner checked in at the Wayside Inn, made famous by none other than Henry Wadsworth Longfellow, and, here I quote, 'stayed awake all night reading mystery stories.'"

Pete plopped down Blotner's book and his own note sheet, at the same time picking up another xeroxed piece of paper. "One final justification, my patient friends."

Pumping jaws and bouncing Adam's apples presented our only visible replies.

On an instructional roll, Pete forged ahead. "When Faulkner's screenwriting colleague from Hollywood, Albert I. Bezzerides, visited Faulkner in Oxford in July of 1947, the two men walked from Rowan Oak to the drugstore on the Oxford square, where Faulkner intended, quoting here, 'to exchange a stack of mysteries for a new stack,' end of quotation. Bezzerides asked Faulkner, quotation, '"Why do you read all of these damn mysteries?"'"

Pete stood and simulated the rapid beating of drum sticks on a tympani. "Mister William Faulkner, our Mississippi oracle and inspiration, replied with these words, ones which I believe provide validation for our forays into literary investigation. AHEM. Quoting Faulkner here, '"Bud, no matter what you write, it's a mystery of one kind or another."'"

With a smug smile of satisfaction plastered across his face, Pete leaned forward in his chair, grabbed a slice of pizza, with bared front fangs ripped a sizable chunk from it, and began to chew noisily. "Smack, smack, grind, grind, swallow, swallow, gulp, gulp."

"Whaddya think of those anecdotes, fellas?" Pete queried, his words muffled by cheese, dough, sausage, and anchovies. "If Sir William of Faulkner was such an avid fan of mysteries and detective novels, then we certainly can feel more fully justified in impersonating detectives as we read his books, right?"

"Ahem, Pete," I intervened, as I wiped tomato sauce from my chin with a paper napkin. "Please remember that one member of our illustrious trio IS an authentic detective and can also boast a prestigious pedigree in the profession of investigation."

Pete was quick to respond. "Of course, of course, Doctor. My groveling apologies, Monsieur Dupin, scion of Gallic ratiocinists. What I meant to convey was my inclusion of you, a genuine detective. . . ."

"Retired, please remember," interrupted Augie, as he set his bottle of Corona on a frayed cardboard coaster displaying the faint logo "Billy Carter Beer."

"Emeritus, then, if you wish, sir," continued Pete, barely pausing to inhale. "I designate the three of us all as amateur readers of Faulkner, but you, Captain, as our investigator extraordinaire."

Augie held up both of his arms, palms outward. "Flattery, when augmented by pizza and beer, will definitely persuade me to deliver on my end of the bargain, Pete. Are you ready for the tentative solutions that I have worked out and run past Speck, the ones centering on young Ms. Quentin's burglary?"

"Most definitely, astute sleuths," boomed out Pete. "Let's toss our paper plates in the trash can, take our beers with us, settle in here"—Pete pointed to his cluttered den and study area—"and, as they say in Arkansas, git down to bidness."

Risky Business at Twilight Time

Augie and Pete hauled their books and papers with them onto opposite ends of the Prefonts' bright orange couch, I cautiously settled into a mustard-colored Lazy-boy rocker-recliner, and Augie, placing his "Detective" cap firmly over his thick reddish-brown hair, launched into the evening's principal topic.

"If you will remember, Pete, the question from your student Davey Titus involves Quentin's theft of her Uncle Jason's hoard of money. Mister Titus essentially wanted you—and then me, assisted ably by my sidekick Speck—to reconstruct the crime, if possible, focusing principally on the questions of when Quentin carries out the theft and how she manages to perpetrate it and to escape discovery or apprehension. At least this is our understanding of Titus's question."

From his seat at the southern extremity of the orange couch Pete nodded in agreement. "That summary squares with my memory also, Captain. And did you repeat to your bespectacled associate here"—Pete waved his right arm in the direction of my Lazy-boy rocker and me-self—"our class discussion concerning the terms 'burglary' and 'robbery?'"

My turn to play butt-in-ski. "Most assuredly Augie did just that, Professor. Since Quentin forcibly enters Jason's locked and unoccupied room, breaks into his locked metal box, and steals cash money from it, her crime technically qualifies as a burglary. But Jason apparently considers Quentin's stealing of the money in his box to be a robbery, because in his outrage he believes that his niece has deprived him personally of his rightful and valuable property, even if the money is not taken directly from his personal control, as customarily occurs during a robbery."

With lowered head Pete read from his notes. "On at least three occasions Jason speaks of a robbery or of being robbed: on page two-eighty-four, when he telephones the sheriff; on three-oh-three, when he visits the sheriff's home; and on three-eleven, when he pursues Quentin and her accomplice, the show worker with the red tie, to the show's next stop in Mottson, before he loses track of them."

Augie took over again. "Correct. Unquestionably Jason believes that Quentin steals his very own precious money, even though we readers know that Jason has been stealing funds from his niece—sometimes as much as forty or fifty dollars per month, money sent to Quentin by her mother Caddy—for most of Quentin's seventeen years. So we can categorize the crime as partly a vengeful burglary and partly an act of justifiable restitution."

I piped up. "And as is typical in Faulkner's fiction, the author does not narrate the central episode—the burglary itself—but only the events leading up to it, and also its aftermath."

Unable to remain ensconced on his cushy couch, Pete hopped up and began his compulsive pedagogical pacing. "Yes, Speck, yes. After Titus asked his questions on the final day of Faulkner class, I looked back at *The Sound and the Fury* and realized the parallels between this episode and the one in *Sanctuary* that you tackled earlier, gentlemen. In both cases, Faulkner focuses the narration primarily upon the consequences of the seminal episode rather than upon the episode itself, and the author challenges the reader to fill in the narrative gaps by employing inference and supposition."

With his back erect and his arms locked straight and clamped on his knees, Augie stared intently at Pete and then at me. "In summary, my detective colleagues, we have before us a crime to reconstruct. Let us commence."

Augie leaned to his right and lifted a legal pad from the center cushion of the orange couch. "Once again, Pete, I have prepared an outline for you, and I will work from it. Satisfactory with you?"

In his circuit of the room Pete was just then passing the wide entryway into the kitchen. "You bet, Augie, yes-sirree-bob. Thankeee, thankeee, *merci, merci.*"

As I chuckled softly, Augie raised his right arm with palm rigidly outward and pronounced patiently, "Okay, Pete. First is the question of the timing of the crime. During your class session we quickly concluded that Quentin must conduct the break-in on Saturday night, April seventh, 1928. By the way, for convenience let's all agree to refer to this novel in some shortened way, okay? Any suggestions?

Pete said, "In Faulkner scholarship the standard abbreviation is TSAF." He pronounced the letters, "TEE, ESS, EH, EFF."

"That sounds good. Shall we adopt its use?" Augie asked.

Nods of assent came from Pete and me.

Augie resumed, "All right, then; TSAF it is. I began searching in TSAF for references to incidents occurring prior to that Saturday night, references that would help us determine whether Quentin might have planned her caper in advance."

Pete abruptly stopped walking and, with slumped shoulders and dangling arms, stared at Augie. "The question of advanced planning has never entered my dim brain, Augie. I guess that I have always assumed that Quentin, in a fit of desperation, saw her sole chance to take the money and took advantage of the opportunity."

I stood and in four strides placed myself alongside the professor. "You have described my own initial reaction, Pete. Now listen to a demonstration of the reason that Captain Dupree is a worthy descendant of C. Auguste Dupin, master ratiocinist, while you and I remain callow rookies in this business of sleuthing."

With an embarrassed smile and a gentle shake of his head, Augie replied, "Don't elevate me yet to the status of Sherlockdom, friend and neighbor. Pete, first I looked through the research materials on Quentin which you sent to me, and I discovered that two critics who write helpfully in other ways about Quentin both assume that her burglary is an act of impulse. One of these critics calls the crime 'unpremeditated.' However, evidence in the novel suggests that Quentin begins to plot the crime at least thirty hours in advance of her carrying it out with stealth and precision.

"On Friday, April sixth, during the noon hour, Quentin confronts Jason at her uncle's place of employment, the farmers' supply store on the Jefferson town square, and demands that he give to her the money that she is aware he has been stealing from her. During this conversation Quentin also hints that she especially needs money at this time for a particular purpose. Gentlemen, look in your copies of TSAF on page two-fourteen."

After I resumed my seat in the rocker-recliner, Pete and I rapidly complied, flipping quickly over to the designated pages and studiously following Augie's references to selected passages.

"Furious that Jason offers her only ten dollars out of what she knows must be a larger amount sent by her mother, Quentin pitifully pleads with her wicked uncle: '"Jason please please please. I've got to have some money. I've just got to. Give it to me, Jason. I'll do anything if you will."' When Jason demands that Quentin, quoting Jason here, '"Tell me what you've got to have money for,"' he becomes instantly aware that she will not tell him the truth. Here I quote again, this time from Jason's thoughts: 'I knew she was going to lie.' But when Quentin weakly replies that '"It's some money I owe"' to '"a girl. I borrowed some money from a girl,"' Jason assumes merely that Quentin has, quoting here, '"been charging things at stores again."' Throughout this heated conversation Jason fails to deduce that Quentin must already be scheming to run away and that she is desperate to possess all of the getaway cash that she can lay her hands on."

Pete waved his left arm. "I'm with you so far, Augie, but when does Quentin hook up with the red-benecked worker from the traveling street show?"

"Glad that you asked, Pete, because I wondered about that joining of forces myself. We know that Quentin has sneaked out of her bedroom window many times by descending the nearby pear tree, because Luster reports that he and Benjy have often observed her nocturnal escapes—page two-eighty-six. We can also conclude that at age seventeen Quentin has become sexually active and possibly even promiscuous, because on Saturday afternoon, April seventh, while searching for his lost quarter, the young Black man Luster finds a 'bright' metallic condom box beneath a bush near the pear tree and says to Mister Red Tie, quoting Luster here, "'I dont keep no track of them,'" with the plural pronoun clearly referring to Quentin's after-hours male companions—see page fifty. So it is not surprising that on Saturday night she runs away with an available and willing masculine accomplice.

"Quentin may have already established a liaison with Sir Red Tie when she begs Jason for money at noon on Friday, April sixth, because she would have had enough time to do so. The show tent is under construction during the interval earlier in the morning when Jason forcibly drives Quentin to school, and we cannot be certain if she attends school for all or only a part of the morning class schedule. Also, she often skips school and is in jeopardy with the school authorities for truancy; check on page one-eighty. Now, Mister Tie of Red first appears in the chronology of the novel at two-thirty on Friday afternoon when Jason sees him and Quentin both sneaking along a downtown alley. Perhaps Quentin forms an alliance with Sir Scarlet Pimp-ernel earlier in the day or between noon and two-thirty, but for certain by the afternoon she has linked up with a partner who offers her the hope of achieving her most cherished desire—escape from the bitter, claustrophobic Compson household and especially from Jason, crass champion bully and woman hater. To her new merger with the show worker she needs to supply only some ready cash."

Augie sat back on the couch and, adjusting his reading glasses, peered searchingly at Pete and me. "Are you two gentlemen comatose yet? Have I buried you in a blizzard of verbiage?"

Taking my cue, I rolled my head to the right as I closed my eyes, fetched up a rasping snore, and for my thespian pains received a wadded paper napkin squarely in my separated upper and lower choppers. Miraculously reviving, I joined Pete in encouraging Augie to proceed. Our host sweetened the offer with another round of Mexican brews, and Augie resumed his analysis.

"Quentin and the show worker spend the remainder of Friday afternoon together, because Jason futilely pursues them into the countryside north of Jefferson; see pages two-thirty-eight to two-forty-three. And Jason doesn't see Quentin again until the supper hour at the Compson house, as recounted on page two-fifty-seven. Also, Benjy interrupts Quentin and Red Tie while the two are together in the Compsons' yard swing on Saturday afternoon. During only these two periods of time—and they possibly could get together at other intervals on April sixth and seventh—Quentin and the Crimson Cravat would have ample time to plan for Quentin to run away when the street show leaves Jefferson after its Saturday night performance."

Listening intently, Pete halted his pacing, spun toward Augie, and clapped his hands. "ERGO——let us assume, compatriots, that with Quentin's motive established and her accomplice identified, all that our heroine now lacks is"—dramatic pause here—"an opportunity to boost the filthy lucre."

Augie smiled and announced, "To the hunt, gentlemen. On to the burglary itself."

At that instant the phone jangled, Pete hurried into his kitchen to answer it, and at our host's nod I reverted to my professional identity and took this call from the medical exchange. As I spoke at length with my patient, Brunhilde Brunthaver, concerning complications of her glaucoma, I could hear Pete and Augie laughing in the front room. When I returned to Faulkner Analysis Central, I politely inquired about the reason for the audible mirth.

Pete and Augie stood side by side in front of the apartment's picture window overlooking the second floor balcony and the asphalt parking lot below. Pete answered my query. "Our discussions of the Friday afternoon merry chase around the countryside indulged in by Mizz Q. and Mister R. T., along with the couple's tryst in the Compson swing on Saturday, have reminded Augie of an incident that occurred on the Moffatt campus this week."

"By all means let me in on the story," I requested of my colleagues. "We have broken our momentum here anyway, so let's take time out for a good old-fashioned Southern storyfest. First, however, I need to partake of your facility, Professor Pete. The old saying goes that nostalgia ain't what it used to be, and unfortunately neither is my aging bladder."

Possibly stimulated by my rapier-like witticism but more likely by the beer that they had also consumed, Augie and Pete in turn followed me to the water closet, and after we had all three resumed our established places on couch and recliner, Pete filled us in on background details. "As you know, Doctor Double-U, Moffatt College has no summer semester, but the campus facilities are available for use by various visiting groups of alumni, business and professional people, or high school students. For three days this week Moffatt was the site of a conference for two hundred and fifty gifted and talented secondary students from all over Arkansas. Augie?"

Our ratiocinist leaned back on the couch and smiled widely at the recent memory. "Speck, it seems that two of these brainy children, ones named Darla Dawn and Luke—both of them upcoming seniors but in high schools located at opposite corners of our state—met on Tuesday morning, became inseparable by Tuesday afternoon, and on Tuesday evening began giving the conference's staff fits by frequently disappearing during programs and seminars. A residence hall director found them in the bushes outside Sturm Hall at eight-thirty p.m. and admonished them, but twice on Wednesday they vanished again and were later found entwined with one another and oblivious to the outside world, once in the woods beside the running track and the other time in the basement of the painting and sculpture building. Despite ardent efforts to keep them separate, Darla Dawn and Luke managed to eat all of their meals together, speak to or look at no one else, and spend their meeting times sitting virtually in each other's laps."

"Sounds reminiscent of the togetherness enjoyed by Ms. Quentin and Sir

Red Tie, although their implied couplings in the novel take place offstage," I interjected.

Pete and Augie exchanged wry smiles, and Pete replied, "An apt choice of words, Speck, as you will soon realize. Continue, please Captain."

Augie sipped sedately from his bottle of Corona and resumed the narrative. "On Wednesday evening all of the conference's participants attended the showing of a film in Kimbrough Auditorium, and of course Darla and Luke sat on the back row and paid no attention to the screen. Their designated chaperone, Dionne Belmont, did become caught up in the film, however, and when she remembered to look over at our young star-crossed lovers, much to her dismay she discovered that their seats were empty."

Pete picked up the narrative here. "Dionne the erstwhile chaperone called Chevy Myers, our campus director of security, Chevy called Chief Buddy Cotham, and Buddy telephoned Augie for assistance, after a routine canvassing of the campus and nearby neighborhoods had turned up no trace of Luke and D. D. The lovebirds had no access to an automobile, so they had to be located somewhere nearby. Right, Monsieur Detective?"

"The conference staff had fruitlessly searched all of the customary lovers' trysting places on the campus," continued Augie, "but I remembered when the Watkinses, Prefonts, and Duprees had discussed my ancestor Dupin's sleuthing skills in 'The Purloined Letter,' and I decided to start my search within Kimbrough Auditorium itself. Consequently, I carried my flashlight and walked to the back of the building where a large garage door can be raised, or so Chevy Myers tells me, to allow deliveries of furniture, stage sets, or musical instruments. Noticing that the lock on the door had been jimmied and the door itself was elevated two inches from the concrete apron on which it should have been resting, I quietly lifted the door just high enough so that I could crawl under it.

"As I entered the darkened back hallway, surely enough I heard what seemed to be moans, gasps, and protestations of undying affection. Cupping my right palm loosely over the flashlight, I tiptoed down the hall to a small storage room, the door to which was slightly ajar. The sound effects of love in bloom became more distinct, so I slipped my left hand through the door, found by touch the light switch on the inside right wall, flipped it on, and asked in a stern voice, 'What's going on in here?'

"Darla Dawn shrieked, Luke shouted 'What the hell,' and as I stepped through the door I observed the young sweethearts frantically disentangling themselves from one another as they jumped up from an ancient sofa sporting numerous exposed springs. Neither of the two young people was wearing a stitch of any type of clothing."

I interrupted, "My goodness, Augie; were you not embarrassed by this skin show?"

"Yes, neighbor, I was, as well as being startled by their loud exclamations. I did have the presence of mind to spot a tattered blanket on a nearby stool and to toss it in Darla's direction, but I was not prepared for Luke's quick thinking and his own attempt to cover himself, so to speak."

Augie chuckled at the memory and continued his narrative. "'Wait, sir!' Luke shouted. 'It's not what you think! Darla and I went on the scheduled hike through the pine forest this afternoon, and we were just now getting around to checking each other for ticks.'"

"No wonder Luke was chosen for this gifted and talented program," I responded between wheezes of laughter.

"My reaction precisely, Speck," said Augie. "But Luke's brazen excuse was not sufficient to prevent the conference staff from telephoning his parents and those of Darla Dawn and then depositing Luke on the first Greyhound bus heading northwest while making certain that D. D. was aboard the next bus going southeast."

Pete's turn came to pipe up. "So you solved another mystery, Detective Dupin, honored sir. At least so far your consulting work for the Murryville

Police Department has not exposed you to any violence."

"Right you are, Professor," acknowledged Augie.

I interrupted at this point. "But Augie certainly has met some ingenious young miscreants, such as Rodger the Dodger Compton and now Lochinvar Luke and Darla Dawn, delicacy of the Delta. I sincerely hope that Darla's home life is happier than that of the unfortunate Ms. Quentin in TSAF. Shall we now attempt to reconstruct the burglary? What say ye, gentlemen?"

Pete immediately offered more beer, but Augie and I decided to switch to iced tea, since I was on medical call and the Captain adhered to a self-imposed limit of two brews in any one evening. Pete served us cold cans of Lipton with lemon flavoring, he himself swigged some Mountain Dew, and with slaked thirsts all around we tackled the interpretive problem before us.

From his seat on the orange couch Augie lifted a thick legal pad out of his pile of miscellany. Over the next several minutes he consulted it frequently. "Gentlemen, we must collect the few scanty clues to the burglary from scattered places in the monologues of Benjy and Jason, and from the novel's final section. Then our task is to reassemble these clues as logically and accurately as we can. When we do, the following scenario emerges.

"Early in the evening of Saturday April seventh, 1928, Luster and Benjy enter the library in the Compson house. Look on page sixty-one of TSAF. Since Luster turns on the light and then Benjy narrates that 'The windows went black,' the sun apparently has already begun to disappear and the time—in northern Mississippi, during early April—likely is between five-thirty and six-thirty p.m. Dilsey the housekeeper calls everyone to supper, and after Quentin comes downstairs and joins the rest of the family at the table she and Jason quarrel about her spending time with the man whom Jason condemns as '"that show fellow."' Look on page sixty-seven, fellows, and be prepared to flip to other parts of the novel."

Augie balanced his copy of TSAF in his left hand while he consulted his legal pad, which he held in place on his right knee. "The Compson family then commences eating supper, and soon Quentin, who is fed up with Jason's ceaseless tauntings of her and can no longer control her volatile temper, inadvertently discloses the central motive for the plans that she and Mister Red Tie earlier have hatched: *'I hate this house. I'm going to run away.'* Not taking her threat seriously, Jason criticizes her savagely, and then Quentin, prevented by Dilsey from throwing a water glass at Jason, shouts *'Goddam you'* at him twice and runs up the stairs."

Captain Dupree paused and looked over his reading glasses at his audience. "Any questions so far, fellows?"

Pete and I affirmed that we understood, agreed with our leader's analysis so far, and were eager to forge ahead. Augie graciously complied.

"Presumably Quentin breaks into Jason's locked room within the next sixty to ninety minutes, because sometime after supper Benjy goes to an empty upstairs room in the house, holds the slipper that once belonged to his beloved Caddy, and immediately is struck by his recurring sensory memory of his long-absent sister. Look on page seventy-two. *'She smelled like trees. In the corner it was dark, but I could see the window'*

"Luster's primary responsibility is taking care of Benjy, but for a period of several minutes after supper he loses track of his charge, finally finding Benjy in the unused room that Benjy has always associated with Caddy. *'Here you is, Luster said. . . . What you doing, off in here. I thought you done slipped back out doors. Aint you done enough moaning and slobbering today, without hiding off here in this empty room, mumbling and taking on.'* At some point during the time period when the Black young man is searching for Benjy, Luster encounters Quentin—possibly in the upstairs hallway, since we have no evidence that she descends the stairs after supper—and receives from Quentin the means by which he can achieve his coveted goal to attend the Saturday night performance of the traveling show. Here I quote again from page seventy-two: *'Look what I got. He showed it to me. You know where I got it. Miss Quentin give it to me. I knowed they couldn't keep me out.'"*

Staring intently at his copy of TSAF, Pete shot his right arm into the air, palm forward. "Hold it here please, Augie. To what does the pronoun 'it' refer?"

"Good question, Pete. I assume that Quentin gives Luster either a quarter, the price of admission to the show, or an actual ticket to the performance, one which Mister Red Tie certainly could have passed on to her. This gift is significant because it reveals that Quentin possesses at least a smidgen of her mother Caddy's legendary compassion and also that she hungers for revenge on Jason in any way that she can exact it. Remember that on Friday evening—check on page two-fifty-five—Jason sadistically burns two tickets to the show right in front of the pleading and then blubbering Luster."

As I reread to myself the specified passage, I suddenly blurted out, "What a gin-you-wine grade-A certified ASSHOLE Jason is. Pete, your student, Miss Muffy, was right on target when she called him a pig."

"Correct you are, Speck. Perhaps you and Muffy even owe an apology to swine everywhere for lumping them with Jason. And say—you may be interested to learn that William Faulkner himself despised Jason Compson the Fourth. Let's see, I have some notes on that topic. . . ."

Pete riffled through his class lecture note cards on TSAF, yanked one of them from the stack, and exclaimed, "Voila! Here we are . . . on Jason. . . . Faulkner regarded Jason Compson as, and I quote, 'the most vicious character in my opinion that I ever thought of . . . . To me [he] represented complete evil.' When a student at the University of Virginia asked Faulkner, quoting now, 'was Jason Compson . . . a bastard?' the author replied, "No. Not an actual one—only in behavior.' And when Cynthia Grenier conducted an interview in Paris with Faulkner in 1955, Faulkner told Grenier that his, quote, 'unfavorite character' was 'Jason. Jason Compson.'"

With his fingers and thumbs spread and forming a steeple in front of his nose and mouth, Augie had been listening quietly to Pete's recitation of scholarship. Dropping his arms to his knees, he spoke. "Thanks for the supporting commentary, Professor. You make even more convincing our commonly held assumption that Ms. Quentin is desperate, or even frantic, to escape the domination of her odious Uncle Jason. Now, let's return to the scenario."

I leaned back in the venerable recliner and raised the leg rest, Pete picked up his copy of the novel, and Augie once more perused his outline on the legal pad. "We are focusing on the period of time during which Quentin likely commits the burglary, the sixty-to-ninety-minute window of opportunity after supper and before the start of the Saturday night performance of the traveling street show. Look again at page seventy-two. After Luster gleefully brags to Benjy that Quentin has furnished Luster with the means to gain admittance to the show, Luster begins to lead Benjy to Benjy's bedroom, admonishing Benjy to get ready for an early bedtime so that Luster can depart for the show tent pitched nearby on a vacant lot just off the town square. Luster speaks: *'Come on here to bed, so I can get up there before it starts. I cant fool with you all night. Just let them horns toot the first toot and I done gone.'*"

Augie paused and looked first toward Pete on his right and then at me, limply sprawled as I was in the mustardish recliner directly across from the couch. The Captain spoke: "Let's talk about the location of rooms on the second floor, fellows. We know for certain that Benjy's room is adjacent to Quentin's, because after Luster and Benjy have entered Benjy's room the two males overhear a conversation between Quentin and her grandmother, Mrs. Compson, who of course is also Benjy's mother. Look on page seventy-three, once again in Benjy's interior monologue. *'Quentin, Mother said in the hall. What, Quentin said beyond the wall. We heard Mother lock the door.'* And this door must be the one leading from the hall into Quentin's room.

"The exact location of Jason's room is not discernible from evidence in the novel, but this room does appear to be some distance away from Quentin's, because on Sunday morning Mrs. Compson leaves Quentin's abandoned room and walks away from the stairs, quoting here from page two-eighty-three, 'on down the hall to another door'—Jason's. Also, on Friday night—check with me on page two-sixty-three—Jason passes his mother's room before going, as he narrates, 'on to my room,' another indication that Jason's room is along the hallway farther away from the stairs than is Quentin's. I stress the issue of location at this point as preface to our upcoming analysis of the break-in itself. But now let's return to the question of timing."

Augie flipped a page on his legal pad. "After Mrs. Compson locks in Quentin, the older woman says goodnight to Benjy and then leaves Benjy in the care of Luster. The young Black man helps Benjy to *'put my gown on,'* as Benjy narrates, and then Luster looks out the window, notifies Benjy *'Here she come,'* and both Benjy and Luster *'went to the window and looked out.'* Those quotations all come from page seventy-four. Next, as they have done several times in the past—refer to pages fifty and two-eighty-six for proof—Luster and Benjy then watch Quentin crawl out of her window, climb down the pear tree, and scurry off into the night. Benjy is again the narrator here, and he is unable to discern Quentin's identity in the dark. But Luster's use of the pronoun 'she' and Benjy's own specification of Quentin's window leave no doubt that Quentin is once more descending the handy pear tree on the way to another nocturnal ramble, this time one from which she never returns. Back to seventy-four, friends. *'It came out of Quentin's window and climbed across into the tree. We watched the tree shaking. The shaking went down the tree, then it came out and we watched it go away across the grass. Then we couldn't see it.'*"

Augie set aside the novel and resumed perusing his notes. "Since the traveling show moves on later that night to Mottson, the next town to the south, and since the show people presumably would want to allow their paying Jefferson customers to eat supper before coming to the show, the night's performance would likely begin no later than seven-thirty or eight o'clock, and we know that Luster still has time to arrive close to the time of the opening curtain as he helps Benjy prepare for an early bedtime." Augie reclaimed his copy of TSAF, opened it, and began, "From page seventy-four again: *'Come on, Luster said. There now. Hear them horns. You get in the bed while my foots behaves.'* Probably Luster is reacting to the trumpets, cornets, and trombones as they blare out the overture to the evening's program."

Raising his left index finger, Augie said, "Let me add one more piece to this time puzzle, guys, and then I will review my original hypothesis. Jason definitely spends the night in his own room—refer to page two-seventy-five—so we can be certain that Quentin carries out the burglary before Jason's bedtime. THEREFORE—Quentin must break into Jason's room through the window after supper, before the opening of the show, and during the interval of time when Benjy squats in the empty room holding the slipper while Luster searches for him. She must then re-enter her own room and be present when Mrs. Compson comes to lock her in, craftily making her grandmother believe that Quentin intends to stay in her bedroom for the duration of the night. After Mrs. Compson falls for the ruse and goes to her own room, Quentin is free to make her escape down the pear tree, carrying a substantial amount of cash with her."

Groaning and creaking, I lowered the leg rest, sat forward in the recliner, stretched my arms, and spoke up. "Let me relieve you for a couple of minutes, Mister Interlocutor. Pete, when Augie and I were reviewing his findings, I remembered that Davey Titus had also asked us to look into the whereabouts of Jason during the break-in. I undertook the task and discovered that the novel doesn't tell us Jason's location or locations during the approximate hour to hour-and-a-half between the end of supper and Quentin's clandestine departure down the pear tree with the coveted cash. However, I have concluded that Jason probably remains downstairs while Quentin steals his hoard.

"If you are willing to bear with me, I will cite commentary from the following pages: two-sixty-three; seventy and seventy-one; two-fifty-one and sixty-six; and two-fifty-four. The preponderance of the evidence appearing on these pages leans in the direction of Jason's being on the premises. Point one: the night before he had sat alone and smoked a cigar after supper, perhaps indicating a nightly pattern of behavior. Two: at Saturday's supper he does not mention plans to go back out during the evening. Three: he would not go back to work, since the farmers' supply store customarily closes before suppertime, and also he implies before Saturday supper that he is home for good from the store on that night. Four: he has no intention of attending the traveling show, even though he has tickets."

Pete arose from the couch, bowed stiffly in my direction, and applauded loudly. "Extraordinary thinking, my dear Watkins," he carefully enunciated in a plausible imitation of a clipped British aristocratic accent. "You are becoming jolly well adept at this sleuthing game, I DO say. Bloody good, bloody good, ahem."

"Old chap, you are MOST kind," I responded, and then, switching accents, I continued. "But we'd bettuh git our bee-hinds back to Miz-sipp-eee and let ole Dew-pree tawk agin, okay, bubba?"

"Thanks for the two-minute version of 'Masterpiece Theater,' and also the epilogue from 'Smokey and the Bandit,' gents," said Augie. "I will take the baton here. Speck, I agree that Jason probably sits and smokes a cigar or reads a newspaper downstairs in the Compson manse while Quentin breaks into his room on the floor above him. Without question Quentin demonstrates commendable courage by taking significant risks during the burglary, and pilfering the stash over Jason's head is just one such risk. The journey that she undertakes between her window and Jason's also is chock-full of danger. We have already discussed the location of Jason's room and concluded that it is likely not adjacent to or even very close to Quentin's. Possibly it lies at the end of the hallway or perhaps even on the opposite side of the second floor."

Pete spoke up. "Have you decided how Quentin travels from window to window? Or"—he turned with a wry smile in my direction and stretched his voice into a drawl—"frum win-dur to win-dur?"

With a slow nod Augie continued his analysis. "I can list three possible ways of traversing the distance, each of which calls for a high quotient of fearlessness if not recklessness, since in a former plantation house as old as the Compson manse must be, the second-story windows and roof would be a sizable distance from the ground."

"Detective Dupin," interrupted Pete," the Compson domicile was built in the 1830's, and the ledges on the second-story windows would probably be at least fifteen feet from the ground."

"My turn to be impressed, distinguished Proff-fess-sewer," I boomed out. "What is the source of this information? I must have missed these statistics in my own careless reading of the novel."

"I'll tell you later, Doctor," replied Pete. "Let Augie stay on track for now."

"All right," Augie complied, "although you have also piqued my curiosity, Pete. The three possible modes of travel. First, Quentin could descend the reliable pear tree all the way to the ground, sneak to the base of Jason's window, and ascend another handy tree, if one exists. Second, she could move from her pear tree to a nearby window ledge or step across two or more ledges in succession, but only if Jason's window is close to hers or if ledges jut out at traversable intervals most of the way along or around the second story. Third, she could somehow climb to the roof, crawl across the roof, and then drop down onto the ledge on the outside of Jason's window."

"A fourth possibility exists," intervened Pete, "and it is suggested by Faulkner himself." The young professor glanced respectfully at Augie and then at me, smiling at our dual expressions of surprise.

"Did yon super sleuth and his humble assistant overlook some evidence in the novel?" I asked in exasperation.

"No, no," answered Pete, with a vigorous shaking of his copious locks. "I'm not playing fair, fellas. Remember my reference a moment ago to the age and features of the Compson house? Faulkner wrote about the history of the house and about many more subjects related to TSAF when in 1945 he composed additional information about the novel and entitled the material in this way."

Pete held up an opened book and pointed to this heading:

COMPSON
1699-1945

"This extension of the novel is popularly known as the 'Compson Appendix,' and Faulkner wrote it to accompany critic Malcolm Cowley's anthology of Faulkner's works, *The Portable Faulkner*."

While Pete was expounding, Augie had been nodding steadily. "I remember that you mentioned the 'Appendix' in class once, Pete," our lead detective said, "but we didn't have time to discuss it any length."

"Right, Augie. I wanted to spend at least one class period on it, but the Benjy and Jason sections bit too large a chunk out of our available schedule. Gentlemen, let me point out that the 'Appendix' can enhance a reading of TSAF but can also cause confusion. Let me explain."

Pete identified the book he had just shown us; it was a paperback edition of TSAF bound in colors of burnt orange and off-white. A magenta photo of Rowan Oak in need of a paint job, with a 1920's-era automobile parked beside it, appeared on the cover. "This is a Norton critical edition of the novel, my pals. It contains not only the text of the novel but also the 'Appendix,' critical articles, and other assorted goodies."

Pete opened the book in the middle and again showed us the "Appendix." He then rummaged in his own pile until he found a tattered note card. "While

Faulkner and Cowley were corresponding in 1945 concerning plans to publish *The Portable Faulkner*, the Mississippi author freely admitted to Cowley that he did not reread his own novel before writing the 'Appendix.' Faulkner wrote, 'I don't have a copy of TSAF,' and he informed Cowley that he was not concerned about discrepancies between various facts in the original novel and those in the new Compson material. This is what I was referring to earlier when I mentioned the causing of confusion. In the 'Appendix,' for example, Faulkner, relying solely on memory, writes that Jason had locked Quentin in her room after dinner on Saturday. The quotation reads, in part, 'the room in which her uncle had locked her at noon.' Actually, as we all know, Mrs. Compson locks Quentin in the girl's room after supper, and presumably after Quentin has already traveled via the windows into Jason's room and back."

With eyes a-squint and lips a-pursed, Captain Dupree and I listened to Pete's exposition, and then I piped up. "But is the 'Appendix' helpful at all, Pete? Does it enrich a reading of the novel? Could it enhance our understanding of the book? Or should we disregard this appendage—I mean 'Appendix—altogether?"

"In order, yes, yes, yes, and no, Speck. I have discovered that some of the information in the 'Appendix' is consistent with material in the original novel and may, as you so accurately state, enrich and enhance our comprehension of it. For example, as Augie was explaining his theory concerning the period of approximately sixty to ninety minutes after supper during which Quentin carries out the break-in, I thought of these two brief passages in the 'Appendix.'"

Pete leaned to his left, pointing to a page in the Norton critical edition. While Augie shifted to his right in order to look on, I arose, leaned forward, and peered at the book. Simultaneously we all read these underlined words: "<u>that spring dusk in 1928</u>," and then Pete flipped to another page with heavy underlining: "<u>and then climbed down the same rainpipe in the dusk and ran away with the pitchman.</u>" Pete explained: "The two uses of the key word 'dusk' confirm Benjy's reference to the time of day, the one appearing on page seventy-two of his interior monologue in the original novel. As Benjy squats in the empty room, he narrates '*I could hear it getting night,*' and two lines farther on '*I squatted there, hearing it getting dark.*' So you are correct, Monsieur Dupin. A few minutes before Quentin descends the pear tree, twilight has passed into deepening darkness. Your estimation of between seven and eight, likely around seven-thirty, seems on target to me, and in 1945, seventeen years after he had written TSAF, Faulkner obviously thought of the getaway time as being the transition between late evening and night—in other words, dusk."

Augie leaned back into a couch cushion, looked straight up at the ceiling, and replied, "Thanks for the confirmation, Pete. But what is the meaning of this reference that you read to a 'rainpipe?' We all know that Quentin climbs down the pear tree."

"Bingo, Captain," exclaimed Pete gleefully. "I admire your perspicacity. You have designated one of the numerous discrepancies in fact between novel and 'Appendix.' Cowley called Faulkner's attention to some of these errors, but Faulkner replied"—here Pete read again from his note card—"'Would rather let the appendix stand with the inconsistencies.' Cowley concluded that Faulkner's— here I quote—'creative power was so unflagging that he could not tell a story twice without transforming one detail after another.' In summary, I believe that we should use the 'Appendix' with caution. If a fact in it is consistent with one in the original novel, then we can perhaps make interpretive use of that fact. If a contradiction exists, we must rely upon the original 1929 text."

Augie's eyes bore in on Pete's. "So the fourth possibility for Quentin's nocturnal—or should I say 'dusk-y'—trip from window to window appears in the 'Appendix,' I presume."

"Right again, Mister Auguste," replied the professor. "Despite the author's faulty memory concerning who locks Quentin in her room and when, Faulkner does provide here a credible means of passage from the outside of Quentin's room to that of Jason: she 'swung herself by a rainpipe from the window of the room in which her uncle had locked her at noon, to the locked window of his own locked and empty bedroom and broke a pane and entered the window. . . .'"

Augie pointed to the "Appendix." "And this is that 'same rainpipe' that Quentin descends during her final escape—in the 1945 version of events that you underlined, not the published 1929 recounting."

"Another hit, my ace detective. Soon you will sink my battleship. Ooops, wrong game. Your host is becoming giddy with thirst and fatigue. Liquid refreshments, anyone?"

Policeman, pedagogue, and physician all soon slurped from refills, and then the evening's cerebral exertions began to push toward their conclusion.

Captain Dupree once more took the floor. "We have only the forced entry itself remaining to discuss. I'll work from my notes again. Let's start at the point when Quentin reaches the window of Jason's room, however she arrives there. We know that Quentin uses care and precision when breaking the pane. The next morning, Easter Sunday, Mrs. Compson points out that the hole in the window appears in, as she says on two-eighty, "'The upper sash, behind the shade'" and, hidden as it is, the broken pane, quote, "'could have been like that a long time. . . .'" Definitely, Jason does not notice the hole until Sunday morning; check on page two-seventy-five. So Quentin must have also carefully picked up the broken glass, likely carried it away with her, and later disposed of it somehow. As she searches Jason's room in the increasing darkness for his stash, Quentin must also use extreme care in replacing every object that she disturbs, because Jason is quite vain about his knowledge of his small domain. Look on two-eighty, when Jason belligerently asks his mother, "'Dont you reckon I know the room I live in?'""

At this point I butted in again. "Augie, I seem to remember that Jason counts his money sometime over the weekend. Apparently he does not do so on Saturday night, or he would have discovered his loss before Sunday morning."

While I was blabbing, Augie was rhythmically nodding his head. "Right you are, my good friend. Here, let me find that reference in my notes. . . ." Flip, flip, flip. "Oh yes, here it is. Jason counts his cash on Friday afternoon shortly after three-thirty, and he goes through it again on Friday night before going to bed. These episodes occur on pages two-thirty-seven and two-sixty-three, respectively. Quentin is simply flat-out lucky that Jason leaves the metal box undisturbed in its hiding place on Saturday night."

Pete took a turn. "Augie, you may be interested to learn that Faulkner's memory in 1945 failed him concerning Jason's secret storage spot for the nest egg of moolah."

Augie looked up from his legal pad, raised his eyebrows, and said, "Oh? We have a clear description in the novel of his clandestine cache; look on page two-eighty-three. The 'metal box,' which also contains assorted papers, normally resides in a space in Jason's closet under, I quote here, 'a sawn section of tongue-and-groove planking' covered by, quoting again here, 'garments, shoes, and a suitcase.' What did Faulkner write in the 'Appendix,' Pete?"

"A plausible explanation, Captain, but not one that squares with the words that you have just read from the original text of the novel. Here is the 1945 version. Ms. Quentin, quoting now, 'with the uncle's firepoker burst open the locked bureau drawer and took the money. . . .' The 1929 version is much more suspenseful, Augie, as we reconstruct it. Jason has scrupulously disguised the location of his metal box under planking covered by ordinary closet paraphernalia. In order to find the box, Quentin must spend several anxious minutes in a disciplined search. Since she well knows her uncle's obsessive personal habits, it also makes sense that she would look for an obscure hiding place rather than break into a bureau drawer. Naaaah; I vote for the original text. As we reconstruct the crime, the first version features much more gut-wrenching tension than does the later one."

"I agree," confirmed Augie, "and let's also remember that Jason perceives no reason for alarm until Sunday morning, and then only because of the broken window—which Quentin would have no way of fixing—and not because of any other visible clue left by Quentin, who must have been meticulous in her search and in her strategy of leaving no tell-tale signs of a breaking-and-entering operation."

"Make the vote unanimous," I pitched in. "Quentin carries out a masterful second-story job. And in 1945 Faulkner apparently forgot that Jason, upon entering his room at bedtime on Saturday night, immediately would have noticed a bureau drawer that had been broken open."

Pete licked his right index finger, raised it high, drew it slowly downward, and proclaimed, "Chalk up one acute observation for your assistant gumshoe, Monsieur Dupin. The good Doctor is becoming an adept student of literary sleuthing. He may yet prove to be valuable to your investigative endeavors."

"Thanks, Pete—I think," was my rejoinder. "So, Augie, is Ms. Quentin through with her revenge crime now?"

"Not quite, Speck, but almost. We can assume that Quentin returns to her own room by ledges, trees, roof, rainpipe, or some combination thereof, and next she provides a cover for herself by replying 'What' to her grandmother during the time when Luster is helping Benjy get ready for bed. Then for Quentin it is down the pear tree, off to the show, and later that night farewell to Jefferson forever, accompanied on her journey not only by Sir Red Tie but also by a substantial amount of cold hard cash."

"Do we know how much loot she got away with?" I asked my companions.

Pete spoke up. "Look on page three-oh-three, Doc Double-U. Jason tells the sheriff that his niece has robbed him of three thousand dollars, but in the 'Appendix' Faulkner claims that Quentin actually steals, quote, 'almost seven thousand dollars,' end of quotation, a figure that makes sense when we remember that Jason has been stealing money from her for most of her seventeen years of life."

"Quentin gets away with the burglary," I said, "and disappears from

TSAF. But does Faulkner tell us in the 'Appendix' what happens to her?"

"The author sums up the girl's fate in these succinct words," answered Pete: 'And so vanished. . . .' Her final appearance in Faulkner's fiction occurs when she descends the pear tree and sneaks across the Compson lawn and into the gathering dusk."

Augie slapped both palms onto his knees, exclaimed, "Mission accomplished, gentlemen," and stood up. "We have analyzed Ms. Quentin's stealthy break-in and have answered Mister Titus's questions to the best of our abilities, I believe. Pete, are you satisfied that we have achieved our objectives?"

Pete bounced up, grabbed Augie's right hand, pumped it vigorously six times, and yelped, "Yes, yes, yes. Boundless thanks once more, my very generous friend. Your detective skills continue to impress me. I will snail-mail young Davey a brief summary of our findings and also contact a few other students from the class by e-mail. Thank you again, also, Doctor Speck, for sharing your wise counsel and fabled wit."

As my vertical companions conversed, I remained horizontal, struggling vainly to extricate myself from the rickety recliner-rocker. After several failed attempts I finally succeeded in clamorously lowering the leg rest—"bang, crash, ping, sproing"—and in wrestling my bloated corpus delicti out of the upholstered Venus's-flytrap. As I finally managed to achieve a standing position—primordial humans probably did not take as long to evolve from semi-erect to erect positions—Pete's phone jingled, our host hurried off to answer it, and he returned to announce, "That was the Mayor, Doc. She says that she and Mrs. Dupree have been at your house for over an hour and that she is glad to learn we three are still here and not throwing up cheap beer in the parking lot of R. T.'s Celestial Country-and-Western Honky-Tonk. Heh heh, heh. In addition, she invites you two stud-hosses to make your way pronto back to Summit Avenue, there to join your girlfriends, who are comparing their mall purchases while they merrily sip wine coolers."

"Sounds suspiciously like our exit cue, Speck," said Augie. "I think that we have imposed on Professor Prefont all that we dare. And my goodness, it's past ten o'clock already!"

"No, no, fellows," Pete pleaded. "Let me wind up the evening by showing you just how much you have helped me. Please take five minutes longer, all right?"

Augie looked at me, I shrugged my shoulders, he nodded in reply, and we guests resumed our seats. Little did I know that we would stay for nearly half an hour.

Pete smiled broadly, said, "Thanks, guys; I'll be brief," and hopped back onto his couch cushion, grabbing note cards as he descended. "Augie," our host spoke hurriedly, "when I was gathering critical material on Ms. Quentin, I found out that during the 1950's, between twenty-five and thirty years after he had written TSAF and a decade after the 'Appendix,' Faulkner frequently had Quentin still on his mind. In 1956 he told a friend that he planned to write a book about Quentin; he mentioned the rainpipe escape and vanishing act again in his next-to-last novel *The Mansion*, published in 1959; and, most intriguing of all, in two separate mid-fifties interviews he called TSAF a 'tragedy of two lost women: Caddy and her daughter.'" Pete looked up from his notes, staring first at me and then at Augie.

Our ratiocinist was the first to respond. "In class, Pete, you told us students that the consensus of critics holds Caddy to be the central character and the principal tragic figure in TSAF. Now you are saying that Faulkner himself awarded equal status to Caddy's daughter?"

"Yes, Augie, and until tonight I never understood fully the reasons for Faulkner's union of both mother and daughter as dual tragic heroines of the book. The more obvious explanation for Faulkner's inclusion of Quentin with Caddy as a 'lost woman' is because of the author's perpetual infatuation for Caddy—he called her 'the beautiful one' and 'my heart's darling'—and because Quentin reminds him so vividly of her mother. But now, Augie and Speck, you have made me realize that Faulkner also kept thinking about Quentin and even put her on the same pedestal with Caddy as the novel's other tragic heroine BECAUSE—"

Pete slowly leaned back, straightened his back, inhaled deeply, raised both arms like a conductor prior to an overture, and intoned, "Quentin is the sole adversary—the ONLY one—who ever defeats that triple-plated son of a bitch, Jason Richmond Compson the Fourth! We have already discussed just how much Faulkner despised Jason, so the author understandably would admire Quentin for getting the best of Jason, that 'bastard in behavior,' who also has so horribly mistreated Caddy. But also Faulkner would lament Quentin's perpetual absence from Jefferson, because she is the only Compson child of the next generation and her loss represents canceled potential for both hope and compassion in the family.

"With Quentin's having, quote, 'vanished,' Jason can now reign supremely in the Compson domain and can piss away any remaining honor, dignity, or integrity still clinging to the Compson name. SO—Quentin is tragic because of the bitter mistreatment that she long endures and against which she finally rebels, and she is a heroine because of her delicious victory over Jason Compson, undisputed 1928 ratfink skunk scumbag of north Mississippi. One more quotation, gentlemen—"

Pete snatched up the "Appendix" and said, "Here is Faulkner's description of Jason's volcanic anger at Quentin after Jason loses track of his niece in Mottson: 'this was Jason's rage, the red unbearable fury which on that night and at intervals recurring with little or no diminishment for the next five years, made him seriously believe would at some unwarned instant destroy him, kill him as instantaneously dead as a bullet or a lightning bolt.'"

Pete closed the book, jumped to his feet, and proclaimed, "Quentin commits the crime, but Jason suffers the punishment."

Applause from Augie, along with whistles and foot stomping from me, brought a huge smile to Pete's face, and at that moment the doorbell chirped.

Pete's stuff-eating grin dissolved into a look of bafflement. "Who could that be?" he muttered. Loping to the door, he opened it to find a smiling, crew-cut, blocky patrolman wearing the uniform of the Murryville Police Department and carrying a large box of Milk-Bone Dog Biscuits.

"Why, it's Arkie Duncan," exclaimed Augie. "Does Buddy Cotham need to see me? Is that why you are here?"

"No, no, Captain Dupree," replied the young officer. "Mayor Watkins called me at ten-twenty-five—twelve minutes ago—over at the duty room, and she asked me to deliver this box to you and Doctor Speck, sir." He held out the Milk-Bones, with their assorted flavors of bacon, cheese, liver, and poultry, no less. Duncan continued, "The Mayor and Missus Dupree said that this food—uhh, these snacks—uhh, these dog biscuits should tide you over just fine as you try out your new backyard sleeping accommodations for the remainder of the night."

Chapter Four

The Case of Quentin Compson's Suicide Site in
The Sound and the Fury

Hospital Street Blues

    Luckily for Augie Dupree and your faithful narrator, our vengeful spouses relented and allowed us to spend the night in our human and not canine edifices, but if we truly had been forced to sleep in the out of doors, the next month would have provided ideal conditions for a campout. Late July, 1995, developed into one of the most climatologically pleasant mid-summer partial months in the memories of weather-obsessed Murryville valetudinarians. Ordinarily unrelenting in heat, aridity, and dustiness, with the dog days of August providing only more of the same, the daytime hours of the shank of this particular July felt more like those of a typical early May—highs only in the middle eighties, lows in the sixties, with tolerable humidity, and a rainy spell every week or ten days so that the Delta farmers did not have to worry about irrigating their crops of cotton or soybeans.

    In the cool, cool, cool of the evenings, rather than hunkering down in front of our boob tubes while armed with intergalactic remote controls—"Zap, Zing, Zowie," most of the residents of Summit Avenue and contiguous streets actually sat on our front porches (if we owned one), strolled around the block visiting neighbors, organized croquet games in the huge side yard belonging to Wally and Verna Wahlquist, and just generally behaved civilly and sociably as had our ancestral Murryvillians in the earlier decades of this century before indolence, apathy, air conditioning, and the cathode-ray tube had combined to make twilight cave dwellers of us all.

    Those Summitteers who enjoyed gardening and yard work were rewarded with field days and bumper crops: impatiens, gladiolas, irises, petunias, day lilies, and roses appeared in rare July profusion, as did gargantuan tomatoes; bushels of beans, peppers, and squash; and the sweetest, stickiest strawberries on record. The couple Watkins reveled in the social and recreational activities made possible by this temperate late July and left the skilled labor accomplished by tiller, shovel, spade, clippers, and mower to our more industrious and emerald-thumbed neighbors. Our sole regret was that Augie had to miss the joy of these salad days because of an unanticipated hospital confinement.

Earlier in the month Augie had battled a persistent cold and had also been plagued with a nagging ache in his right leg, the one that had been hit with bullets while Augie was a Memphis detective. Checking with Pablo Ziegler, his internist, Augie was dismayed to learn that he had somehow developed separate infections in lung and leg and would have to spend several days in the Churchill River Medical Center (recently upgraded in nomenclature status from merely Churchill River Hospital), while Pablo and some other specialists combined their expertise in treating his problems. Dividing her days between visits to C. R. M. C. and pre-school meetings with her teachers and staff, Mary Alice squeezed in time to soldier on in the Dupree flower beds; Jackson Burton from down the street took scrupulous care of Augie's prized azaleas, crepe myrtles, mimosas, and Japanese maples; and I, yours truly—Mister Saint Augustine-Bermuda-Zoysia himself, TA DAH!—gladly sent to the residence next door the crew members from Brown's Landscaping Service after they had mowed my yard. It was my earnest pleasure to pay them to tend to Augie's prize lawn.

Admittedly I was handier with my aqua-tinted checkbook than I was with Augie's lime-green Lawnboy, but I compensated for my botanical indifference by spending considerable time with Augie while he was incapacitated at C. R. M. C. located on, would you believe it, Hospital Street. Demonstrating the quirkiness that can make small-town life so colorful, the people living or working along the avenue leading from the edge of the river district straight north to our burg's medical complex had successfully avoided the Town Council's campaign for upward social mobility and had managed to retain the street's century-old and customary title.

Despite the sad irony of his having to be indoors when Murryville was blessed with a rare mild period in this July, Augie characteristically did not mope but made productive use of his forced confinement by tackling student Miriam Littlejohn's question concerning the second section of *The Sound and the Fury*, the male Quentin Compson's interior monologue entitled "June Second, 1910."

On Wednesday, July 26, at 9:30 a.m., I completed my oral report to Katie and Dan Pollard concerning their toddler daughter Melissa's successful strabismus surgery and strolled, still in my garish puke-green surgical scrub suit, through the hallways from the outpatient surgical wing of Churchill River M. C. and then up the elevator to the seventh floor, where Augie was reluctantly occupying a bed on the internal medicine ward. As I turned into the open doorway of his room, I overheard his voice and that of a female engaged in what sounded like some type of disagreement.

"Now Captain Dupree, you just go ahead and expel that gas. Doctor's orders, you know. Doctor Ziegler specifically asked me to be certain that you got rid of as much intestinal gas as possible before he comes in to examine you around ten. Come one, now, let it go."

To the left of Augie's bed Nurse Geraldine Coker stood with locked legs. She was bending stiffly at the waist and vigorously kneading my friend's exposed lower stomach. Red in the face and holding his breath, Augie steadily shook his head from side to side. Spotting me, he gasped, sat halfway up in bed, and yelped for assistance.

"There you are, Speck, thank goodness! Tell Mrs. Coker here that her request is uncalled for. You're a doctor. Tell her, please. She won't listen to me."

Amused by my neighbor's predicament despite my best professional instincts, I approached the right side of the bed and replied, "Augie, if Pablo gives Geraldine orders, then you had better follow them. Go ahead, if you can."

"But Speck," Augie growled, "I can't do that with a lady in the room, no matter what my doctor says. My whole life I have never—er, uhh, you know, done THAT in front of a woman, not even Mary Alice or Valerie at home. I was raised in New Orleans and Memphis to try at all times to be a Southern gentleman. Give me a break, please."

Geraldine maintained her rhythmic massaging. "Captain, remember that I am a professional person and that this is my calling as well as my job. Thank you for thinking of me as a lady, but for now just consider me to be your nurse."

Augie's face deepened into a darker shade of red. "I can't, Geraldine; I just can't. Leave the room for a few seconds, and I'll happily comply."

"Captain," knead, knead, knead, "if you will just pass gas it will be a feather in my cap," said Geraldine.

Pushing himself up on his elbows, gritting his bared teeth, and staring intently at the nurse, Augie hissed these words: "Madam, if you will step outside that door, I will gladly make you an Indian princess!"

I never learned who won this battle of wills because at that moment Pablo Ziegler waltzed energetically through the door, I greeted my medical colleague cordially and made my exit after promising Augie that I would stop in again after my office hours, and Geraldine backed away from the bed and began her report to Pablo. When I returned at 5:45 that afternoon, a berobed Caesar Augustus Dupree V was sitting in a recliner in the corner of his room, his color was normal, and neither of us revived the subject of the morning's skirmish. The patient has just completed his low-calorie hospital dinner and seemed to be pleased with my company.

"Augie," I asked, "is there anything I can bring you from home? Any errands that I can run for you?"

"Thanks, thanks, Speck, but no. Mary Alice was here most of the afternoon, and she is taking care of all of that. But I'll tell you what you could do. . . . Give Pete a call, and the two of you decide on an evening when the three of us can get together here for a little Faulkner chat. Pablo says that I will be here probably until Sunday—the infections are both clearing up well, thank goodness—and if you and Pete can come in, we can fill up some of my idle time with talk about *The Sound and the Fury.*"

In my visitor's chair I recrossed my legs and said, "But the last time I talked on the phone with Pete, he told me he had found an article in the Faulkner criticism that answered all of his student's questions about the Quentin section. Do you want us to meet just to go over that essay?"

With lowered head and a tight-lipped smile that communicated modest satisfaction, Augie softly replied, "Well, yes, I do want to talk about that article, but I have some further thoughts on Miriam's questions about where Quentin kills himself and if our knowing the location really matters." Raising his head and looking directly at me, Augie asked, "Will you indulge your bored friend here and join Pete and me for one night later this week?"

"Of course, Augie, of course. And your words about 'further thoughts' are quite intriguing. Methinks that ratiocinist Dupin has been engaged in some detective work once more. Am I correct?"

"Well. I guess that you could say that, friend. Admittedly I have had a large quantity of idle time while I waste away in this room and exasperate my caretakers, so naturally I have tried to keep my dimming brain occupied and agile. Now, how about Friday night? Saturday? My social calendar is full of blank pages."

Bridge Over Tempting Waters

Friday turned out to be the evening of choice, because Julianna had already asked Mary Alice to join her in feasting their middle-aged, lascivious eyes on Kevin Costner as he cavorts semi-naked in and out of oceans in "Waterworld," a film epic then showing on the giant screen at the Cinema 180, and Ellie was delighted when the Mayor and the Principal invited her to join them for this visual lust-fest. I was content to change from my seersucker business suit into a red polo shirt and black Docker slacks, eat a meatloaf sandwich, and wait for Pete's arrival.

In his belching, ancient beige Volkswagen beetle nicknamed "Herbie Junior," Pete, wearing a Cleveland Indians baseball jersey and faded jeans, soon picked me up at home and chauffeured me along Hospital Street to Churchill River Medical Center, where we two junior sleuths entered the private room of our superior, Captain C. Augustus Dupree, at 7:20 just as Dr. Bobbie Sue Middlebury was leaving. Dr. Pablo Ziegler had brought in Bobbie Sue, a pulmonary specialist, to work on the persistent infections in Augie's right lung, and she had prescribed treatments that were clearing up the problem.

A diminutive, perky, freckled redhead who had set up her practice in Murryville only two years before, Bobbie Sue had quickly become successful through her sincere concern for her patients and her excellent diagnostic skills. Board-certified in internal medicine before she sub-specialized in pulmonary diseases, she often was consulted on difficult cases and had built a reputation as our area's best medical detective. Meeting her at the door, I greeted her warmly.

"Doctor Middlebury, good evening to you. Let me introduce Doctor Peter Prefont, English professor at Moffatt, my new friend and also Augie's."

Shaking hands with Pete and then with me, Bobbie Sue replied, "Yes, Speck, I have heard of Doctor Prefont from Captain Dupree here. Our patient"—Bobbie pointed her left thumb toward Augie, who had already started up from his seat in the corner recliner—"tells me that the three of you have been engaging in some investigative work together. In fact, he has now drawn me into the conspiracy, at least on the periphery." Turning toward Augie, Bobbie said, "I will call my friend in Cambridge, Captain, probably tomorrow, and tonight I'll ask Ollie about that second question that you posed to me. When I stop in to see you Sunday morning before you check out, perhaps I will have answers to both of your inquiries."

From the corner Augie bowed elaborately. He was dressed as presentably as he could be, given his current status as a patient on the medicine ward. He wore bright red cotton pajamas and a medium-weight dark-blue robe. "A thousand thanks, Doctor Middlebury. You are most kind to help me—I mean us, actually—in this unusual endeavor."

Pete and I looked at each other in puzzlement, I shrugged, and Pete spoke: "Well, Speck, I suppose that Monsieur Dupin will fill us in on this development in due time. Nice to meet you, Doctor Middlebury."

Bobbie paused at the door and replied, "Same to you, Professor, and farewell, Speck. Captain, perhaps on Sunday somebody can also explain the fractured French and that change in the last syllable of your name. But I'm late to a dinner meeting with my partners, so I must scoot. Later...."

The last word echoed toward us from the hallway as young Dr. Middlebury jogged away toward the elevator, her white hospital coat flapping behind her and her stethoscope bouncing leftward with each hard landing of a hurrying foot. Augie asked Pete and me to sit in plastic-cushioned straight chairs, apologizing as he crossed the room for the Spartan furnishings of his temporary domicile while acknowledging, "At least Pablo and the other doctors don't have me hooked up to those annoying tubes any longer. I was beginning to feel like the dupe in a science fiction experiment. But I have been told to reside either in this recliner or in bed, so I'm afraid that you guys get stuck with the interrogation seats."

Pete and I both clucked that we were fine, Augie thanked us for coming to keep him company, and then he reached to his bedside table and pulled out a thick set of photocopied pages. "This article, 'June 2, 1910: An Historic Day,' with which you kindly furnished me, Pete, is an elaborate reconstruction of Quentin Compson's itinerary on the last day of his life. I found it to be exhaustive in its attention to geographical details and highly illuminating in its interpretations of Quentin's final activities." Augie fell silent and stared at Pete and me.

"The unspoken word hanging in the air here is 'BUT,'" I interjected. "Since you have summoned your two earnest assistants here tonight and also have persuaded Doctor Middlebury to gather intelligence data for you, I assume that this essay"—I leaned forward and thumped the stack of papers in Augie's right hand—"needs to be corrected in a few details. Right, Mister Detective?"

With a curt nod Augie replied, "I would say in only one major detail, Speck." Holding out his left hand, palm upward, toward Pete, Augie inquired, "Professor, when you discussed the Quentin section of TSAF (TEE, ESS, EH, EFF) in class, did you talk about the issue of place of death?"

Pete sat erect in the metal chair, palms on knees, elbows rigid, arms straight, and eyes locked on Augie's eyes. "Wellll, Cap-uhh-tun, duh, ah don't rightly recollect . . . . Uhh"—a vigorous slap to the forehead—"let me concentrate now. I guess that we did not directly discuss this specific problem. In fact, Miriam's question on that last day of class surprised me, as I think back on it, because the place of Quentin's suicide always seemed to me. . . ."

Augie's stare at Pete intensified. "Yes, go ahead. You were saying. . . ?"

Pete threw up his hands, leaned back in the chair, and replied, "Oh hell. I might as well step into the trap and spring it. I have always assumed that Quentin kills himself by jumping from a bridge somewhere near the Harvard campus. Am I wrong, Monsieur Detective Man? Have the steel jaws of the trap seized me by the ankle?"

"Yes, I believe so," stated Augie mildly, "but you may take comfort in knowing that the author of this painstaking plotting of Quentin's journeys on June second, 1910"—here Augie waved the thick packet of photocopied pages—"draws the same conclusion, as do several other critics, and I think that I know the primary source of this commonly held misinterpretation."

With his left index finger and thumb Augie lifted a book from the table and held it high in the air like a laboratory specimen. "Remember our good friend the 'Compson Appendix?' On page two-twenty-nine of this Norton critical edition of TSAF, under the heading 'Quentin III' in the 'Appendix,' Faulkner includes these words: 'Committed suicide in Cambridge, Massachusetts, June 1910. . . .'

"Pete, last month you told Speck and me that Faulkner stubbornly refused to reread the original text of TSAF before he wrote this additional commentary and narrative about Quentin and the other Compsons. Unlike Mister Bill the author, I own a copy of the novel—remember he wrote in 1945 that he did not—and here in this dull hospital I have had much more available time to fill up than Faulkner must have had back then. So I methodically re-examined the Quentin section of the original text and concentrated on the question of location, remembering Miriam's disquietude upon her own second reading of the section. Also, I looked through some of the other critical material that you graciously furnished for me, Pete, and I asked Mary Alice to go to the Moffatt library in order to find further information in some journals and to check out some books for me, mostly various editions of TSAF and biographies of Faulkner."

"Augie, you have been one busy beaver," I exclaimed. "I had no idea that you had become so industrious during your time here at C. R. M. C."

"Beats the hell out of counting the flowers in this wallpaper or rotting my brain with daytime trash on the t.v., Speck. A sane person can stand only so many televised pleas from misunderstood nymphomaniacs about their constitutional rights to have carnal relations with any barnyard animals of their choice," replied our favorite patient of the moment.

"True, true," I responded, "and what is your conclusion, friend? About

Quentin on June second, 1910, I mean, not about nymphos."

"Yes," interrupted impetuous Peter P., "are you claiming that Faulkner erred in the 'Appendix' about this issue of location?"

Holding both arms in front of him with palms down, and gently patting the air with his palms, Augie replied, "Now, now, Pete; I wouldn't say 'erred.' After all, Faulkner is the deity of Yoknapatawpha, or at least its 'sole owner and proprietor,' as he calls himself at the base of his map of Jefferson that you showed us in class. I would prefer to put it this way: in 1945 the author apparently overlooked the fact that in the 1929 edition of the novel itself, as well as in the main texts—not the 'Appendix'—of all succeeding editions, Quentin Compson carefully chooses a remote bridge out in the countryside away from Cambridge and Boston as the place where he terminates his own existence. Faulkner must have created this rural location out of his vivid imagination and not drawn it from any personal experience gained in Massachusetts, since I could find no evidence in any of the principal Faulkner biographies—the definitive one by Joseph Blotner, of course, but also life studies written by David Minter, Stephen Oates, and Frederick Karl—ummm, no evidence that Faulkner had visited the Cambridge-Boston area before he wrote TSAF in 1928." For the names of the latter three biographers Augie consulted a note card on his bedside table.

Pete continued to look perplexed. "Augie, when I conducted my first search through the Faulkner criticism for commentary on this subject, I found a modest amount of information, all of which I passed on to you. But the major article presenting any specific assertion on the topic is that one." Pete pointed to the thick copy of "June 2, 1910: An Historic Day." "Most of the rest of the criticism seems to approach the topic of location and then veer away from it."

"Right you are, Professor," responded our chief detective. "Apparently the published critics of TSAF have taken Faulkner's reference in the 'Appendix' to Cambridge as the place of Quentin's death to be correct, because neither you in your initial search nor I in a subsequent look have been able to find anyone who has questioned Faulkner's listing of Cambridge. Admittedly, the question usually just doesn't come up. In my search, based on photocopies supplied by librarians Doris Towson and Jane Millard of the Moffatt Library staff and delivered to me by my faithful Mary Alice, the majority of the published commentary on this exceedingly complex Quentin section seems to focus, and quite sensibly I would say, on four main topics."

Augie picked up another note card from the stack on his small table. "Ahem. I have summarized the four topics as the following: Quentin's hopeless obsession with an intellectual concept of purity; his inability to fulfill his self-appointed role as Caddy's protector; his morbid fascination with time; and his infatuation with thoughts of his own impending death. Fellow investigators, in building my case I have focused mostly on Quentin's words in his interior monologue that speak to this fourth topic—his upcoming death—because the other three topics are discussed mostly in expressions of Quentin's memories, whereas the fixation with death develops both out of memories and from Quentin's accounts of his actual experience on June second, 1910. And these final-day activities provide us with the pieces to the puzzle in narration that lies before us."

Augie paused, looked up from his note cards, shook himself like a golden retriever that had just run through a lawn sprinkler, and earnestly said, "I am sorry, my friends. In this hospital version of solitary confinement I have become accustomed to talking to myself too much. Have I lost your attention totally?"

The first to respond, I blurted out, "I'm with you so far, Augie," and Pete affirmed, "Me, too. Or I should be mindful of my professional status and say, 'I, also.'"

My turn again. "Augie, let me ask a question here. Am I remembering the end of the Quentin section correctly? Faulkner does not present the death scene, or even Quentin's final trip to the suicide bridge, wherever that may be. Let's see—" I leafed hurriedly through Augie's handy copy of TSAF. "Yes, here we are. Page one-seventy-nine. Quentin's interior monologue ends just as the young man is preparing to leave his dormitory room at Harvard." I looked up. "Hell, Pete, I didn't even realize that Quentin kills himself in this book until you mentioned the word 'suicide' during one of our discussions back in May."

"An excellent point, Speck," exclaimed Augie. "Once again Faulkner has left unnarrated a central event in a novel, just as he does with the beating of Clarence Snopes and Ms. Quentin's second-story job. And Faulkner has challenged us readers to figure out how the event occurs."

Augie placed his left index finger in front of his lips and stared at the floor. "Gentlemen, tell you what. Let's all attempt to take an intellectual leap backward and place ourselves in the identities of first-time readers of TSAF. When—at what place in the novel—can a first-time reader become certain that Quentin commits suicide on June second, 1910?" Enthusiasm oozed from Augie's voice. "What I'm suggesting here is that any reader—or even a seasoned critic—who attempts to gather the available facts about Quentin's suicide has a difficult enough time even finding confirmation of the act of self-annihilation itself, never mind the apparently trivial issues of where or when it takes place. No wonder everyone simply accepts Faulkner's word from the 'Appendix' and thinks: 'Cambridge, of course.'"

"Okay, Augie," replied Pete. "We three fans of Faulkner have bent the covers and pages of this novel pretty often in the last couple of months. Let's take a few minutes and start skimming, looking for—what? Evidence of Quentin's death?"

"Right, Pete," replied Augie. "And let's add more: for the first proof that he dies by his own hand, and then in what way. Pete, I see that you have your own edition of TSAF with you. Speck, here; use this extra copy that Mary Alice brought to me on one of her trips of mercy. We should start on page one-eighty, where the Jason section begins, just after we witness, at the very end of the second section of the novel, Quentin's preparation to leave Harvard and head for the bridge." Augie then stood, walked seven steps to the small closet of his room, and took from a shelf his "Detective" baseball cap. "I'd better don this, if I want to keep my luck going," he said.

"I'll play along," I said with reluctance evident in my voice. "But then will we get back to your argument about country over city, Augie?"

"Most certainly," my friend responded. "Originally I intended to make our session tonight a quick one, but once more Mister Faulkner has loosened my tongue and kept it flapping. Pete, one day in class you mentioned that Faulkner's mesmeric appeal to some readers lies partially in the fact that he grabs hold of their brains and won't let go of them."

"That can be a curse, also," I grumbled, and agreeing by their laughter, Pete and Augie joined me in an intense scanning of pages in TSAF. As we flipped, stopped, went forward, leafed backward, chewed lips, and bobbed heads in concentration, Pete filled the auditory void. "Shoot, fellas, even before my students start reading TSAF they know that Quentin drowns himself. It's part of the accepted knowledge about the novel available in conversation to all high school and college kids, since so many of them are compelled to read it for class assignments. Hmmm, just like the situation with *The Scarlet Letter*, I would say. All of my students in the survey course who have not read the book beforehand know that Arthur Dimmesdale is the dude who knocks up Hester Prynne. No big secret there."

Determined to establish myself as a worthy participant in this literary colloquy and joust, I concentrated as assiduously as if I had been performing an ocular examination. Scan, flip, skim. . . . "Whoa—here we are, guys. Look on one-ninety-six." Rustle, rustle of pages. "Quoting our favorite Mister Congeniality here, Jason Compson: 'I says no I never had university advantages because at Harvard they teach you how to go for a swim at night without knowing how to swim.'"

Pete arose in a crouch from his chair, balancing his copy of TSAF on his left knee, and shook my proffered hand. Then he turned toward Augie and proclaimed, "A fine bloodhound the good doctor has become, don't you think? I was just about to cite page two-oh-two, but this earlier reference hints at place and method, and mine does not."

"Oh, let's look at yours anyway," I pronounced with elaborate magnanimity now that I was a full-fledged member of the Faulkner Bureau of Investigation—at least in my own mind.

"Yes, go ahead, Pete, please," requested Augie.

"All right, I will," replied our compliant professor. "In this scene on two-oh-two Jason encounters the solitary, partially disguised Caddy among the Compson family gravestones in the Jefferson cemetery on the day of their father's funeral in 1912. Quoting Jason's monologue here: 'She looked at the flowers again. There must have been fifty dollars' worth. Somebody had put one bunch on Quentin's.' Therefore—first-time readers of the novel can now be certain that Quentin does die on June second, 1910, as it appears certain that he will at the end of his own interior monologue."

"Eureka!" I shouted. Heady with my earlier success, I had moved past Pete's quoted passage and had been skimming feverishly. "Guys, look on two-thirty-three. Jason fills in the last essential piece of the puzzle here. He is speaking of his three siblings, first Benjy, then Quentin and then Caddy: 'one of them is crazy and'"—I raised my voice almost to a shout—"'ANOTHER ONE DROWNED HIMSELF'"—with voice lowered again, "'and the other one was turned out into the street by her husband. . . .' Jason irrefutably confirms what these earlier two clues cumulatively suggest."

"Wonderful, wonderful," bespoke our evening's host, rubbing his hands together in satisfaction. "Thanks so much, my colleagues in investigation. You have just demonstrated how difficult it is in this bedeviling book even to know with certainty that the male Quentin dies and, if so, then by what cause. Therefore, as I asserted earlier, the 'where' of the matter understandably gets lost in the shuffle."

I wiggled my right index finger at Augie and pronounced in a childish whine, "Tee-chur! You promised! Now kin we tawk about WHERE?"

Chuckling indulgently, Augie nodded his head vigorously and agreed. "Certainly, master Watkins, unless you need to make a potty stop first. No? Then let's go back to the summary of Quentin's itinerary presented in the 'Historic Day' essay." Augie picked up the thick packet to which he had earlier referred.

At that moment a very attractive young brunette nurse whom I recognized as Penny Lou Swann walked briskly into the room and asked, "May I do anything for you, Captain Dupree? Time to take these pills." She handed Augie three pills of assorted colors and shapes, along with a plastic cup of water. "Why are you wearing that baseball cap indoors? You have another half hour until I must shoo your visitors out—oh hello, Doctor Watkins. I didn't recognize you with your casual clothes on."

"Good evening to you, Ms. Swann. And this is Professor Prefont from Moffatt College." An exchange of "Pleased to meet you" and "Thanks, you too" followed, and Augie politely declined Penny Lou's offer of any further assistance. As she pulled the door shut behind her, Pete and Augie both snorted, guffawed, and directed several barbs at me: "Casual clothes, eh?" "How does she usually see you, honored practitioner of the healing arts?" "Have you been playing doctor and nurse, Speck?" "A little episode of comparative anatomy, by any chance?"

"ENOUGH!" I shouted. "I just knew that you two clowns wouldn't be able to pass up the chance to jump on that innocent straight line. Now, may we hear your Faulkner discovery of the night, Augie, before Pete and I get unceremoniously evicted?"

"Yes, Speck, yes," said our Captain. "I'll settle down. Now Pete, you shouldn't have leered that way at me. I don't need to laugh so hard, in my delicate condition—ahem. Anyway—back to Mister Faulkner's book. The summary presented in here"—Augie held up 'An Historic Day'—"about Quentin's movements during the morning of June second, beginning with the young man's awakening and his early activities in the dormitory room at Harvard, and continuing with Quentin's trips to the nearby post office, various sites in Boston, and then back to Cambridge, seems accurate. But I have a problem with this next part. I quote: 'This bridge at the foot of Boylston Street (now known as J. F. Kennedy Street) could only be the one in the area that Quentin crossed several times and eventually jumped from to his death.' The reference here is to the Larz Anderson Bridge, a structure spanning the Charles River adjacent to the Harvard campus."

Augie looked up from his notes and said, "I disagree with this designation of bridge. Evidence from the novel demonstrates that Quentin could not have chosen the Larz Anderson Bridge or any other bridge in the immediate Boston-Cambridge area as the place of his death by drowning."

Augie held up his copy of TSAF. "Speck, Pete: grab your novels once more tonight, and follow me through some page references, please," he politely requested. "Look first on eighty-five. During the morning of June second, after he has eaten breakfast in Boston, Quentin first goes to a jeweler's shop and then to a, quoting here, 'hardware store . . . across the street," in the latter of which he purchases, quoting again, 'two six-pound flat-irons' that 'felt heavy enough together.' A few hours later, after he has ridden trolleys and interurban trains that travel in several different directions, he disembarks at a stop where—look on one-twelve—'A road crossed the track. . . . The road went into trees, where it would be shady.' Now go to one-fifteen. Quentin follows the road away from the tracks, into the woods, and toward the beckoning waters of the Charles River, until he discovers a bridge."

"Aha!" I exclaimed. "So here we are in the countryside, at a bridge. Sniff on, leader hound of the Murryvilles!"

"You might be wise to eschew the canine metaphors, Doctor Double-You," Pete interjected. "The hour is growing late, and remember what happened when we three discussed TSAF until nearly eleven o'clock just last month at my place."

"'Zounds' rather than 'hounds' then, I say," was my reply. "Lead on, MacDupe. We have now reached the key bridge."

"Right, Speck," spoke Augie, with an indulgent shake of his head. "Listen to Quentin's poetic description of the span. We are still looking at page one-fifteen. 'I began to feel the water before I came to the bridge. The bridge was of gray stone, lichened, dappled with slow moisture where the fungus crept. Beneath it the water was clear and still in the shadow, whispering and clucking about the stone in fading swirls of spinning sky.' Quentin's scrutiny of the bridge proves it to be satisfactory for his purposes. On one-sixteen: 'Where the shadow of the bridge fell I could see down for a long way, but not as far as the bottom.' And Quentin hides the flat-irons in a secluded place where any casual passerby would be unlikely to find them: 'I hid them under the end of the bridge and went back and leaned on the rail.'"

Pete spoke up. "Captain, are you assuming that this is the suicide bridge, because later that night Quentin uses the twelve pounds of flat-irons to keep him beneath the surface of the Charles River until he drowns?"

"Right, Professor," eagerly responded our chief detective. "We know from Jason's caustic comments we read earlier this evening that Quentin waits until after dark to drown himself." Augie read again from his copy of TSAF: 'because at Harvard they teach you how to go for a swim at night without knowing how to swim.' However, Jason, who as far as we know never goes near Massachusetts in his life, must have been speaking in general terms with that reference to Harvard. Jason is correct about the chronology—'at night'—but incorrect about the specific locale. This bridge cannot be the Larz Anderson or any other actual structure but instead must be a fictional bridge created by Faulkner and placed by him in a remote area, away from the urban congestion of Cambridge proper or greater Boston,"

Frowning deeply, I looked intently at Augie and spoke. "Your argument seems plausible, but I'm still not certain that I am convinced. . . ."

"Wait please, neighbor Watkins, and let me present you with two more clusters of evidence from the text, ones that I hope will fully convince you."

"Tallyho—oh hell, I mean sally forth, my good man," I spluttered.

"Right on," replied Caesar Augustus Dupree. "Look on one-seventeen. As Quentin stands on this stone structure, looking down into the water, quoting here, 'Three boys with fishing poles came onto the bridge.' Quentin asks these boys two questions. See one-nineteen: quote, 'how far it was to the nearest town. They told me." And, 'Are there any factories in that town?' If this bridge were the Larz Anderson or any other bridge near it in the Cambridge area, Quentin would have no reason to ask such questions about the city that serves as the site of venerable Harvard. He would know that he could quickly walk to his dormitory at the University from the Anderson Bridge or other nearby spans, and after nine months of residence in Cambridge he would surely be aware of the presence of any nearby factories."

Augie looked at Pete and me, smiled at the nodding of our heads, and plunged onward. "Now for point two. Later in the afternoon, when Quentin is apprehended by Anse the local marshal and questioned about the alleged kidnapping of the silent Italian girl, Anse escorts Quentin to the office of the local 'Squire'—look on one-forty-three—and the Squire asks Quentin, '"What are you up to, coming out here kidnapping children,"' with the key phrase 'out here' clearly pointing to a jurisdiction a considerable distance away from Cambridge.

"MOREOVER: one Mrs. Bland, whose entourage Quentin soon coincidentally encounters, also reinforces by her words the assumption that Quentin has journeyed out into the countryside west and possibly south of Cambridge before he comes upon the ideal bridge, meets the Italian girl, and experiences his skirmish with the local rural, and not urban, constabulary. As she whisks Quentin away to a picnic taking place within walking distance of a farm house with a pump in its yard, Mrs. Bland haughtily says—check on page one-forty-five: "'Quentin Compson. . . . What would your mother say. A young man naturally gets into scrapes, but to be arrested on foot by a country policeman.'"

Augie took another deep breath, this one for purposes of recuperation, leaned back in his recliner, and asked, "Well, gentlemen? Have we solved this geographical puzzle?"

Raising both fists high in the air, Pete proclaimed, "Two and a half for the Captain: RAH, RAH, UHHH!" Then he bounced to his feet. "Allow me to be more formal, dear sirs. Monsieur Dupin, you have proven your case. The bridge that Quentin chooses for his suicide appears in a rural and obscure location rather than an urban and public one. I will notify Miriam Littlejohn of your findings. Case closed!" Pete slammed together the covers of his copy of TSAF.

"Thank you, thank you, Pete," Augie humbly replied as he bowed in his chair, "and also to you, Speck," acknowledging my staccato applause. "But there remains Miriam's other question: does all of this matter? So what if Quentin drowns in the Charles River away from Cambridge rather in the middle of the city?"

"Well? Do you have more entertainment for us mystery addicts tonight?" I queried.

"Not tonight, Speck, but perhaps I will by Sunday, when I will gain my parole from this antiseptic penal colony. Remember that Doctor Bobbie Sue is conducting a brief inquiry for me, and perhaps in two days I can wrap up the entire case for us all." Augie finished speaking just as Nurse Swann sashayed through the door once more.

"Visiting hours are over, please, Doctor Watkins, and Professor. This patient and I need to be alone. Captain Dupree, you be a good boy now, take off that robe, and drop your pajama bottoms. It's time to. . . ."

Penny Lou stopped speaking, turned toward Pete and me, and stared with dropped jaw as we irreverent interlopers whooped, snorted, and yuk-yukked our ways out the open door, bumping into each other and stumbling as we exited.

Turning into the hallway, I heard Penny Lou say to Augie, "Now what in tarnation is wrong with those two, and Doctor Watkins on the medical staff here, if you please. What's so funny about a routine rectal temperature? Oh my, Captain Dupree. Why are you holding that book up in the air like that? No, don't throw it at your friends. They've already gone. . . ."

Tracking the Troubled Mississippian

Eliciting universal gratitude from the citizens of Crowder County, the unusual cool spell continued right through the transition between July and August, months ordinarily cursed throughout our part of America for their steadily dreary weeks of incessant heat and oppressive humidity. On Sunday, July 30, the residents of Summit Avenue were delighted to welcome Augie Dupree back into our fold, grateful as we were that he would not miss enjoying these halcyon days altogether. Pablo Ziegler, Bobbie Sue Middlebury, and also Phil Luther, the orthopedist treating the infection in Augie's right thigh area, collaborated in agreement that Augie was fit to return to his home, and they put no restrictions on his activities other than to caution him not to overexert himself and to retreat indoors in the afternoons if our weather returned to its normal inhospitable temperatures.

Consequently, Augie spent the early part of Sunday afternoon inspecting his yard and consulting with neighbor Jackson Burton about the latter's expert substitute care of his foliage and shrubbery. And then at three o'clock the Captain and Mrs. Dupree came through the gate separating their yard from the Watkins estate and spent the next few hours happily ensconced in lawn chairs in the shade of a capacious red gum tree next to our swimming pool as a steady stream of friends from all over Murryville stopped by to take refreshing dips, swill various beverages, and schmooze with the Dew-prees.

By six-thirty, once the welcoming party had dwindled to a few lap paddlers with apparent aspirations for the Olympics and two or three garrulous story tellers, Augie took advantage of the departure of one sweet but particularly talkative widow and motioned me over to his honored reception throne. "I'm feeling energetic tonight, Speck, despite all of the jawing I have already done," he informed me. "How about if you, Pete, and I use our time together tonight and wind up this Quentin Compson business, before Pete takes off on his August trip to Ohio with Ellie and you and Julianna fly to Boston for that convention of mayors? We may not have another chance to chat until September."

"Dandy with me, neighbor," I cordially responded. "I'll see if Pete and Ellie can stay for supper also. Julianna has stored several filet mignons in the freezer, and I'll just add two more to the four that are thawing right now. The other hangers-on should depart soon."

Luckily, the Prefonts had no other pressing engagements and were persuaded to stay by the promise of choice grilled beef, baked potatoes, Caesar salad, assorted beverages, and double-chocolate brownies for dessert. The meal went off splendidly, and after dinner the six of us lolled around on the Watkins's railed back porch, burped (discreetly, of course), reveled in the comfortably cool evening, and sipped French hazelnut coffee. Fortunately, Ellie had donned a knee-length cotton beach shirt that covered her tantalizing hot-pink string bikini and allowed me to avoid staring dumbfoundedly at her as I had already done too many times—or so Julianna's arched eyebrows told me—during the late afternoon.

From the near-railing side of our suspended porch swing Coach Ellie said to Augie and me, "Guys, you all are so nice to help Pete with these Faulkner puzzles and readings." She placed her left hand on her husband's nearby right knee. "Honey, have you told Speck and Augie that you might try to write up some of these interpretations and see if you can get them into print?"

Pete switched his coffee cup to his left hand, patted Ellie's slender paw, and responded, "Sweetheart, you have just notified them of my scheme. And I would like to do that, if they do not object. I'll give them all due credit, of course."

"A capital proposal, Pete," boomed out Augie from his reconfigured lawn chair. "Just remember to spell our names correctly; right, Speck?"

"Make that a unanimous vote," I said with sincerity. "If we can help your scholarly career in any way, then I will be truly delighted."

"Thanks for the approval, friends," Pete spoke, as he nodded and smiled in contentment. "I'll use our notes and your offered outlines, Augie, and tackle the

Macintosh word processor early this upcoming fall semester. I'll probably need to consult you two detectives often before I mail off any potential articles. If or when I hear from any journals, I'll certainly let you know."

"The best of luck, Pete," spoke up my fair bride. "I just hope that you can make publishable sense out of the gibberish dreamed up by these two enfeebled, self-anointed Sherlocks."

Sitting on my spine in a lawn chair, I immediately straightened my back, sloshing my coffee, and proclaimed, "Watch thy tongue, you brazen hussy! You knoweth not of what you speak. And remember, Monsieur Dupin is a recuperating invalid, and I am possessed of an exceptionally fragile artistic temperament."

"Oh, horse hockey!" the Mayor replied. "Archie, you lost any delicacy or fragility you might have ever had at about the same time you lost your. . . . Oh, never mind."

To my eternal gratitude, Augie redirected the conversation. "Speck, if we are to be of real help to Pete on TSAF, we had better wind up the discussion that we started on Friday night, when I was still behind bars in the Churchill River Medical big house."

Mary Alice took the opportunity to speak. "Ladies, we could walk next door to my house, catch Sylvester Stallone in "Demolition Man" on the Sunday night t. v. movie, and let these allegedly scholarly sleuths jaw away to their mandibles' content. What do you say?"

"Oh, goodie!" blurted out Julianna. "But isn't Wesley Snipes in that movie too? I just LOVE his pectorals."

"I'll come with you and try to decide which of those hunks is cuter," concluded Ellie. "It will take me at least two hours to reach my conclusion." I averted my eyes as Ellie placed her gorgeous legs into motion, walking saucily away from the swing.

"It's flick time for us sorority girls," squealed Her Honor, descending our steps rapidly, Mary Alice and Ellie in her wake. "Come join us AFTER our movie is over and ONLY when you have wound up your boring literary chit-chat."

Shaking my head as the women departed, I said, "Pete, I just hope that those two Summit Avenue beauty-shop babes don't corrupt your new wife with their middle-aged brainwashings. Ellie should limit her exposure to their propaganda concerning the inherent shortcomings of the male gender."

"Not to fret, Doctor Dub-Ya," spoke back the professor. "Ellie considers your wives to be her wise mentors in the subject of how to tolerate a perpetual man around the house, but believe me my little sweetums will ALWAYS do her own thinking about any subject. Oh, here's Augie, back already."

Following discreetly several steps in the aft of the prancing pompon squad, Augie had gone to his house and brought back his brief case containing two copies of TSAF, the Norton critical edition featuring the "Appendix," his notes on cards and paper, and his outline, the latter meticulously plotted as usual on several consecutive sheets of a legal pad. He had also switched headwear, from his black-and-gold New Orleans Saints cap to his blue one reading "DETECTIVE" in gold letters. I went into my library in order to retrieve my copy of the novel, and upon my return we were fully prepared for FAULKNER TIME.

". . . Three, two, one. You're on, Monsieur C. Auguste Dupin the Fifth," I enunciated in my best Ed McMahon imitation.

From his lawn chair situated three feet from the porch swing, Augie inclined his head to the left, responded "Thankee, thankee, thankee, or should I say "*Merci*?'" Pete and I had taken seats on opposite ends of the swing, and we slowly rocked in unison, the weight-bearing chains softly sounding, "Sproing, sproing, sproing."

Our chief detective commenced. "Pete, Speck, do you remember that I asked Bobbie Sue if she would kindly do some research for me? Well, this morning when she agreed that I could be released from solitary confinement, she came through with the requested information. I'll fill you in on that as we go along." Augie shifted in his chair, and, with left elbow on his arm rest, raised his left index finger. "We stopped at the point when we were just about ready to consider Miriam Littlejohn's original question of, if I may abbreviate it, SO WHAT? Does it matter if we prove the conventional wisdom to be wrong and we realize that Quentin's suicide does not occur in Cambridge but actually takes place a considerable distance away from Harvard University? Obviously 'Yes,' I assert, or as you fellows are certainly aware, we would not be here tonight, flapping our jaws about one of the most difficult major novels of the twentieth century—or so you termed it in class one day, Pete, and I heartily agree with you."

Augie leaned back and crossed his arms across his chest. "I won't coyly tease you tonight, friends. Here is my central argument. An awareness that Quentin Compson ends his life immersed in the waters of the Charles River beneath a fictional bridge in an imaginary rural locale presents a plausible motive for the young man's final journey on June second, 1910, around the metropolitan Boston-Cambridge area and outlying regions." Augie then leaned forward, raised both hands two feet apart with palms inward, and locked eyes with first Pete and then me. "The motive is this: Quentin is seeking an obscure and infrequently traversed bridge from which he can clutch his purchased flat-irons—or pocket them, possibly—and leap unobserved and unhindered into the lethal depths of the Charles River." Augie elevated his chin and awaited our reactions.

Pete spoke first, which was salutary, because at that juncture my mind was a whistle-clean slate. "You use the word 'motive,' Augie. I have always assumed that Quentin had no motive for his wanderings on this day, other than to—let me think. Oh, yeah—finish out the Harvard term."

Chopping the air vigorously with both inturned palms, Augie stated, "Precisely! Professor, you have summarized the commonly accepted interpretation of Quentin's activities on his last day of life. For part of this assumption, we can thank our old friend"—finger and thumb on book, specimen once more held high, our three voices sounding in unison, "the 'APPENDIX!'"

Quickly flipping pages, Augie requested, "Please listen to this passage from the section headed 'Quentin III': 'waiting first to complete the current academic year and so get the full value of his paid-in-advance tuition.' Faulkner goes on to write that Quentin filled out the year in this way as a form of tribute to, quoting here, 'his youngest brother, born an idiot.'" Augie looked up from the "Appendix." "Well, guys, it is no surprise, is it, that Mister Bill's memory failed him again here?" From a rubber-banded packet in his briefcase Augie pulled out a note card. "As Malcolm Cowley writes, Faulkner, quote, 'could not tell a story twice without transforming one detail after another.'"

Twice Augie flipped the Cowley card with his right thumb and index finger, "Snap! Pow!" and picked up another card. He looked at his listeners and continued: "June second, 1910, was a Thursday, an unlikely day on which the Harvard academic term would end." Augie lifted the note card to chest level and perused it. "Critic Arthur Geffen mentions a reference by Quentin's Harvard roommate Shreve MacKenzie to an eight a.m. psychology class—look on pages seventy-seven and seventy-eight—and thus concludes that final examinations at Harvard could not yet have begun. Geffen also notes the numerous references in Quentin's interior monologue to the Harvard-Yale boat race, scheduled to be held a week in the future, as evidence that the 1909-1910 academic year is still in session on June second, 1910; the race is a traditional sporting event marking the end of the spring term."

I filled the auditory void. "Then we can assume that the motive Faulkner attributes to Quentin in the 'Appendix' is not consistent with the facts in the original text. But Pete, didn't you also say something about Quentin's having no motive for his—was the word 'wanderings?'—on his last day alive?"

Gradually sliding his head backward, his eyes enlarged and focused on Augie's peepers, Pete responded, "Yes, I did, Speck, but I sense that rattlesnake Dupree is coiled and preparing to sink his fangs into that unwary prairie dog of an idea, also."

Laughing softly and shaking his head, Augie sat back and responded, "Am I that transparently predatory, Professor? Well, you are right. I do plan to disagree with the word 'wanderings,' but let me hastily assure you that many critics who have published commentary on TSAF presume that Quentin spends June second, 1910, in purposeless or ineffectual activities. Here are three representative examples.

Flick . . . another note card came out of the packet in Augie's open brief case. "Quentin engages in, quote, 'aimless wanderings to fill out the day.' Another: Quentin, I'm quoting here, 'wanders on the subway and interurban trolley lines.' Three: his movements around the area are, quotation, 'circuitous excursions,' end of quotation, during which, quoting again, 'Quentin fritters away time.' Summary of assumptions? Quentin is killing time until he can kill himself."

"And you obviously disagree, Monsieur Dupin," interjected Pete. "Certainly it is more logical for Quentin to possess a method to his madness during this bizarre last day of his life than it is for him merely to be wasting senselessly his few remaining hours, but how can you prove just what that motive is? Does Quentin ever clearly let us readers in on his secret purpose?"

As I listened to Pete's question, in the dimming light I watched Augie's face, and the Captain slowly allowed a glimmer of a smile to glide through his mouth and eyes. "Monsieur Dupin will prove his case," I said, "just as he has with *Sanctuary* and with Ms. Quentin's burglary: that is, by piecing together clues and reconstructing a crime, this time a suicide. Am I correct, my detective friend?"

"Yes, you are, neighbor," was Augie's response, "although please amend the words 'will prove' to 'hopes to prove.' You two will serve as my jury and render the final verdict concerning the persuasiveness of my argument. But before I begin my peroration, let me tell you about one tangential bit of intelligence that Doctor Middlebury gathered for me.

"You may know that Bobbie Sue completed her undergraduate work at

Harvard. She graciously called a friend who lives in Cambridge, and the friend obligingly took a short trip to the Larz Anderson Bridge. Two published critics mention that some devotees of TSAF had placed a commemorative plaque on the actual Anderson Bridge, but Bobbie's friend could find no trace of it. So that minor mystery remains: what has happened to the plaque?"

I growled, "Maybe Jason Compson materialized magically, appeared in Cambridge, and with his bare teeth ripped it off the bridge facing."

Augie laughed and agreed, "Perhaps the phantasm of Jason did make a ghostly guest vengeance appearance at Harvard. But now it's time to dive into TSAF, my companions."

"Before we start, does anyone want more coffee?" I inquired. "Augie, this is decaf, so it won't keep us old poots up too late tonight."

All three of us chose to sip more hot dessert java while we were out in the refreshing air, and with cups in hand or on a nearby wicker-and-glass deck table we picked up our copies of TSAF, Pete and I looking expectantly at our leader.

"I have consulted two categories of sources in the Quentin section for the information that I am about to outline for you," began Augie: "first, Quentin's private thoughts as expressed in his monologue that often is quite intimately 'interior'; and second, his overt actions, as he narrates them. When combined, both sources provide evidence revealing that Quentin decides to spend June second NOT in meandering purposelessly around the Cambridge-Boston area but in searching until he finds an ideal place for his death by drowning. Look on page eighty. While in his Harvard dormitory room and after he has evaded Shreve's admonition to attend the early psychology class, Quentin subtly reveals through his mental references to 'bones,' 'deep water,' 'the flat-iron,' and the Deity that he has already decided on this day to drown himself."

Pete stared intently at the designated page. "So this early in the day, Quentin has already made up his mind to take the leap of annihilation," he muttered.

"So it appears," Augie responded. "Let's look at the entire quotation in context. Here Quentin creates a fleeting visual fantasy in which, during an indeterminate future time, he views his own physical remains at the place of his death and learns that on Judgment Day his soul will not ascend but that the metal instruments aiding his death will. 'And I will look down and see my murmuring bones and the deep water like wind, like a roof of wind, and after a long time they cannot distinguish even bones upon the lonely and inviolate sand. Until on the Day when He says Rise only the flat-iron would come floating up.'"

Looking up from the book and drawing a deep breath, Augie continued his analysis. "Quentin's very next expressed thought reveals that June second will be the appropriate day for his death, not because he has finally succumbed to despair but because he has developed the certainty in his own mind that he will be able to act alone, and successfully, in accomplishing his morbid objective: 'It's not when you realise that nothing can help you—religion, pride, anything—it's when you realise that you dont need any aid.'"

"Wowee, Sir Caesar Augustus Number Five," I exclaimed, "you have become one whizbang of an interpreter of complex Faulknerian sentences. Whaddya think, Pete? Could Augie qualify as one of your English majors?"

"He's ready for a graduate degree right now," Pete stated admiringly. "I AM impressed."

Setting aside his copy of TSAF, Augie swung his outstretched arms together in front of himself and back to his sides in a baseball sign of "Safe." "Thanks for the positive strokes, friends," he said with sincerity, "but if either of you were to lie prostrate for ten days in a dreary hospital room, you can bet that you would find ways to occupy your restless brain. The alternative is to go stark raving mad, so my choice was an easy one. Concentration on a tricky problem helps the time to pass. ANYWAY—back to the book. Could we use a little more light, Speck?"

Hopping up from the swing and flipping a nearby wall switch, I turned on the three lights recessed in the porch ceiling and then flopped back into my seat on the swing. Augie asked us all to turn to page eighty-one, and he resumed his analysis.

"Here Quentin makes preparations for his last day on Earth: packing his clothes and sundry other possessions; stacking some of his books on a table; addressing a label on his trunk; bathing, shaving, and dressing; and then writing notes, one of them intended for Shreve. Later in the morning he purchases the flat-irons—page eighty-five—that have already been on his mind—page eighty. Quentin assures himself that the flat-irons will keep him under water for a sufficient period of time—eighty-six, toward the top of the page: 'But they felt heavy enough in the air.' Now Quentin can begin his scouting expedition for a location suitable for a clandestine and private drowning."

Augie reached down, pulled 'An Historic Day' from his briefcase, and held it out flat in front of him. "In these pages we can read a place-by-place summary of Quentin's journey during the next two to three hours around the Boston and Cambridge areas. During this time period Quentin explores the vicinity surrounding the Longfellow Bridge and the nearby MBTA Bridge, structures that did exist in 1910. Look on pages eighty-nine and ninety in TSAF. As Quentin smells the nearness of water, touches through his coat letters intended for Shreve and for Quentin's father, and then, from the Longfellow Bridge, observes his own shadow on the water below, he clearly is sizing up this span as a possible site for his final leap. He thinks twice of the word 'drowned' and once of 'submerged,' refers to the flat-irons again by alluding to the package in which they are hidden, and then conjures up images of the romantic allure of oblivion in—look in the middle of page ninety—'the caverns and the grottoes of the sea.'"

Glancing up. Augie politely asked, "Still with me, guys?" Pete and I responded "Yes" simultaneously, guffawed together also, and both ducked our heads once more into the pages of TSAF.

Augie resumed. "Quentin's mind then turns to a practical problem of physics—still on page ninety, guys. Quoting here, 'The displacement of water is equal to the something of something . . . and two six-pound flat-irons weigh more then one tailor's goose.' Gentlemen, I looked up 'tailor's goose' in my dictionary. The term means a ten-pound piece of specially shaped iron, a device once used for pressing clothes, and it has a gooseneck handle. Now . . . let's see. Oh, here we are. Still on ninety. Quentin's next thoughts leap ahead to the laments that he imagines will be expressed by Dilsey back in Jefferson when she learns of Quentin's death, and also to Benjy's visceral fear of sensed death: 'What a sinful waste Dilsey would say. Benjy knew it when Damuddy died. He cried. *He smell hit. He smell hit.'"*

A pause for a sip of coffee, and then steady as he goes. "At the Longfellow, Quentin has found a candidate bridge, and the pull of death is strong here. But this location lacks one essential characteristic." Augie looked at us two stooges. "Pete? Speck?"

The Professor won the kewpie doll. "Privacy. There are too many people around."

"Keee-rect, kind sir. Now flip between pages eighty-nine and ninety, my friends, and cite some examples, if you please," Augie directed.

A moment's silence. Then . . . "Here on eighty-nine," yelled Pete. "Quentin disembarks from a streetcar full of travelers."

"Also on eighty-nine," I shouted. "Sailors on a schooner that is being towed by a tugboat."

"Ninety," blurted out Pete. "Several rowers, including Quentin's schoolmate, Gerald Bland."

"Wun-dur-full, wun-dur-full," responded our most excellent detective but mediocre imitator of Lawrence Welk. "You guys have listed my own examples of evidence. Now look on ninety-two, and you will see that Quentin rejects this bridge and continues his quest. Quoting Quentin here, with the pronoun 'it' referring to his own shadow: 'I walked it into the shadow of the quai. Then I went east.'"

Augie kept on keepin' on. "Onward to page ninety-nine, please. After a return to Harvard and a conversation with the elderly Black named Deacon to whom he entrusts a note intended for Shreve, Quentin eventually heads west on an interurban train, staying close to the Charles River and disembarking at a rural intersection where—page one-twelve now"—flip, flip, flip—"I quote here, 'There was a wooden marquee with an old man eating something out of a paper bag.' Quentin then walks along the nearby road leading into the trees until he finds the, quoting here, 'bridge of gray stone,' and as he investigates this promising location, ironic images of his soul's possible resurrection occur to him again, just as they had at the Longfellow Bridge. I'm reading now from page one-sixteen, near the middle: 'And maybe when He says Rise the eyes will come floating up too, out of the deep quiet and the sleep, to look on glory. And after a while the flat irons would come floating up.' But this time he concludes that he has found a suitable spot, and as we discussed on Friday night, he hides the flat-irons in a secure place, quote, 'under the end of the bridge.'"

I looked up from my concentrated stare at page one-sixteen, "So why doesn't he go ahead and jump at this juncture, Augie? We know now that Faulkner's 'Appendix' statement about Quentin's wanting to end the Harvard term is a bogus interpretation, so Quentin doesn't really need to fill out the hours of the day here."

As I babbled, Augie keenly observed me and slowly nodded. Then he shifted his eyes to Pete. "Professor? Your opinion?"

Our youngest detective sat hunched forward, with the tip of his left thumbnail ensnared between his bare upper and lower front teeth. "Too many people around again, just as was true at the Longfellow Bridge."

"Well, SHI...," I exploded, "er, I mean SHINOLA! Of course. The three boys with the fishing poles on page one-seventeen."

"Correct, Doctor," stated Pete mildly. It was evident that he wished to avoid another game of one-upmanship with me, his rapidly aging host. "To go back to your original question, Speck. Quentin must now wait until night, after full dark sets in, when from this remote and seldom-visited span he can plunge into the Charles River and be reasonably assured that he will be neither restrained from jumping nor rescued from drowning."

"Yes, yes," I affirmed, rocking back and forth more vigorously. The chain sang "Sproing POP! Sproing POP!" I jumped back into the conversation. "At the Longfellow and MBTA Bridges, schooners or tugboats with their crews and streetcars with their passengers could appear at almost any time, day or evening. So this gray stone bridge possesses the number one desirable feature. As Pete earlier put it, privacy, at least of the nocturnal sort.

"Now we are all thinking alike," smilingly spoke Augie as he rubbed his hands together in approval of the functioning brains of his companions. "Pete, you mentioned Quentin's determination not to be rescued from drowning. Bobbie Sue also kindly supplied me with some helpful information on the topic of death by drowning. By serendipity, her husband Ollie, who is also an internist—"

Rude as usual, I barged in. "Yes, Doctor S. Olaf Middlebury is recognized in our medical community here in Murryville as a top researcher and contributor to medical periodicals. A very scholarly and knowledgeable doc, my friend Ollie."

The Captain politely waited until I had run down my wound-up-toy motor mouth, and then he resumed in mid-sentence—"has written an article for the *Journal of the Arkansas Medical Society* on the subject of death by drowning. Bobbie Sue passes on this expert information to us." Augie pulled another note card out of his banded bundle. "Here is a summary of Ollie's scientific opinions on this subject. 'Quentin Compson will require only a short passage of time before he drowns, with the immediate cause of death being the lack of oxygen to his brain. If Quentin does not hold his breath, his lungs will quickly fill with water, oxygen cannot enter his bloodstream, and he will die within three minutes, and likely sooner.'"

"But what if he holds his breath?" I inquired. "Whether he intends to or not?"

"Ollie reports that if Quentin does hold his breath, 'within a short time under water he will breathe reflexively, and his lungs will inhale water. In this second scenario, he could live no longer than four to five minutes, and probably fewer.'"

Pete pursed his lips, nodded emphatically once, and stated, "With the flat-irons assuring that he will stay beneath the waters of the Charles, then, Quentin will need—at the longest—five minutes in which to accomplish his ardently desired death. And it appears certain that this dark, secluded bridge will give him his maximum of five minutes."

My turn again. "So what does he do to occupy his time until night sets in? Let's see, there is the accidental encounter with the silent Italian girl. . . ." As I talked, I rapidly turned pages in the novel and scanned them.

Augie took over. "Right, Speck. This episode, along with its subsequent farcical legal entanglements, supplies one answer to Quentin's dilemma of what to do with the rest of his day, and the equally coincidental meeting with the Bland picnic party adds another time-filler to his waning hours." Augie picked up TSAF again. "Now, during the picnic Quentin sinks into a lengthy reverie, remembering both his confrontation in late summer 1909 with Dalton Ames at the bridge back in Mississippi near Jefferson and also his own numerous ineffectual attempts to serve as Caddy's self-appointed protector. This reverie extends from one-forty-nine to one-sixty-four."

"Oh, yeah," I piped up. "This is where Quentin and Gerald Bland duke it out with their bare fists."

"At the picnic he does box with Gerald," affirmed Augie. "Quentin loses badly and suffers a black eye and episodes of bleeding. And then after Quentin separates himself from the group of merry picnickers and alone boards the trolley heading back into Boston, he begins once more to feel drawn toward the oblivion offered by water. Look on one-sixty-nine and one-seventy: 'the road going on under the twilight, into twilight and the sense of water peaceful and swift beyond. . . . This was where I saw the river for the last time this morning, about here. I could feel water beyond the twilight, smell. . . . I could smell the curves of the river beyond the dusk and I saw the last light supine and tranquil upon tide flats like pieces of a broken mirror. . . .'

"Almost finished now, fellows," Augie told us, raising his head from TSAF. "Let's see, by my watch it's nine-thirty. Do you think that the movie is about over?"

"Probably by ten or shortly after," I replied, "so we should have enough time to finish off Quentin—OOPS, sorry, guys, bad accidental pun—before our girlfriends return from lapping up the Muscle Beach review."

For most of the evening Pete uncharacteristically had remained in a seated position on the swing, but at this moment, with the novel lying open in his left hand, he abruptly arose and began his professorial perambulation. Augie leaned leftward toward me and whispered, "Earlier he was mostly listening. Now, he is thinking, and intensely."

I nodded in agreement, observing Pete as he cerebrally strolled in an uneven pattern all around my railed porch.

"Shall I continue, Pete?" inquired Augie.

"Please do, sir," replied our earnest scholar, waving his right hand absent-mindedly in our direction.

"Okay," said our leader, "we now have followed Quentin back to his room at Harvard. Look on page one-seventy-two. Here he cleans his own blood from his vest with gasoline. . . ."

"HOT DAMN!" bellowed Pete. "Waaa-HOOO! I've got it. You bet your sweet arse. I truly DO!"

Augie flinched, I jarred myself to a sudden stop in the swing, and both of us older gents stared at our junior colleague in surprise.

"Captain! Doctor!" Pete yelled at us as he leaned almost within touching distance of our startled faces. "When I taught this novel in the spring, I spent several hours trying to make sense of this one crazy italicized passage on page one seventy-two, and I never could. Follow along as I read it. *'seeing on the rushing darkness only his own face no broken feather unless two of them but not two like that going to Boston the same night then my face his face for an instant across the crashing when out of darkness two lighted windows in rigid fleeing crash gone his face and mine just I see saw did I see not goodbye the marquee empty of eating the road empty in darkness in silence the bridge arching into silence darkness sleep the water peaceful and swift not goodbye.'"*

Still on his feet, Pete stood straight, pounded twice on the inner spine of TSAF, and excitedly spoke: "Augie, your lengthy analysis of Quentin's motive for his many geographical changes of place on this last day of his life has furnished the mental light bulb that illuminates this passage. And I believe that it is the final piece in your puzzle. May I tell you what I am thinking?"

"Most assuredly, Pete," replied our chief detective. "I studied those words but was content simply to agree with the summation of the very helpful critic Edmond Volpe when he writes"—Augie read from yet another note card—"'Image: Ride Back to Bridge.'"

"Co-oh-oh-rect you are, sir. In this passage Quentin's mind flashes rapidly through a series of images that amounts to a visual preview, or plan, of his upcoming return trip to the chosen rural suicide bridge with the flat-irons hidden beneath the end of it."

Throwing back his shoulders and unconsciously assuming a formal oratorical stance, with opened novel in left hand as he gestured and pointed with his right, Pete, now in command, barked out orders and explications to the senior contingent. "Turn back to one-sixty-nine and follow along with me please, gentlemen. Within the preceding hour, during his recently completed trip back from the countryside, first to Boston and then to Harvard, Quentin had sat with his face toward the window—because he is self-conscious about his recently acquired black eye—and had watched his own reflection—'The lights were on in the car'—and that of 'a woman across the aisle' whose hat has 'a broken feather in it.' From his own room mentally retracing his route in reverse, Quentin thinks of various reflections of how his own face had looked. Now go forward to one-seventy-two again, and I quote, with the second use of the word 'face' referring to Quentin's memory of his image as it appears in the train window: *'my face his face for an instant across the crashing'; his face and mine just I see saw did I see.'"*

Pete orated, paced, gestured dramatically, and totally surrendered himself to the spell of Faulkner's poetic prose. Augie and I followed along with Pete, smiling frequently at each other in agreement with his acutely accurate analysis and in amused acknowledgment of his enthusiastic response to great literature.

Peter Edward Prefont: "Then Quentin's mind locks on the image of the marquee at the rural intersection as it will appear after dark, *'empty of eating,'* with no old man dining from a bag, as happened at mid-day. The marquee and its surrounding area will be devoid of other human beings and hence safe, with no one nearby to deter him from achieving his destructive objective. Likewise, the country road will be free of potential unwanted Samaritans: *'the road empty in darkness in silence.'*

"In the most attractive image of all to Quentin, the bridge itself will be ready for him so that he may end his torment by merging sleepily and peacefully into the water: *'the bridge arching into silence darkness sleep the water peaceful and swift.'* The final two words of this intense reverie—*'not goodbye'*—stress that Quentin has deliberately avoided saying words such as 'goodbye' or 'farewell' to any person, family member, friend, or mere acquaintance, so that no one will know of his firm intention to kill himself. His good-byes will be expressed after his death through the written messages to his father and to Shreve that he plans to leave behind."

Pete fell silent, dropped his head, and then gradually raised his eyes and fixed them on Augie and me. Simultaneously the Captain and I broke into applause, and then all three of us were startled to hear additional clapping emanating from the patio below us, along with shrill whistling and cheers: "Say it, brother." "Sing to my ears." "You the man, Pete." "Huzzah, huzzah." "Yowzer, wowzer." Our perilous Paulines had returned and again were satirically showering us, or at least one of us, with a demonstration of approval, just as they had done in April when *Sanctuary* was the novel of the moment.

Quite visibly blushing, even in the moderate light of the porch bulbs, Pete gulped, sat on the swing, and said, "Thanks, everyone—I guess. Augie, have I helped to prove your case?"

"Definitely, Professor," replied Augie. "You have supplied the final piece in the puzzle. Now Quentin stands poised on the verge of leaving his dormitory room, irrevocably determined to return to the ideal suicide location discovered during his earlier scouting expedition. Quentin knows that at the top of any hour he will be able to board an interurban train that will take him back out into the countryside and on his way to the chosen bridge. We all know what he does next, and he does it with grim finality."

By this time our wives had joined us on the porch. Julianna grabbed my hand and pulled me to my feet. "If you haven't finished your b. s. session yet, boys, too bad. Our movie is over, and we coeds need to head to our boudoirs and start having dream fantasies about virile studs dressed in berets, sleeveless flak jackets, and tight trousers."

Meekly, we three literary detectives followed our spouses down the porch steps of the Watkins manse, past the swimming pool, and around the house to the driveway where Herbie Junior was sedately parked. As Pete opened the passenger door for Ellie and cordially thanked Julianna and me for the evening, Ellie hugged Augie, welcomed him back, and also hugged the other three remaining nifty fifty-year-olds.

A large halogen streetlight, recently installed by the town's Public Works

Department as a gesture of appropriate—ahem—homage to the Mayor, flooded our section of Summit Avenue with illumination. While Ellie was passing warm fuzzy squeezes all around, Pete took notice of a bright red Ferrari that was pulling into a driveway across the street from my house. In the driver's seat sat a tall, strikingly handsome man in his late twenties, with razor-cut, wavy, thick brown hair and a slender, muscular physique that was tastefully complemented by an elegant gray pin-striped Italian silk suit. Next to him in the Ferrari sat the ravishingly beautiful blonde daughter of our neighbors Connie and Herb Wilks. Jamie Wilks wore an electric-blue cocktail gown and an exquisite peach-colored scarf over her hair. Looking at Ellie, then at himself, then at Herbie Junior, Pete cupped his right hand around the side of his mouth and shouted in the direction of the Wilks's driveway: "Hey, buddy. You wanna trade lives?"

The last we Summit Avenue residents saw of the Prefonts that night, Ellie was sprinting along the center stripe of our street in hot pursuit of her husband, swinging her fists at him in near-miss swats as she shouted, "Trade wives, huh? TRADE WIVES? You ingrate! I'll penalty-kick you right in the big hurt. . . . Huh? You said 'LIVES?' So what the squat is the difference? I'll . . . I'll . . . cram that insult right where the sun don't shine. . . . You lousy pseudo-comedian. COME BACK HERE!"

Chapter Five

The Case of Addie Bundren's Mathematical Bequest in *As I Lay Dying*

Bare-Chested Running Choir

"Do you hear singing coming from somewhere to the east, Augie, or am I beginning to conjure up imaginary voices as I slide further into my anecdotage?"

"Yes, Speck, I also am hearing what sounds like many voices raised in song, but I can't understand the words. Perhaps this momentary mystery will resolve itself as we draw closer to Moffatt, since my ears are telling me that the music is drifting toward us from that sector of town."

On Monday, September 4, 1995, at 7:20 a.m., Captain C. Augustus Dupree was once again accompanying your humble narrator on a morning exercise walk. Augie and I had taken the liberty of commencing our jaunt not at our customary six a.m. but at a later hour on this Labor Day, since I had closed my office for the long holiday weekend and Augie had no pressing plans other than a date with Mary Alice later in the morning during which the Duprees would meticulously prune their prized shrub rose bushes. Julianna and I predictably had found a solid reason to avoid any yard work that might beckon to us from our surrounding lawn or foliage, for Her Honor the Mayor had been invited to serve as the principal speaker at the traditional Crowder County Labor Day fish fry, which would commence at 4 p.m. in River Bend Park.

Every ambitious politician (pardon the redundancy) in the County, ranging from assistant superintendent of solid waste services up through members of the Town Council and then ascending to County Commissioner and to Julianna, eagerly awaited this annual fish fry and spent several hours each Labor Day glad-handing with constituents, pretending to be humble in the presence of the proletariat, and reminding segments of the electorate of actual or hypothetical accomplishments beneficial to particular voting blocs or other special interest groups. My role at the picnic was to make certain that Julianna conversed, however briefly, at some moment during the afternoon or evening with every attending member of Murryville's business and professional establishment. The modest working class could certainly provide votes, but the executive stratum supplied the money, clout, and other lubricants essential to the continued operation of the Julianna Murry Watkins well-oiled political machine.

At 7 a.m. Augie and I had moseyed out of our neighborhood in the older near-northwest residential area of Murryville and had guided our feet to the east and then the northeast, aiming for the contiguous campuses in the north-central sector of our burg on which sit Churchill River Medical Center and Moffatt College. Both institutions reign serenely on large parcels of land dedicated solely either to the hospital or to the school. Surrounded by woods, three trout-stocked ponds, and undulating lawns, C. R. M. C. looms majestically over one hundred acres of rolling hills into which streets enter from six different directions, with not one of the six streets passing all the way through to the opposite side. The Medical Center acreage thus preserves its sanctity and aura of unusual serenity. Hospital Street, which leads northward from the downtown area and dead-ends into the C. R. M. C. acreage, is lined with medical office buildings (including my three-thousand-square-foot freestanding edifice) and pharmacies along the four blocks closest to the main entrance into the C. R. M. C. estate. College Avenue, three blocks due east of Hospital and its parallel thoroughfare beginning at the northern edge of downtown and continuing to its termination at the entrance to the Moffatt campus, features along both of its sides a mixture of older cottages, larger homes mostly now reconfigured into student apartments, fast-food outlets, video stores, and T-shirt shops. Walking eastward on Williams Lane, Augie and I had crossed Hospital Street and soon were approaching College Avenue when we again heard some voiced notes of music.

Now more curious than ever, we nodded to one another, in lock-step turned left at College Avenue, and, determined to discover the source of the mysterious choral entertainment, walked straight toward the main entrance leading into the Moffatt campus.

We did not have to wait long for a repetition of the music that we had now heard twice. As we stepped onto the sidewalk beginning at the edge of the campus and leading toward Shoemaker Hall, where Pete Prefont continued to impersonate "Phantom Professor of the Opera" by maintaining his solo office behind the elevator shaft, Monsieur Dupin V and I jerked our heads abruptly to the left at the sudden sound of multiple feet pounding softly on the asphalt running path snaking through the thick, dark-green carpet of Moffatt College lawn. We instantly stopped and awaited the arrival of approximately twenty-five young men, all of them attired in white nylon Umbro soccer shorts with black trim, black triple-white-striped training shoes, and nothing else visible; nary a shirt, tank-top, or scrap of cloth covered any runner's upper torso. The Moffatt College men's soccer team was circumnavigating the perimeter of the lushly landscaped campus on its customary morning training run, and Augie and I took two steps backward so that the runners on the southern edge of the staggered pack, with three to four runners abreast, would not have to deviate from their prescribed route.

A muscular six-foot athlete sporting a blonde pony tail, presumably the team captain, paced steadily at the head of the group, frequently turning his head to the left or right in order to shout words of encouragement: "Only one more mile to go, Bulldogs! Pick it up, freshmen; you're in college now. No stragglers allowed! Beat Southeastern!" Erratically antiphonal responses echoed in the wake of the leader's yells: "Right on, Cap!" "Bulldogs, bulldogs, ruff, ruff, ruff!" "Whip those Polecats!" As a loyal Moffatt alumnus, I felt a tingle in my spine and a swelling of my vain chest in reaction to the sight of these youthful warriors preparing to line up on the soccer pitch in stout opposition to the Bulldogs' traditional opponents. I glanced at Augie, who smiled and said softly, "Makes you want to join them in battling the Polecats; right, Speck?"

I had no time to respond to Detective Dupin's most recent invasion of my thought processes, because as the leader spotted us two interlopers standing to the side of the running path, he raised his right arm and shouted in rhythm, "One, two, three." Then the entire group of runners joined the blonde choirmaster in straggle-breathed a cappella harmony:

[musical notation]

Good morn-ing, good morn-ing, how'd ya like to bite my ass?

[musical notation]

Good morn-ing, good morn-ing, how'd ya like to bite my ass?

The parade of vocalizing runners swept past us two forlorn spectators, continued pacing steadily into the sunrise bringing the promise of another 90-plus degree day of high humidity, and resumed its pattern of solo shouts from the leader followed by collective responses from the pack. Startled by the volume of the choral tribute as well as the unexpected lyrical content, Augie and I initially reacted in wide-eyed surprise and then in mutual laughter punctuated by his elbows in my ribs and my left hand slapping my left knee. "What a hoot, Augie," I said between guffaws. "Now we know the source of the enigmatic music we have been indistinctly hearing this morning."

"Yes, neighbor," responded the Captain, "and we can also conclude that this choir more properly belongs in a stag locker room than it does in a church sanctuary."

"Augie! Speck! Oh good honk, fellows, so it is you two prominent citizens standing over here. I am so sorry for the behavior of the Bulldogs and for that song."

Peeling off from his posterior place in the pack, a profusely perspiring

Professor Peter Prefont paddled over to our path-side positions while pointedly panting his apology. "Hey, guys," he enunciated between heaves of chest and raspy gaspings for breath, "the soccer boys meant nothing disrespectful" . . . wheeze, wheeze . . . "by that ditty. Rest assured that on their runs they sing it to whomever they encounter: grounds crew workers, coeds, townspeople, deans, stray dogs or cats, and even—perish the thought—professors." Pant, pant, pant. "I've had it sung to me more times than I can count."

"Pete, my good man," I shouted at my young friend of half-a-year's time, "shake my hand. No, don't recoil; I care not one whit if you are sweaty. I am also somewhat stinky. After all, this is the morning exercise period for the Captain and me. It's good to see you again after this long time." As my machine-gun motor mouth fired off its incessant ammo, I succeeded in clasping hands with Pete, slapping him on his drenched, shirtless back, and presenting him to Augie. "See here?" I babbled onward. "The Terrific Trio of inTerpreters has convened once more. Look out, William Faulkner scholars, wherever ye may be."

Shaking his head in begrudging acceptance of my fraternity-pledge good cheer, Augie warmly grasped Pete's right hand, assured our friend that no apology was necessary, and once again reverted to his customary interrogative mood. "Did the soccer team invent that chant in a fit of collaborative inspiration? Did the players find it written on the wall of a bathroom stall? What is its source, Pete?"

Lifting high each knee alternately while steadily rotating his hips and arms, Pete moved efficiently through a process of cooling down while he conversed with us. He was dressed (or underdressed) like the other runners except that his soccer shorts were bright red with white striping and a large white letter "W" (for his alma mater, Wittenberg University in Ohio) on the fabric above his right thigh. Lowering his hirsute head and slowly shaking it in amusement, Pete replied, "Much to his enduring chagrin, Tom Michaels, Ellie's counterpart in his role as coach of the men's soccer team, brought that song with him when he joined the faculty here at Moffatt ten years ago. Tom first heard it—and sang it many times—as an undergraduate at Randolph-Macon College in Ashland, Virginia. He told me that at least once every fall semester the entire freshman class gathers very early in the morning, proceeds en masse to the home of the College's president, and serenades the Randolph-Macon head honcho and his family with numerous pre-dawn repetitions of this invitation to—well, you heard the words. Tom absent-mindedly boomed out the 'Good Morning' song one summer morning six years ago when he was showering near the soccer locker room after a solo run through the woods and thought he was alone. But he told me that his goalkeeper had come in unannounced to dress for a voluntary workout and overheard him. Imagine Tom's surprise during the first training session that August when the team graced him with a full-throated rendition of this ditty from the Old Dominion. The song now has become an integral ritual in morning runs and practices here at Moffatt."

Delighted with the story, I first chortled and then remarked, "Tom probably wishes now that he had sung 'Tennessee Waltz,' 'Wabash Cannonball,' or some other country classic while he was soaping himself in the shower. But at least his goalkeeper didn't catch him in an impromptu performance of 'Roll Your Leg Over' or 'No Balls at All.' Then Tom really would have found himself buried in deep cow flop."

Augie smiled and gestured toward the twisting and stretching Pete. "Perhaps Speck and I had better resume our walk before the team finishes another circuit of the campus perimeter and bestows a second vocal mixed greeting upon us. Would you care to join us, Pete, for a short distance or for the remainder of our route back to Summit Avenue?"

Pete elaborately bowed from the waist and replied, "Why, thanks, Captain, I will happily accompany you two detectives extraordinaire if you are headed in the general direction of my apartment. I told Ellie that I would wake her up when I got back from my run and that I would treat her to a late country breakfast at Story's. She gave her women's team the day off after their game yesterday against Treesap Tech."

The three of us amiably chatted while we strolled diagonally across a series of connecting campus sidewalks. We headed in a northeasterly direction toward Pete's apartment located three blocks beyond the Moffatt athletic complex—field house, running track, indoor swimming pool, baseball park, intramural fields, and soccer pitches—on the corner of the campus farthest away from the medical center acreage. When we reached the base of the metal steps leading up to Pete's second-floor honeymoon suite, the Professor invited us in for coffee, but Augie and I politely declined, being well aware that Ellie would be in no mood to entertain visitors before she had even arisen from her bed of bliss. Not without the gaining of some insight into feminine psychology had each of us older gents been married for more than a quarter-century. As we bade farewell to Pete and expressed hope that we would encounter him later on that evening at the Labor Day picnic, our shirtless companion started his ascension of the stairs, stopped, and pivoted toward us.

"Augie, Speck, one more minute if you don't mind, please. Did you guys get a chance to read *As I Lay Dying* during August?"

Late on the July morning following our final session on *The Sound and the Fury*, Pete had telephoned my office to inform me that fifteen minutes of silver-tongued oratory—followed by three hours of groveling, toadying, foot-kissing, and servile apologizing—had gained him a begrudging absolution from Ellie for his "trading lives" indiscretion. Flushed with excitement from our mutually satisfying forays into the first two Faulkner novels, I had asked for a recommendation for the next Yoknapatawpha book that Augie and I should match our brains against, and Pete had quickly specified *As I Lay Dying*. During the remainder of the summer, as we all went our separate ways (Ohio for the Prefonts; Memphis and Atlanta for the Duprees; Boston, Dallas, and Little Rock for Julianna and me), Augie and I independently had read slowly through *As I Lay Dying* and had conversed about the novel on three occasions when we were both in Murryville.

"Yes, Pete, we did, upon your recommendation," replied the Captain. "Would you have any free time coming open soon when we three could chat about this complicated book? I would be grateful to continue my literary education during these first months of my retirement."

Half-turned toward Pete's stairs, I waved my left arm and added, "A second for that motion. You simply name the time, Professor."

Pete's entire face seemed to brighten two shades of pink. His eyes widened and sparkled, his eyebrows crept rapidly upward onto his forehead, and a mammoth grin that stretched completely across his visage appeared almost to connect the corners of his mouth with his earlobes. "Captain Dupree, Doctor Watkins, you are truly princes among men. For a month I have been worried that I have imposed on your time and civility far too extensively. Are you really ready to tackle another Faulkner headache-inducer?"

This time I spoke first. "Pete, during the spring and early summer we three developed a productive pattern that called for stimulating—and rewarding—mental activity on our parts. Earlier this very morning on our exercise walk, Augie and I were talking about how eager we are to dive into the Faulknerian quicksand again."

"Vigorous cerebral exercise helps us keep excessive wrinkles off our aging foreheads, Pete," affirmed Augie. "After this recent lengthy period of vegetating, we are ready to tackle another case in Faulkner whenever you say the word."

Standing on the third step of the metal stairs, Pete began bouncing from foot to foot, assumed a long-jumper's crouch, suddenly leaped forward, shouted "The word! The WORD! Now! Let's do it!" and landed squarely—PLOP!—eighteen inches in front of the smiling detective and your startled narrator. Twirling 360 degrees, Pete initiated a high-five somewhere in the hills of the next county to the west and slapped palms loudly—WHAP!—with Augie. The professor then took aim at my hand, but I squeaked a request for an exemption. "I plan to operate on a ninety-year-old woman's cataract tomorrow morning, Pete, and I need all of my appendages to be in full working order. Here; how about a modest handshake?"

Pete settled for a slap on the back of my unprepared left shoulder—"OUCH!"—and for several reiterations of "All right": "Alllll riiight; Awwwwlll right; Alll mighty right!" Then he straightened his back, assumed a more serious pedagogical posture, and gained about as professional an appearance as a person could muster at 8:15 a.m. on an already hot September day while he is attired only in sweat-stained soccer shorts, ankle-high socks, and well-worn running shoes. "Gentlemen, once more I humbly seek your expert assistance in trying to solve a mystery. I am reviewing *As I Lay Dying* in preparation for assigning the novel this fall as part of the second half of the American lit survey course. The entire text of the novel is included in the anthology that Carter Modlin, Dottie Campbell, and I all use in our various sections of the survey. Last year when I first taught *As I Lay Dying,* I couldn't understand one particular passage—hell, I couldn't understand bunches of passages, but this one in particular really bumfoozled me. It seems to present what our friend Edgar Allan Poe would call 'a mystery all insoluble.' I asked Carter about it, and he gave me one answer. Then I talked to Dottie, and she gave me another interpretation. So I just told myself to forget about it, and I did just that, until I started reviewing the book a couple of weeks ago. Monsieur Dupin, your solutions to problems in *Sanctuary* and *The Sound and the Fury* give me confidence that you can figure out this one, also."

Augie held up both hands, palms outward, in his habitual gesture of modesty. "Pete, we have been lucky so far, but I am willing, with the help of you two capable investigators, to try again. Now, which passage puzzles you? If you can tell me approximately where it appears in the book, I'll look it up when I get home. We won't solve any problems this morning out here in the heat of the rising sun, but in the shade of my sugar maple tree I will feel more worthy of impersonating a literary sleuth."

"Agreed, agreed, Captain," hastily interjected Pete, "and I have detained you too long anyway. I can definitely locate the passage for you; it is the next-to-last paragraph of Addie Bundren's only interior monologue. Actually, I have studied this passage so often recently that inadvertently I have memorized it and also the page number—one-seventy-six—on which it appears in the Vintage International Edition of the novel. Addie is the 'I' in the title of the novel, and her mind and voice are also represented here by the first-person singular pronoun:

> I gave Anse Dewey Dell to negative Jewel. Then I gave him Vardaman to replace the child I had robbed him of. And now he has three children that are his and not mine. And then I could get ready to die."

Since I—Archibald Fulmer Watkins at your service—had not exercised my brash vocal chords in at least three long, painful minutes, I did not hesitate to butt right into the colloquy between Pete and Augie. "I vividly remember that paragraph, Pete. At least twice Augie and I have talked about these four strange sentences, along with other bewildering words in Addie's monologue."

Nodding in agreement, Augie added, "I am still stewing over the identity of, as Addie expresses, 'the child I had robbed him of.' Is that the question bothering you also, Pete?"

The professor swung his head abruptly in my direction, dropped his jaw, looked back at Augie, and stammered, "How did you know? Can you read my mind?"

Throwing my head back and chortling loudly in the direction of three distant fleecy clouds, I intervened once more. "It is about time that Swami Dupin started messing around with somebody else's brain besides mine. Pete, Augie has been peeking into my secret mental closets ever since I have known him. Welcome to the club of mere mortals. I am delighted to have company in this fraternity of dimwits."

"Now, now, neighbor," Augie said in a placating tone as he almost imperceptibly walked in place, rhythmically raising first the balls and then the heels of his feet while he remained stationary. "All that I do is to observe people closely and then make guesses. Luckily, I hit the target on this one."

"When did you last miss the center of the bull's-eye, Robin of Locksley?" I asked my good friend. "Anyway, Pete, don't feel offended or invaded. Just be grateful that you are not the guest of dishonor in an interrogation room at Memphis Police Headquarters when Augie is the grand inquisitor."

Pete bowed in Augie's direction and concluded, "Monsieur Dupin, once more I humbly plead for your assistance. Some critics think that this mystery 'child' is Jewel, the third Bundren son; others nominate Cash, the oldest child; and a third group concludes that no specific child is represented in Addie's thinking. The temptation exists to dismiss the identity of the child as being forever ambiguous, but I am just not ready to give up the search yet."

"Nor am I," responded Augie. "Pete, please repeat the paragraph's first sentence for me."

"Sure, Captain. 'I gave Anse Dewey Dell to negative Jewel.' Okay? What are you thinking, sir?"

Augie stood with his head bowed, his chin pressing into his upper chest, and his arms folded across his stomach. "Are you acquainted with anyone in your college's Department of Mathematics, Pete?" Augie asked pointedly with a sudden rise of his head and a direct stare at the professor.

Pete nodded his own hairy skull sharply once. "Well yes, I have met all eight of the number crunchers in Math, and one of them in particular is a pretty good friend. Why do you ask?"

But Augie had already turned toward the street as he said to our friend the bare-chested runner, "I'll call you later in the week, Pete, and tell you what I am tossing around in my head. Speck, we had better hot-foot it on home before our wives send out a posse in search of us—or worse, a pack of Saint Bernards with Milk-Bone Biscuits in the containers around the poochies' necks."

Count No Count

East on Williams Lane, north on College Avenue, east again on Ridgecrest Road (the street bordering on the south both C. R. M. C. and Moffatt College), northeast onto a narrow blacktop road leading into the campus of my glorious alma mater, and looming before me were a nearly full parking lot, an energetically voluble crowd of approximately 300 soccer fans sitting in aluminum bleachers or roaming the west sideline of the pitch, and a blur of team colors (silver with black trim and orange numerals versus purple with gold numerals and trim) mixed with bouncing blonde, brown, black, and auburn pony tails. The Moffatt Silver Streaks, Coach Elvira Prefont's female futbollers, were hosting the Lady Witnesses of Zelotes Baptist University located in Immersion, Oklahoma.

On Friday, September 8, at 5:30, after a typically bustling day in my office filled with vision screenings, diagnoses of ocular pathology, and treatments of eye injuries, I had hurried away as soon as May Ellen would release me and had managed to arrive at Moffatt in time for the final twenty minutes of the game. As I slid into a distant parking spot, shed my chocolate-brown sport coat and gold patterned tie, disembarked from my Explorer, locked the vehicle, and then trudged toward the shouts of the crowd, I began searching the stands and sidelines for Augie, who had agreed to meet me here in order that we might converse with Pete after the contest and decide how to proceed on the problem of Addie Bundren's enigmatic language in *As I Lay Dying*. Already by phone we three self-styled sleuths had decided to adopt a sensible acronym for this novel as we had done earlier for *The Sound and the Fury*, so *As I Lay Dying* in our discussions became enshrined as AILD (EH, EYE, ELL DEE). Minor progress, perhaps, but at least it represented a tentative baby step toward a desired understanding of another Faulknerian mystery.

Rounding the corner of the bleachers, I spotted Pete, Augie, and Mary Alice standing together in the shade of a large river birch tree near the corner flag on the southwest edge of the soccer pitch. I walked in their direction and turned my attention to the game, in which the visiting team clearly had gained the upper foot. During the two minutes that it took for me to stroll from stands to standing friends, the Lady Witnesses took four shots at the Moffatt team's goal and scored on the final attempt in the sequence, a low, screaming rocket off the powerful left foot of a tall, olive-skinned brunette who shouted words of joy in a language unrecognizable to me as she high-fived with her teammates following her impressive shot into the upper right corner of the net.

Gritting his teeth and throwing both arms high into the air in a gesture of obvious disgust, Pete shouted, "Oh, bull. . . . Oops"—here a sideward glance at Mary Alice—"I mean *Bullfinch's Mythology, Bullfinch's*. That makes ten goals for Zelotes, seven of them in the second half. Why are those alleged 'Ladies' running up the score like this? PHOOEY!"

In deference to Pete's diatribe, I slowed my approach. Soon I was tiptoeing into place slightly behind the left shoulder of Augie, leaning forward, and whispering to both Duprees as I avoided Pete's sweeping gaze of the playing field. "Pssst. Howdy, neighbors. I assume that our friend Professor Pete is none too delighted with the progress of the contest."

Turning their heads rapidly in my direction, Augie and Mary Alice greeted me quietly but cordially. Then Augie grasped my right upper arm and led me five strides out of the shade of the tree and away from the pawed turf of Pete the raging bull. "Pete is justifiably upset because the coach of the Lady Witnesses seems to be ordering her players to pile on the points," Augie informed me sotto voce. "Our girls held up well until the end of the first half, when the score was only three to one. But for the last several minutes our overmatched players have not been able to clear the ball out of our defensive end, and Z. B. U. has been enjoying target practice at our net."

"Come on, Immersion, make this contest fair! Surely you can tell that the outcome is no longer in doubt. Your girls on the bench haven't played even one minute yet. Send in some of your subs!" Pete windmilled his arms, shouted his imprecations directly at the purple-and-gold contingent on the opposite sideline, and drew no response other than a frantic wave from Ellie along with a right index finger held firmly to her lips. Earlier I had spotted Ellie prowling the sideline in front of the Moffatt bench situated farther north of the Z. B. U. group. In a seething fury Pete turned abruptly toward Augie, Mary Alice, and me.

"Friends! I ask you—what kind of sportsmanship is this? Oh hello, Doctor Speck. Glad you could come, although our girls don't deserve to be humiliated like this, and I had better zip my loose lip before Ellie or the Dean or some authority figure calls out the campus SWAT team on my head."

Our group of four fans reunited under the shade tree, and after shaking Pete's hand I asked him about the apparent disadvantage under which Ellie's team was laboring. "These Baptist babes look like professional players, Pete. Good gosh!" I pointed toward the pitch. "Look at the sprinter's speed on that one. She looks as if she could run on our Olympic dash team."

With both hands buried in the pockets of his khaki shorts, Pete slumped his shoulders and dejectedly replied, "She might well make the Olympics, Speck, but not on the U. S. A. team. That is Isabella, one of several Brazilian exchange students on the Zelotes squad. She has scored four goals already—Oh no, c'mon—whew, she just missed another one with that bicycle shot—and so has number ten over there, Evita—scored four goals today, I mean. As you may know, some soccer players in Brazil often use only a first name—Pele, Romario, or Bebeto, from Brazil's World Cup men's teams, for example."

Moving my head up and down in enlightenment, I replied, "So that is Portuguese that I hear mellifluously flowing from the lips of several of the Witnesses. Pete, how did so many young women from Brazil wind up enrolled in a college located on the windy plains of northern Oklahoma?"

Throwing both arms outward from his sides, Pete replied, "Scholarships, Speck. Zelotes is an NAIA school, and athletic scholarships are allowed. The school's administration pays retainers to Baptist missionaries all over Latin America who serve as scouts for soccer talent, both male and female. A steady flow of speedy midfielders, accurate strikers, and rough defenders enters the pipeline below the equator and pops out in—surprise! Immersion, Oklahoma."

I raised my eyebrows and gently tapped my left palm on my jaw. "And Moffatt belongs to the NCAA, Division Three—no athletic scholarships allowed. So we are truly at a competitive disadvantage here. Why does Ellie's team play the Lady Witnesses, Pete?"

Shaking his head, Pete answered, "Ask Tom Michaels, the athletic director. He schedules only D-Three opponents for his Bulldogs, but apparently the Z. B. U. women's coach is a friend of his, so he accommodated his pal. But Ellie has asked to schedule only our conference opponents and other non-scholarship schools for next season, so this is the last time that we will be whipped like yard dogs by that Zelotes bunch. Look at that!"

Number four, the woman identified by Pete as Isabella, had just whizzed past our spectators' positions beneath the river birch tree, juggling the ball variously on either foot, either knee, her feet again, and twice off her forehead, touching the ball eight times without letting it hit the ground before she dropped the ball to her right foot and sent a twisting screamer directly at Rose Hummerly, the Streaks' goalkeeper, who managed to block the shot and then fall on the ball. Isabella spat in the air, shouted "Luck-eeee" followed by several oaths in what must have been Portuguese, and then trotted arrogantly back toward midfield.

Pete stomped along the sideline near the corner flag, muttering, sputtering, and asking all of us as he rambled past our stationary positions, "What can I yell that will get that other coach's attention? During the early part of this half I shouted at her so often, telling her to put in her subs and make the game competitive, that Ellie banished me to this corner of the pitch. What will make that pious church lady listen to me? Ellie told me that Coach Magdalene—Mitzi Magdalene—is a Baptist deaconess as well as the Z. B. U. soccer coach. What words would break through her hard shell?"

"Call her Christianity into question, Pete. In my political life I've learned from sad experience that the only words capable of penetrating the self-righteous shield of a religious fanatic are ones that challenge the authenticity of a true believer's behavior."

Along with my three companions, I whirled around and spied Mayor Julianna Watkins regally poised ten feet behind us. "Why dear," I said in surprise, "when did you arrive?"

Dressed for Town Hall in a turquoise jacket and skirt with a pearl-white blouse matched in color by her shoes, Her Honor walked toward us and waved her right arm in an imperious command of approbation. "Proceed, Pete. I'll back you up, no matter what you say."

At that moment the center referee blew her whistle, play halted on the pitch, the Zelotes coaching staff ran onto the playing area in order to tend to a fallen fullback who apparently had twisted her ankle, and the crowd fell silent. Pete stared intently at Julianna; the Mayor raised her chin, stood at attention and curtly nodded to the professor; and Pete pivoted until he directly faced the Z. B. U. head coach, who was kneeling at the eighteen-yard stripe directly in front of the Moffatt goal, only some thirty yards away from us. Cupping both hands tightly around his mouth, Pete rocked back onto his heels, gradually shifted his weight forward onto his toes, and trumpeted a command that probably shattered windows in Butler County, thirteen miles to our east:

> HEY, BAPTIST COACH!
> WITNESS FOR CHRIST!
> RUN UP THE SCORE!

For the count of three, absolute silence filled the northeastern quadrant of the Moffatt campus. With mouth agape I stared at Pete, who leaned slightly forward from the waist, his balled fists tightly pressed against the sides of his legs. Chin jutting forward in defiance, Pete squinted his eyes in intensity and locked his orbs on those of Coach Magdalene, who, suffering from a momentary paralytic shock, remained immobile next to her now reviving player and gazed with a blank expression and drooping jaw at her adversary. For a few seconds the scene resembled the E. F. Hutton television commercials of the 1980's, as players, officials, and fans ceased all speech and motion in order to stare collectively at Professor Prefont, malefactor of the moment. Among the assembled masses only Ellie, who dropped her head into her open hands, failed to look directly at imPetuous Pete the pellucid polemicist. As I was one of the first gapers to break my fixed look and to survey the tableau, I spotted Ellie's sideline show of chagrin and felt the stab of an instant fear that Pete might have succeeded in eliciting some type of sanction meted out by the center referee toward the Silver Streaks.

However, my anxiety turned out to be a false alarm, because in the next instant the world once more unfroze. It seemed that everyone in the area simultaneously began to move about and to talk, and waves of laughter originating in the Moffatt student bleachers washed over the five of us who stood haphazardly near one another within ten yards of the southwest corner flag. Cocking her ear toward the sounds of frivolity and the accompanying shouts of support such as "Yeah, Coach, be a good sport," "Show us what you're really made of, Baptists," and "That's telling her, Prefont" (with this last cheer causing a visible shudder in the now nonanonymous Pete), Coach Magdalene of the Lady Witnesses slowly rose to her feet, shuffled toward her sideline, searchingly looked back once at Pete, and then began to march briskly back and forth in front of her team's bench, pointing at player after player and waving them en masse onto the pitch.

An ear-splitting roar arose from the Moffatt supporters as the Z. B. U. starters reluctantly exited the game, raising their eyebrows, upturned palms, and shoulders in gestures of incomprehension and protest. Several of them began chattering in (I assume) Portuguese at Coach Magdalene, but the Coach continued to stretch out her right arm and draw it slowly back toward herself in a gathering gesture until she had cleared the pitch of seven of her starting eleven, two of whom collaborated in kicking over a sidelines Gatorade container in mutual mute protest.

"Congratulations, Pete. You accomplished your objective." Julianna grabbed Pete's right hand and pumped it six times, simultaneously holding his upper right arm with her petite left hand.

"Yes, Professor," I jumped on my wife's bandwagon, "now we can watch a few minutes of a game with evenly matched sides."

Augie and Mary Alice added their words of support, and Pete began to relax, shaking his head sharply four times and then resuming his perusal of the skirmish on the turf while he paced the sidelines near our corner flag. During the remaining seven minutes each team scored a goal, with the Silver Streaks notching a tally off a corner kick via a splendidly redirected header by Denise Meyer, the talented Moffatt center midfielder.

When the referee blew her whistle, members of both teams mingled in the center circle, congratulating each other for waging a spirited contest, and Ellie warmly shook hands with Coach Magdalene, gesturing toward Pete and apparently, as interpreted from our distance, apologizing for her husband's outburst. The Zelotes coach shook her head several times, smiled over her shoulder at Pete, patted Ellie on the back, and sprinted in the wake of her team toward the distant visitors' locker room.

Ellie jogged over to our spectators' corner, raised her left eyebrow while staring with a half-grin at her wary husband, and blurted out, "Can you believe it, Pete? Mitzi actually told me to thank you for pointing our to her that she was straying from the true path of proper Christian conduct, and in public at that. Cheesh, will wonders never cease to amaze me? Oh well, you big loudmouth, you got away with one that time." Ellie concluded her gentle admonishment with an artificial right cross to Pete's exposed jaw, and then she turned toward the senior contingent. "Thanks for coming to the game and cheering us on, folks. We are now two and two for the year, and Zelotes is six and zero, but the Silver Streaks will start their comeback next week as we enter conference play. Maybe I'll see you at our next home game." With a wave to us and a powerful hip-bump with Pete in which she won the advantage, Ellie ran briskly in the direction of her departing players.

The Duprees, the Watkinses, and one relieved but chastened Prefont walked slowly toward the parking lot, chatting amiably along our way about soccer, Ellie, and Pete's brush with disaster. As we sauntered across the asphalt in search of our scattered vehicles, Mary Alice reached her left arm in front of her husband and grasped the professor's elbow. "Say, Pete, why is Ellie's team called the Silver Streaks and not the feminine equivalent of Bulldogs—Lady Dogs, for example. . . ? Oh, I think that I just answered my own question." Mary Alice stopped, placed her left hand over her mouth, and laughed softly. Then, in an accurate imitation of Gilda Radner on the old *Saturday Night Live* skits, she concluded with the soprano statement, "Never mind."

Pete responded in a most diplomatic manner. "Yes, Mrs. Dupree—uh, Mary Alice. When Ellie and I came to Moffatt and she started the women's team from scratch, she consulted with Tom Michaels and other people in authority before eventually deciding that a totally different team name would be the best choice."

My turn came to pop in. "I suppose that she didn't want to take a chance on having her players becoming subjected to an opposing fan with the temperament and anti-feminine vocabulary of a Jason Compson."

"Well, la dee dah," chimed in Her Honor. "Listen to how my erudite hubby adroitly drops a Faulknerian literary allusion into the conversation. See what a broadening effect you are having on him, Pete? Hmmm . . . although if he grows much broader, I won't be able any longer to wrap my waif-like arms around his circumference."

"Hush up, you vote-mongering shrew!" I demanded. "Look at the thanks I get for taking into my comfortable home you, a starving working girl, an ingénue once so humbly grateful but now so viper-tongued. . . ."

"Oh, blow it through your nose, pill pusher," retorted Julianna, but fortunately we just then reached our vehicles, which were parked three spaces apart, and the most recent episode of *The Bickersons of Murryville* TV sitcom came to an unlamented conclusion. Mary Alice hitched a ride with the Mayor for the trip to Summit Avenue, since Augie and I had expressed interest in conversing further with Pete, and after Julianna peeled out of the lot in her silver Miata convertible, her self-styled "middle-ager's toy," I turned to my genial companions and shared an anecdote from the old memory bank.

"All of this talk about team names reminds me of the contest dreamed up and conducted by my Moffatt classmate Dakota Dan Ludwig in . . . must have been the winter of 1963. In order to try to defeat the cold-weather doldrums, Dan challenged students and faculty alike to match an existing college or university with its most appropriate team name—for example, the Yale Locks, the Hiram Walkers, or the John Brown Bodies."

Pete and Augie both chuckled, and then they asked if I could remember any more entries in the contest. "A few," I replied, "including my own submission, the Rice Pilafs. Several hundred combinations wound up in Dan's hands, and I can dredge up three or four more. Let's see, here are two that came from a keenly intelligent female pre-med student whose name I have deliberately forgotten because she always beat me on exams in Organic Chemistry or Genetics. Her contributions were the Xavier Souls and the Harding Arteries. The only other ones that I can come up with are the Tulane Highways, the Furman Sasquatches, and the Grand Prize winner, submitted by my pal Scotty Laird—Taaa Daaah!— the Vassar Ectomies."

"Whew," Pete said between chuckles, "and a formerly all-female college too. I agree that the Vassar name wins the blue ribbon."

"Well, gentlemen," Augie spoke as he rubbed his hands together in anticipation, "shall we discuss how we plan to proceed with AILD?"

"Of course! Yai-yuss!" Pete yelped, hopping in the air, turning slightly in mid-flight, and landing directly in front of Captain Dupree. "Great idea, Augie. Say— Wait here just one minute." Without another word Pete loped away in the direction of the nearly deserted soccer pitch. "Are you in a hurry, Speck?" politely inquired Augie. "I don't want to detain you from any medical, social, or political obligations."

"No problem, C. A.," I cheerfully replied. "The J. woman and I have no specific dinner plans, and the medical exchange can reach me via my pocket pager. Oh, here comes Pete back toward us, and who in the world is that giant with him?"

Talking as he walked, Pete approached us, but the Captain and I paid absolutely no attention to our sleuthing partner because we were unabashedly staring at his companion. Imagine, kind readers, a man combining the height (six feet, ten inches) and muscular physique of Larry Bird, the Boston Celtics perennial all-star basketball player; the frizzy, profusely unkempt dark hair of a young Albert Einstein; the square face, high cheekbones, sunken eyes, and flat nose of Boris Karloff; the elaborately waxed, lengthily curlicued moustache of Salvador Dali; and the attire—black trousers, cape, shoes, and even cane, all set off by a white ruffled shirt—of the Count, a Muppet regular on *Sesame Street*. If you can wrap your mind around this description and visualize one breathing person assembled from all of these disparate parts, you will have attained a clear impression of the man being escorted toward Augie and me—as clear an impression, that is, as my feeble prose can deliver.

As this odd couple came within earshot, Pete stepped forward and spoke with gusto, "Captain Dupree, Doctor Watkins, please allow me to introduce my Moffatt College colleague Professor Boris Lothar Schuller. Herr Doctor Schuller is a member of the Mathematics Faculty at the University of Graz in Austria and is here at Moffatt filling a two-year appointment to the Henry Distinguished Chair of Mathematics and Physics."

Cordial handshakes followed, or in my case I should say a hand-swallowing, since Herr Schuller's paw completely enveloped my average-sized mitt and released it back into view only after several vigorous pumpings of my (lucky for me) still-attached right arm.

Pete continued, "Boris is a lifelong soccer enthusiast—he played goalkeeper for many years in Austria—and he has graciously volunteered his services as a way to assist the keepers on both Ellie's team and the Bulldogs. I have told him that you would like to converse with a mathematician, Augie, so I brought you our school's star numbers man."

"No, no, Pete," interjected Doctor Schuller with a rapid wagging of his raised right index finger. "Remember that I rarely use numbers in my work. My principal interest is abstract mathematics. I prefer theories, symbols, and hypotheses. A mathematician I am, but not a numbers man, as you employ that dubious title."

Patient readers will understand that my unsophisticated skills in narration do not allow me to deliver a precise recounting of Boris's polished Austrian accent. As you encounter his dialogue, place heavy accents on the vowels, especially the "e" sounds, draw them out extensively, and you will gain a plausible perception of his precisely enunciated patterns of speech. Any other attempt on my part to imitate his impressive traditionally Austrian oratorical skills will only demean them.

Augie seized the initiative by warmly thanking Doctor Schuller for being willing to talk with us and asking the tall professor if he could say when he might have enough time to answer a question that could possibly bear upon his academic specialty.

"I will be happy to talk with you now, Captain Dupree, on our drive to Crocodile. And if that is not sufficient time, then we can visit again at your convenience."

Pete quickly explained. "Speck, Augie, I didn't think you would mind that

I took the liberty of offering Boris a ride home—or actually, to the suite of rooms in which is temporarily residing while he holds the chair at Moffatt. Boris doesn't fit comfortably into Herbie Junior, and Ellie is using our pickup truck to haul some of the soccer nets and flags to the storage area. . . ."

"No problem," I chirped, "let's all four hop into my Explorer. Plenty of room for everyone, and we can talk as we motor to the metropolis of Crocodile in fair Butler County, our contiguous principality on the western edge of the Delta. Here, let me unlock the doors. . . ."

Soon we were all proceeding due eastward on state highway 96 through the flat country known locally as the Bottoms, shortened from "Churchill River Bottoms." Directly behind us the sun was creating an orange, pink, gray, and purple extravaganza as it sank behind the first foothills of the Ozarks, and through the slightly lowered car windows we could discern the aromas of smoke from a distant grass fire, cottonseed oil from a nearby processing plant, and freshly turned dirt in fully harvested soybean fields that were being prepared for the inactivity of the long winter ahead.

My pernicious nosiness manifested itself before we had passed the eastern town limits of Murryville. "Why do you live thirteen miles from the College, Herr Professor? Do you mind if I ask?"

"No, I certainly do not mind, Doctor, and I can state my reason in two words." Professor Schuller slowly turned toward me from the front passenger seat, which he had slid backward to its limit before he had tilted the seat's backrest also as far as possible. Augie sat uncomplainingly behind the huge Austrian and did not seem to mind being almost squashed. Enunciating slowly and quite distinctly, our foreign guest continued, "The two key words are 'DRY COUNTY.'"

"Ah," I responded, with an echoing "Ah" filtering our way from the occupant of the right rear seat. Herr Schuller was referring to the legal stratagem peculiar to Bible-belt states in which an entire county can ban the sale of all alcoholic beverages. "Local option" is the legal term, but the familiar metaphors of "wet" and "dry" are consistently used by peon and potentate alike.

Boris resumed his narrative. "When I arrived at the Little Rock airport in August of 1994, Dean Christianson met me and drove me to Murryville, never informing me of the BARBARIC reality that Crowder is a DRY COUNTY. While Christianson was helping to get me moved into my apartment near the campus, I asked him for the location of the nearest bierhaus, informing him that the time had arrived for my customary afternoon stein of Gosser Stiftsbrau. Only then did he notify me that while in Crowder County I would not be able to purchase ANY brand of beer—or any other alcoholic beverage, for that matter. Imagine such an UNCIVILIZED deprivation. In this county there is not a single bierhaus, tavern, pub, or even what you Americans in the South call a 'honky tonk' or 'juke joint.' *Gross Gott! Himmelfarbe!* I still cannot comprehend the concept of a dry county. Grrrr—Aaaaarrrgh. . . ."

From the backseat Dupree the traveling diplomat spoke up. "Rest assured that many of us native Southerners disagree with the hypocrisy of 'dry' and 'wet' counties also, Professor Schuller."

"Please, please . . . Boris, call me Boris. Do not be formal, all right?"

We quickly initiated Boris into the First Name Club, and Pete finished the explanation. "Boris demanded a reservation on the next plane out of the Little Rock airport heading in the direction of the continent of Europe, but Frank Christianson hastily devised a solution. As we all know, Butler County blessedly is wet, and the hamlet of Crocodile sits just over the line separating Crowder and Butler counties, with only thirteen miles of this very highway standing between Moffatt College and Crocodile."

Before I spoke, I negotiated a gradual curve to the right, or southeast, and ahead of us appeared a fading glimmer of the Churchill River. "When I was a Moffatt undergrad, my buddies and I became well acquainted with the granddaddy of this road. It was narrower and bumpier way back then during the Pleistocene era, but old 96 was still traversable. On many a moonlit evening I have made the round trip between chaste Murryville and the sinful liquor stores or alluring honky tonks of Crocodile, Arkansas, yes sirree; but not in recent decades, I might hastily add."

"Of course not. No, never, Speck," replied Pete from directly behind me. "Anyway—Frank immediately got on the telephone to George Uehgandt, the prominent landholder in the Crocodile area, and George was happy to make a suite of rooms in his farmhouse available to Boris."

I piped up. "George was my classmate at Moffatt—1964. What a lucky man. George Goodwin Uehgandt, heir to twenty-eight hundred acres of the richest land this side of the valley Nile. We all called him 'Gorgeous George' because of his wavy blonde hairdo. The coeds all swooned over him."

"George is indeed a most congenial host and dear friend," Boris affirmed. "Since his children are all grown and are living elsewhere, he and Karen had closed up several spare rooms that they have now graciously allowed me to air out and inhabit. And the Uehgandt hostelry is certainly not DRY. To the contrary, it is exceptionally WET. George and Karen love their beers, also, and malt liquors. I have been able to introduce them to several stout Austrian and German brews that I bring back with me from my periodic trips home to Graz, and they have just about succeeded in convincing me that some American brands are strong enough to provide an authentic beer taste. So my residential situation has improved from unacceptable to highly satisfactory."

Pete resumed the narrative. "Boris doesn't drive, so initially transportation was a problem. But you soon solved that problem too, right, Count?"

I jerked my head to the right. "Pete, did you say 'Count' and not 'Boris?'"

"I'll explain the nickname in a moment, Speck. Tell these Southern good old boys how you get around the countryside, Boro."

"Sure, Pete-o. Heh, heh. Yes, well, I am a lifelong early riser, so on an ordinary week day at 6:30 a.m. I catch a ride into Murryville on the Holsum

Bakery fried-pie truck driven by Buddy Bob Banks, a most entertaining Southern raconteur. Usually I stand in the well of the truck on the steps to Buddy's right, so that I can stretch to my full height. Also, the sliding door makes entrances and exits quite manageable. In the afternoons someone usually offers me a lift home, as you gentlemen have today, but on the few occasions when I have not been able to encounter a student or a faculty colleague who is heading to Crocodile for a round of civil sipping, then George has sent one of his farmhands to—I think that the phrase is to 'fetch me.'"

I held the steering wheel firmly with my left hand, raised my right arm, and politely asked, "Professors Schuller and Prefont, will you please explain the nickname 'Count?'"

Boris glanced at Pete in the left rear seat, and Coach Ellie's husband spoke up. "Some of the students at Moffatt saw Boris wearing his Austrian aristocratic attire—a version of which he has on today—last winter, on some special day—right, Boris?"

The Austrian nodded in agreement. "I was invited to the President's mansion for an evening reception, so I dressed early for the occasion in the traditional attire of a nineteenth-century Austrian opera spectator. On many regular school days I still dress this way, just to play my role. Some student named Rodger...."

"Rodger Compton," Augie and I spoke in unison.

"Yes," Boris continued, "this Rodger saw me in the campus center and shouted, 'Oh ho ho ho. Eeet eeez zeee Count. Oh ho ho ho.' And then Dennis Southman, one of our math majors, added the words 'no count' to the title, since I am an abstract mathematician and rarely use actual numerals in my teaching or research. Hence 'Count No Count,' my favorite nickname among the several that I have inspired during my short time at Moffatt."

"What are the others?" I nosily inquired.

But at that moment Augie patted Boris on his nearby left shoulder and commented, "A smooth pun on the meanings of 'count' there, Boris. And now may I tap your area of expertise for just a moment? Could I ask you a question about a word that might have a meaning in mathematics?"

"Most assuredly, Captain Dupree—er, uh, Augustus, I mean. Please proceed."

"Thank you, Boris. Perhaps Pete has summarized for you the discussions that he, Speck, and I have enjoyed since last April concerning some of the major novels of William Faulkner."

Turned halfway to his left so that he could maintain selective eye contact with all three of his fellow Explorer passengers, Boris nodded and softly replied, "Yes, yes, he has."

"Then may I ask you please to read the four marked sentences on this photocopy of a page from *As I Lay Dying*—the novel we abbreviate as AILD?" Augie handed to Boris Addie's penultimate paragraph, and the Austrian asked me to switch on the overhead light so that he could clearly distinguish the wording. After a few moments he looked up from his reading of the page and nodded to Augie.

"The word about which I am the most curious is 'negative,' Boris. Used as it is in that sentence—'I gave Anse Dewey Dell to negative Jewel'—the word makes me suspect that Addie Bundren may privately be expressing language that has particular meaning in the discipline of mathematics."

"Yes, I think that you are correct, Augustus. This woman—you say her name is Addie?—seems to be utilizing a standard mathematical procedure involving an entity known as the additive inverse."

I had to jerk the wheel back left to keep us from spraying gravel from the highway's shoulder, for in my surprise I had veered too quickly to the right as I stared first at Boris and then at Augie. "Did you say 'Addie-tive inverse,' Boris? Is this term named after the deceased Mrs. Bundren of Faulkner's novel?"

"No, no, Speck," reproved Augie. "You are merely responding to Boris's

Austrian accent. He is saying 'additive inverse,' and the fact that the name of Faulkner's character seems to resonate there is a coincidence—or perhaps a super-nifty Austro-American pun."

Boris was ignoring both my sophomoric interruption and Augie's rejoinder while he continued to stare intently at the printed paragraph. Then he quickly turned over the paper, and, whipping a ball-point pen from his shirt pocket, he hastily scribbled on the paper's reversed side. Silence prevailed in the car for approximately sixty seconds, and then Boris handed the paper to Augie, who extricated his reading glasses from the case in his shirt pocket, leaned to the left so that he could make use of the overhead light, and reacted, "Ahh. Just as I thought. Thank you, Boris. If I may keep this piece of paper, I would like to think further about your contribution to our deliberations before I can discuss with you its full implications."

"Certainly, certainly, Augustus. Whenever you are ready. And Doctor Speck, here is the county line. Next we enter the grand metropolis of Crocodile. Please deposit me here at Jack's Beer Joint, where I have promised to sample the tavern keeper's newest brand of beer, which is curiously labeled 'Red Dog.' Peter, Augustus, Doctor Speck, many thanks for the taxi service and for the intriguing conversation. I eagerly await further discussions of this linguistic and mathematical mystery in Mister Faulkner's novel."

Boris slowly unfolded himself from my passenger seat, swung his legs out the door, and gradually stretched to his full height. He shook his shoulders, twisted the left end of his moustache, and proclaimed, "*Auf Wiedersehen, meinen Freunden.* Until next time"—then, with a malicious grin and a fair country imitation of a Southern drawl, "See y'all, good buddies."

From my Explorer we three Murryvilleans watched as Crocodile, Arkansas's, most cosmopolitan honky-tonk man, waving his cane like a conductor's baton, contentedly ambled through the flapping screen door of his carefully selected Friday night Arkansas bierhaus.

New Slant on an Old Testament

"Are you certain that Boris specified this place, Pete?"

"Yes, Speck, yes. Last night over the phone he definitely said 'Dib's.' And even if he decides on another eatery, we won't have to have walk very far."

"And the time was. . . ."

"Yes, Speck, six-thirty. But please remember that many Europeans pay much less attention to the precise sweepings of a second hand than do—ahem—type-A Americans. I expect him to come strolling or rolling along at any minute now."

At 7 p.m. on Tuesday, September 19, Pete, Augie, and I sat on the benches of three triangularly arranged picnic tables beneath a huge magnolia tree in the sideyard of a popular Crocodile cafe. Pickup trucks, motorcycles, and an occasional passenger car filled the contiguous gravel parking lot, and the air was heavy with the piquant aroma of barbecue sauce mixed with the powerful complementary scent of deep-frying animal fat. On state highway 96, fifty feet to our north, traffic arriving from the west slowed as it entered the village limits of Crocodile, Butler County, State of Arkansas, U. S. of A., and the drivers of the vehicles headed westward flipped down their sun visors, honked or waved at the citizens in oncoming trucks or cars, and began to accelerate as they left this final outpost of civilization in Butler County and entered the stretch of thirteen miles of Crowder County soybean, rice, and cotton fields lining both sides of the road all the way to the edge of Murryville.

I shrugged my shoulders in response to Pete's admonishments and glanced to my right and behind me, where loomed our dining establishment of the upcoming evening. A ramshackle series of haphazardly connected wood-frame rooms squatting beneath a roof of peeling green shingles, Dib's featured a forty-foot long railed front porch graced by six ancient wooden rocking chairs, flashing neon beer advertising lights in every window ("Bud Wei Ser," "It's Miller Time,"

"Tap the Rockies—Coors Light"), and a rear deck that perched precariously on wooden legs sunk into Simon's Swamp, which oozed within a few feet of the backs of most of the business establishments—liquor stores, car repair shops, convenience stores, other eateries—that lined the south side of 96 all the way along the 1.6-mile east-west length of the duchy of Crocodile. Over the main entrance of our cafe stood a sign promoting Coca-Cola in one corner and the name of the place in the remainder of the available white space:

DIB'S RIBS AND FIBS
BARBECUE, BURGERS, BEER, BULL SESSIONS
EVERYONE WELCOME, SOUTHERN OR OTHERWISE
DO DROP IN

Augie rubbed his left index finger once along the side of his nose and offered his opinion. "Speck, it's possible that Boris could have stopped at one of the other places on his way over here, but Pete is right. The Count will be along soon. Anyway, our wives likely will be out later than we are tonight, so we are facing no curfew on the home front."

The first and third Tuesdays of each month marked the customary meeting times for the Murryville Town Council, so I never saw Julianna on alternate Tuesdays until she had wound up the pressing public business of our fair municipality for a particular fortnight. On this third Tuesday in September, the Council was considering a controversial resolution to appropriate funds from the town budget in support of recently formed weekend girls' athletic leagues in basketball, volleyball, and soccer, with competitions held at the local civic recreation center. Kingsford Smockley and a few other troglodytes on the Council still believed that sports were best left to rowdy boys and that girls should stay at home and learn domestic science from the mamas and grandmas, so a potential battle royal loomed. Naturally, Julianna favored the resolution and was working diligently to secure its passage, and she had invited Mary Alice and Ellie to dine with her in town at Chip Schmidt's German Restaurant before they all went to the Council meeting. Mary Alice was slated to speak in favor of the resolution because of its benefits for the female students of Waggoner Elementary School, and Ellie planned to address the Council on the positive effects of competitive sports on a girl's sense of self-worth. Little did Smockley and his kindred crustaceans know that a powerful triple-driven steamroller was poised to flatten them.

I stood up from the picnic bench and walked slowly across the yard of crab grass and weeds until I had nearly reached the highway. To my left, in the west, the sun was beginning to fade away across the Delta fields and drop into the Ozark hills, and to my right I could view a series of signs making up the roster of the Crocodile Chamber of Commerce: Sadie's Stop and Shop; R. T.'s Celestial Country-and-Western Honky Tonk; Brock's Garage—We Love Older Cars; Discount Liquor Store; The Trashfish Cafe—Gar and our Specialties; Jack's Beer Joint; Clem's Church Key; Walt's Transmission and Muffler Repair. . . . I could see no farther in the fading twilight. But as I mutely contemplated free enterprise in this Arkansas hamlet, I spied a four-door, highly polished silver Dodge Ram pickup truck with an extended cargo space and huge dual side mirrors pull out of the driveway entrance into George Uehgandt's plantation spreading across the north side of the highway, turn right onto 96, travel approximately 200 yards, and then turn left into the parking lot of Dib's. The oversized truck rolled regally across the lot straight into a reserved parking spot near the entrance to Dib's, and as I walked back across the yard I observed both front doors open, with Boris disembarking from the passenger side and Gorgeous George Uehgandt from behind the wheel.

"Gorgeous, my good man. King of the Class of 1964, the year that the stars and comets crossed the heavens above Moffatt College. How in the world are you? I haven't seen you in a coon's age." As I approached the killer truck, I shouted my effusive greetings to my friend and classmate.

"Eh? What's that? Do I hear a squeaky voice coming from somewhere? Ever since my last trip to the eye doctor, I haven't been able to see a damned thing. Is somebody calling me?" George erratically waved his arms around and pretended to stumble as he slowly turned in a circle.

George was one of the few men among my wide local acquaintance who nearly matched Boris Schuller in height, and the planter exceeded the Austrian in poundage. Six feet, eight inches tall and happily confessing to 325 pounds of weight richly earned at many a dining table, my classmate had grown very little upward or outward since our college days when he drove his 1960 Chevy Impala from Crocodile to Moffatt College, enrolled as an economics major, occupied a corner room in the basement of Martini Hall, and took over the center spot on the Bulldogs basketball team for four memorable years. After his graduation he had moved back to Uehgandt Farms, a year later married an Independence County girl named Karen Crutchfield with whom he eventually produced four daughters, and increased both the acreage and the productivity of the family's agribusiness dramatically during the past three decades. Moreover, he had remained loyal to his alma mater and now served as the ideal host to visiting professor Schuller.

I met George's satire with a pointed comment of my own. "Gorgeous, if you weren't still so vain you would wear those bifocals that I prescribed for you. Your blonde pompadour is silver now anyway, so no self-respecting barstool buxom bunny would take a second look at you."

Dressed similarly in extra-extra large blue denim work shirts, capacious jeans, and muddy work boots, George and Boris smiled as I approached them and then introduced George to Augie and Pete, who had strolled over from the picnic tables. Both pickup truck riders wore farmer's baseball caps, George a green-and-gold "John Deere" standard issue, and Boris a bright red one advertising "Bama Feeds."

"Mighty glad to see all of you guys here in Crocodile," boomed out George. "Captain, Speck has told me many lies about you, but please remain his pal anyway. He usually alienates most of his friends within a few months, so stay tolerant of his decaying soul for as long as you can. And Professor, Boris appreciates your many kindnesses to him, as do I. Just don't let him drink you under the table tonight. Glad to see you, fellas."

George shook hands with Pete and Augie, slapped Boris and me each on the back (inducing a spasm of coughing from me), and turned toward his truck.

"George, aren't you staying for dinner with us?" I inquired.

"Here in the country we call the evening meal 'supper,' you city slicker. Naw, Speck, I promised to accompany Karen to the Town Council meeting over in Murryville. Our daughters were all on swim teams or did gymnastics in town while they were growing up, and they really enjoyed the experiences, so Karen wants to back Julianna in this resolution to support recreation programs for girls."

"Smockley, eat your heart out," I concluded. "You are a defeated man now, for sure."

Pete touched George on the upper right arm. "Mister Uehgandt, before you go, would you tell me how your village here"—Pete pivoted left and right with outstretched arms—"gained its quaint reptilian name?"

"Sure, son. My great-grandmother Gretchen Uehgandt deserves the credit. She and Big Dad, my great-grandfather, migrated here from Kiel, Germany, in 1881 and settled on this land"—George pointed north across the highway—"when it was mostly hardwood forests or swamps. Big Dad cleared acre after acre of trees and drained some of the smaller swamps in order to start planting cotton on the reclaimed land, and Grandma Gretchen helped him all along the way, except she would go nowhere near the swamps. She was adamantly convinced that all of the damp areas were filled with crocodiles—not true, of course, but all she could talk about, nearly, was the crocodiles in the swamps. My daddy thinks she had read too many books about guys like Burton and Speke trekking through Africa while searching for the source of the Nile River. Anyhow, she talked so much about crocodiles that the word became associated with the place and eventually became official. Sounds more exotic than 'Uehgandt' anyway, now don't it? Har, har."

"George, this is my first time to hear that story. I learn more local esoterica the longer I reside in this mysterious part of the globe," contributed Boris.

"Right, right," said our farmer friend. "Gotta go now, fellas. Karloff, these gentlemen will see that you get home safely. Adios, now!"

With shards of gravel pinging off his truck's undercarriage, George steered his Ram out of Dib's parking lot and onto highway 96. We remaining four patrons sauntered into the evening's restaurant of choice, settling ourselves at a large, round, metal-legged, Formica-topped table offering ample room on its surface for plates, glasses, and cutlery as well as the legal pads, stacks of note cards, and four copies of *As I Lay Dying* carried collectively by Pete, Augie, and me. Dib's Ribs and Fibs was filled nearly to capacity with convivial customers who sat at tables scattered over the grimy hardwood floor, who stood leaning on the bar presided over by Mister Dib himself, or who played shuffleboard or billiards in the nearest connecting room. A corner jukebox blinking alternately in red and green lights contributed renditions of several country classic songs, such as "Give My Love to Rose," "You Win Again," "Amelia Earhart," and "Miller's Cave."

Boris spoke up. "Mister Flowers—Dib—graciously stocks my favorite beer from Graz, Gosser Stiftsbrau, as well as a large array of American brands. May I offer all of you a bottle of my Austrian choice as we commence tonight?

Postponing the issue of who treated whom until later in the evening, we all followed Boris's suggestion and soon were enjoying sips of our visitor's stout hometown brew. Raising his bottle in tribute to the math professor, Augie said, "A great suggestion, Boris. Now please satisfy my rampant curiosity. Did George call you 'Karloff,' or did my battered ears deceive me?"

Wiping foam from his moustache by moving his crooked left index finger from right to left across his spiral-tipped facial hair, Boris chuckled, looked with raised eyebrows at Pete, and inquired, "Do you mind explaining the names, Peter Edward?"

"Happy to, Boris Lothar," responded Pete with a wide smile. "Augie, as you can readily understand, Moffatt does not attract teachers of Boris's . . . uhh, shall we say, uh, impressive appearance every day." With these words Boris dropped his chin in modesty and raised his bottle in tribute to Pete's tactful choice of descriptive language. "So when Boris donned his opera garb—cape, ruffled shirt, long black cane, and all of that—for the President's reception, Rodger Compton hung the title of 'Count' on him, and later that honorific became 'Count No Count.' Then another student, C. Y. Hollowell, Junior, claimed that Boris bears a resemblance to the Hollywood star of Frankenstein films, so along came the names 'Karloff,' 'Frankenstein,' and even sometimes the diminutives 'Franken' or 'Frank.'"

"What a list of nicknames," I offered after I had swallowed a cold mouthful of Stiftsbrau.

"And that ain't all," replied Pete, lapsing into Crocodilian dialect as he unconsciously shifted to relaxed Delta patterns of speech, including a drawl. "One of Ellie's soccer players couldn't keep straight Boris's country of origin, and she still refers to him as 'the Australian.' And Rose Hummerly, the goalkeeper who has been coached by Boris, calls him 'Mister Goalie Man,'" in tribute to his soccer expertise.

"I answer to all of these titles," genially interjected Boris, "and also to Pete's favorite. . . ."

"I call this dude 'Doctor Nickname,'" responded Pete, "and that one also seems to be catching on around the Moffatt campus. As you can tell, Boris has quickly become a contemporary legend at your alma mater, Speck."

"And perhaps tonight we will add 'Mister Faulkner Man' to the list of appellations," suggested Augie. "Shall we order our food and then chat about the novel while we munch and slurp?"

The Captain's idea received unanimous approval, and soon we were all enjoying variously sized orders of Dib's special barbecued pork spareribs, supplemented with onion rings, baked beans, sliced garden tomatoes, and Texas toast. Boris lined up several empty bottles of Gosser Stiftsbrau during the evening's duration, but the other three of us switched to potent iced tea served in mason jars after we had consumed two Austrian beers apiece. By the time that most of our dinner debris had been cleared from the table, including four large stacks of cleaned rib bones, and we were topping off the Southern banquet with fresh blackberry cobbler a la mode, Augie had reviewed some basic information about AILD for Boris, who, as he himself phrased it, was "not personally acquainted with the literary masterpiece under scrutiny tonight." Not trusting my scattershot memory, I jotted down on a legal pad a summary of Augie's commentary.

> Settings: the Bundren farm in rural southeastern Yoknapatawpha County; various stops along various roads on an erratic funeral journey through first Mottstown (Mottson of TSAF) to Jefferson; Jefferson, cemetery and town square. Time: July of a year impossible to pinpoint but likely around 1919 or 1920. (p. 254—"Darl had a little spy-glass he got in France at the war." Must be World War I. Also, automobiles share the roads with wagons—p. 228). The Bundrens: Anse, the father. Addie, the mother (her death—p. 48, and her funeral journey, pp. 104-237). Children: Cash, Darl, Jewel, Dewey Dell, and Vardaman. Dewey Dell is definitely 17 (p. 200). We don't know the exact ages of the others but can estimate, based on what Cash tells us on p. 234, that Cash is approximately 28 to 30, Darl 27 to 29, Jewel 19 or 20, and Vardaman 6 to 8. Addie is the biological mother of all the children—pp. 170-176—and Anse is the biological father of all except Jewel, who is sired by Whitfield, a hypocritical minister (pp. 174-175, 177).

As I glanced up from my notes at my supper companions, Augie surveyed the group and asked, "Is everyone ready to look closely at Addie's enigmatic paragraph?"

Rubbing his stomach with his left hand while with his right one he used a minted toothpick to extricate a morsel of meat from between two back molars, Pete sighed and answered, "You betcha, Augie, but this meal has made me think about one of my other favorite novels, *The Dixie Association* by Donald Hays, who lives in Fayetteville, Arkansas, up on the Ozark plateau. Anyway, in this novel the narrator, one Hog Durham, a first baseman for the Arkansas Reds baseball team, refers to an African-American Reds pitcher named Genghis Mohammed, Junior, who has become a devout Muslim, when Hog remarks, and I quote, 'How can a man let religion stand between him and barbecued spareribs?'"

"I agree, Peter," confirmed Doctor Nickname, alias Boris L. Schuller, with an accompanying chuckle. "This meal is delectable enough to convert the most devout vegetarian to the savory pleasures of carnivorousness. Upon my return to Graz, I shall greatly miss these Southern meals at Dib's place and at Karen Uehgandt's bounteous board."

Mildly slapping both palms on our dining table, Augie convened our plenary Faulkner session. "All right, gentlemen; you will remember that the current investigation began with Pete's puzzlement concerning the next-to-last paragraph in Addie's one and only interior monologue. Here, let me read it again— page one-seventy-six, remember.

> I gave Anse Dewey Dell to negative Jewel. Then I gave him Vardaman to replace the child I had robbed him of. And now he has three children that are his and not mine. And then I could get ready to die."

Pete held up his right hand, waving his pork-tipped toothpick, and proclaimed, "Monsieur Dupin, I have always considered this passage to be one of the most important paragraphs in AILD, principally because in its four intense sentences Addie reveals two of the dark secrets of her embittered soul: that she conceives her two youngest children, Dewey Dell and Vardaman, solely for totally selfish reasons, and that she considers three of her five children to be irrevocably alien to her."

"Precisely stated, Professor, and very insightful," replied Augie. "You are certainly correct about the centrality of these sentences in their hidden place among the most deeply private of Addie's attitudes toward her husband and her offspring." Then, with a sideways glance at Boris, Augie asked, "And have you mentioned to the Count here about. . . ?"

"Oh yes, Cesar Auguste Dupin the Fifth," volubly affirmed Professor Schuller, the Man of Multitudinous Monikers. "Peter has told me of your distinguished French lineage. I would be more impressed if your family were native to Vienna and not Paris, but. . . ."

Booming "Har, har, har" while he slapped Augie resoundingly on the left shoulder, Boris drew a barely perceptible wince from Augie, who drew in a deep breath and said, "Fine, then. Let us continue."

Our leader lifted his top legal pad, adjusted his reading glasses on his nose, tapped the small button at the apex of his blue "Detective" cap, and pronounced, "Pete has already told us how some of Faulkner's critics disagree about the identity of, quoting here, 'the child I had robbed him of,' and how the temptation exists for all of us amateur readers to bypass this mystery and go on to some other conundrum conjured up by Mister Bill. But with the assistance of Boris here"—Augie nodded to his right, and Mister Goalie Man acknowledged the tribute by closing his eyes and modestly lowering his chin—"and based upon a careful reading of the paragraph and of certain correlated passages in the novel preceding the paragraph, I have concluded that Addie does indeed have in mind one, specifically ONE, of her children when she mentions 'the child I had robbed him of.'"

Looking around the table and observing that all of us did not appear to be flummoxed or asleep, Augie continued. "Addie slyly disguises her meaning in this paragraph through an obscure use of an already arcane term—'to negative.' By doing so, she constructs a form of mathematical equation involving all five of her children, and an analysis of this calculation demonstrates that Cash, the eldest, must be the unnamed child."

"Aha!" shouted Pete, drawing startled glances from various barbecue sauce-besotted carnivores at nearby tables. "So this time you have given us the answer first, or have provided the equivalent of pulling the purloined letter out of the drawer, as your ancestor uncle does with a flourish in Poe's story. Will you further emulate C. A. Dupin the First and now explain to us humble groundlings how you reached your bold conclusion?"

"Most definitely, Professor," replied the Captain, "and I am truly flattered by your linking my modest detective skills with those of my illustrious ancestor. I do hope that I can make a plausible case for my hypothesis. My goal is to clarify the meaning of Addie's penultimate paragraph by placing Cash's name in the proper place in our presumed equation. Moreover, I assert that this solution reached by plugging in Cash's name should also serve to correct a persistent error in some of the criticism on AILD that Pete graciously supplied to me last week." Now Pete took his turn to nod in acknowledgment. Augie continued, "I refer to a recurrent misconception concerning Addie's abiding attitudes toward Cash and Jewel. Finally, I believe that my solution will also reveal the answer to another mystery in AILD: the primary reason for Jewel's seething jealousy of his older brother."

Stretching my arms out widely, I addressed my tablemates. "A full intellectual menu that should keep our mental gears grinding until our bloated stomachs process this Crocodilian ambrosia." Once again I staked out an irrefutable claim to the title of King of Mixed-Metaphor Mountain.

"Yes, well, let's get into the explication," suggested our ratiocinist, with sidelong glances and a subtly repressed smirk directed at the other two members of our foursome. The Captain picked up his copy of AILD. "Look on pages one-sixty-nine through one-seventy-one, gentlemen. When Anse proposes to Addie—on one-seventy-one, and I'm quoting Anse here, '"That's what I come to see you about"'—Addie is a teacher in rural Yoknapatawpha County, and presumably she would be familiar with the pedagogical terminology of mathematics. Now look at the key words 'to negative.' Several critics assume that this verbal, or more precisely this infinitive—thanks for the condensed grammar review last week, Pete"—nod, responsive nod— "umm, that this infinitive means 'to negate, cancel, or nullify,' that is, to wipe the action off the record as it if never occurred. Here is one critic's opinion on the issue. 'She gives Anse Dewey Dell to negate Jewel.' However, the conception and birth of Jewel definitely do happen, and with major ramifications. In the *Oxford English Dictionary* I found another definition for the transitive verb 'negative.' And I quote...." Augie lifted a note card from a loose pile on the table and read from it. "'To render ineffective, neutralize.' I believe that this definition more precisely fits the logical construction of the paragraph's four sentences. And this is where Boris can provide vital assistance."

Smoothly taking his cue while with his right hand stroking his impressive moustache, Boris said, "Pete, Speck, you will remember that after the soccer game, while we were driving to Crocodile, in answer to Augie's query I mentioned the term 'additive inverse.' I agree with our detective here"—left thumb pointed hitch-hiking style at Augie—"that Addie appears to be using her own personal variation of a standard mathematical procedure involving the entity we math jocks—Pete's name for us—know as the additive inverse. Let me recite a definition for you."

Boris sat up straight, towering regally in his metal-legged chair, closed his eyes, and spoke in clipped syllables: "The additive inverse of a real or complex number 'a' is the number which when added to 'a' gives zero." The Count opened his eyes and slowly surveyed his minions. "The procedure can be stated in the formula—"

As Doctor Nickname reached for a blank note card hastily proffered by Pete, Augie informed me, "This is the formula that Boris wrote out for me when I was riding in the back seat of your Explorer."

I nodded and then read the following from the card held up to view between the lengthy left index finger and thick thumb of Count No Count:

$$a + (-a) = 0$$

-a denotes the additive inverse of a.

Augie took over again. "When Addie Bundren says 'I gave Anse Dewey Dell to negative Jewel,' she means that the act of bearing Dewey Dell renders ineffective, or neutralizes, in her mind the adulterous conception of Jewel."

Now Boris wrote on another blank note card while saying, with his head bent over the card, "Dewey Dell represents the additive inverse, the minus 'a,' and Addie uses the conception and birth of Dewey Dell to 'negative' the same actions regarding Jewel, the 'a.'" He held up the card:

a	+	(-a)	=	0, or a status of
Jewel		Dewey Dell		neutralization

Augie concluded, "By bearing Dewey Dell, Addie balances the bottom line of what one astute critic calls her 'moral accountancy.' Addie does not cancel out the significance of Jewel's birth but rather in her own mind morally justifies it."

Leaning back in his wobbly chair, Augie looked intently at first Boris on his right, Pete across from him, and finally your humble narrator man to his left. "Any questions, gentlemen? Shall we move to the second sentence of the paragraph?"

Vigorous nods and pursed-lipped expressions of approval from the other residents of our table provided all of the body language that Augie required. "All right. Some eight to ten years after the birth of her only daughter, Addie apparently decides that she has not fulfilled to her own satisfaction all of the terms of her highly personal mathematical equation. As she says, 'Then I gave him Vardaman to replace the child I had robbed him of.' Since Jewel is already accounted for—morally as well as mathematically—in the first step of the equation, and since Dewey Dell and Vardaman are conceived and born solely to counterbalance Jewel and this unnamed child, then only two children remain as candidates for this 'child I had robbed him of.'"

Pete hastily stood up from his chair, knocking it backward to the floor with a resounding "Clang," glanced around sheepishly, muttered "Sorry, folks" to the surprised patrons at nearby tables, set his chair upright with its backrest touching the edge of our table, and slowly sank into his seat, with his chin resting on lanky arms that were folded lengthwise atop the back of the chair. His accidental sideshow at an end, he quietly offered, "Detective Dupin, you have reduced the usual suspects to a mere two. Only Cash and Darl have not so far been designated by Addie."

"Yes, Pete, you are correct," patiently affirmed Augie, "and I contend that Addie alludes to the tragic Darl in this key paragraph only in the third sentence. Addie is secretly apathetic toward Dewey Dell and Vardaman, but in her most private heart of hearts she harbors only unalleviated anger toward Darl. In an earlier passage, Addie makes clear that she cruelly ostracizes Darl from her maternal love even before he is born. Look on pages one-seventy-two and one-seventy-three."

> Then I found that I had Darl. At first I would not believe it. Then I believed that I would kill Anse. It was as though he had tricked me, hidden within a word like within a paper screen and struck me in the back through it. But then I realised that I had been tricked by words older than Anse or love, and that my revenge would be that he would never know I was taking revenge.

I stared at my copy of the opened novel as the import of the words filtered into my sluggish brain. "Is Addie saying here that she avenges herself on the innocent Darl for perceived wrongs that Anse has inflicted upon her?"

Inclining his head an inch or so, Augie looked with raised eyebrows across the table at Pete, and the professor spoke up. "You are partially correct, Speck. At first Addie blames Anse for tricking her into her second pregnancy, but then it seems that the villain in Addie's mind becomes harder to define. Probably she is the most furious at the prevailing custom that her roles as wife and mother demand of her in rural Yoknapatawpha County: the assumption that she will bear as many children as her husband wants. So she secretly vows to take revenge—not on Anse, but on Darl, a completely innocent child. Apparently Addie treats Darl decently in front of the other Bundrens or other farm families in the County, but in subtle ways that only she knows and controls, she withholds genuine, abiding affection from him from the day of his birth onward. Only she and Darl are aware of the situation. Look on page—hold on while I flip to it. Page ninety-five. Here Darl thinks, quotation, 'I cannot love my mother because I have no mother.' For all of his life he has had a biological mother, but not one who nurtures him or provides him with the unquestioned adoration that any child deserves from his or her parent. And Darl suffers an encompassing alienation that eventually degenerates into an incurable mental breakdown. See his harrowing final monologue on pages two-fifty-three and two-fifty-four when he foams at the mouth while he is locked behind bars in the state mental asylum in Jackson."

"Thanks, Pete," Augie acknowledged. "Now let's all look at another key passage, this one on page one-seventy-two. Here Addie reveals that she had shut Anse out of the unique relationship existing between Cash and her, thus 'robbing' Anse of their eldest child by claiming Cash completely for herself:

> I knew that . . . my aloneness . . . had never been violated until Cash came. Not even by Anse in the nights.
>
> He had a word, too. Love, he called it. But I had been used to words for a long time. I knew that that word was like the others: just a shape to fill a lack; that when the right time came, you wouldn't need a word for that anymore than for pride or fear. Cash did not need to say it to me nor I to him, and I would say, Let Anse use it, if he wants to. So it was Anse or love; love or Anse: it didn't matter."

"Augie," intervened Pete, "let me add to our explanation an observation that may assist Speck and Boris in their brave attempts to follow what we are summarizing. Guys, please be aware that throughout her life Addie is afflicted with a pervasive, debilitating sense of morbid isolation. Look on page one-sixty-nine, the first page of her monologue. Listen to the overwhelming emotional claustrophobia suggested by this statement arising out of the depths of Addie's soul. Quoting here: 'I could just remember how my father used to say that the reason for living was to get ready to stay dead for a long time.'"

"Whew!" I continued. "I am reminded of the premature burial of Madeline Usher in Poe's story. And oh yes, of the wicked entombment of Fortunato by Montresor in 'The Cask of Amontillado.'"

In visible disgust vibrating his entire body from the waist upward, Boris quite effectively expressed agreement with me. "I also think of coffins and crypts, Speck, and of Austrian folktales about unfortunate wretches who are presumed to be dead but who eventually try to break out of their coffins. *Gross Gott*, I am becoming queasy." With his final remark Boris chugged half a bottle of Stiftsbrau, wiped his moustache and mouth with the back of his right hand, and sighed, "There; now I am feeling better."

Pete continued, "Let me finish this point, guys, and then Augie can get us back on the math fast track. Now, about Addie and her overwhelming sense of isolation. Please be aware that Addie periodically uses forms of physical assertion as ways of temporarily staving off her endemic loneliness. We can discern three categories of these physical means. First, she sometimes beats her pupils, forcing them into an unavoidable recognition that she exists and possesses control over their lives. Look on one-seventy. Here I quote: 'I would look forward to the times when they faulted, so I could whip them. When the switch fell I could feel it upon my flesh; when it welted and ridged it was my blood that ran, and I would think with each blow of the switch; Now you are aware of me! Now I am something in your secret and selfish life, who have marked your blood with my own for ever and ever.' Second, she marries Anse, participates in conjugal sex with him, bears children, and suckles them; look on one-seventy through one-seventy-four. And third, she engages in the torrid affair with Whitfield, with Jewel as the issue; see pages one-seventy-four and one-seventy-five."

"Again my thanks, Pete, for that helpful summary," Augie said, claiming the Faulknerian floor once more. "Gentlemen, please remember the two passages that I read earlier, first the one about Darl and then the one centering on Cash. Let's now think about Addie and Cash, her oldest child. When Addie becomes pregnant for the first time, the possibility for love—with Anse, certainly with the developing child in her womb—exists in Addie's heart and mind, and the birth of Cash represents one of two high points in her lifelong battle to stave off isolation. Look on page one-seventy-one. Here I quote from Addie: 'And when I knew that I had Cash, I knew that living was terrible and that this was the answer to it.'"

"What is the second time, Augustus?" queried Doctor Nickname. "May I know now, or will you keep me in suspense for some indeterminate time?"

"No, no, Boris," replied Augie, with a gentle waving of both outturned palms. "The second high point occurs when she engages in the affair with Whitfield and then bears his child, Jewel. Approximately a decade after the birth of Cash, Addie experiences a second temporary surcease of her pervasive loneliness. Follow along as I read from pages one-seventy-four and one-seventy-five. Here Addie symbolically alludes to the various times during which she secretly couples with Whitfield in their clandestine trysting place:

> I believed that I had found it. I believed that the reason was the duty to the alive, to the terrible blood, the red bitter blood boiling through the land.... While I waited for him in the woods, waiting for him before he saw me, I would think of him as dressed in sin.... I would think of the sin as garments which we would remove in order to shape and coerce the terrible blood to the forlorn echo of the dead wood high in the air."

Augie held up his right index finger and then his second finger. "First, Addie holds back the loneliness by conceiving and bearing Cash, and second by doing the same for Jewel, but of course she makes her third baby with a different daddy."

"Many thanks, Captain Dupree—or Dupin, let me say," responded the Count, who bobbed his chin sharply once as he sat erectly in his chair. "Pray proceed with your close explication."

"Yes, yes, I will," spoke Augie, as his eyes roamed the scribblings on his legal pad. "All right; back to our mathematical equation and the relevance of Boris's suggestion of the additive inverse. Our awareness of Addie's rejection of Darl and her lifelong feelings of adoration for Cash leads to the conclusion that Cash must be the unnamed 'child' and also that Addie has given her youngest child, Vardaman, to Anse solely as a replacement for Cash, whom in her heart she has claimed totally for herself. Vardaman thus represents the additive inverse of Cash, the minus 'a.' Boris, would you mind writing on another note card the next step in the equation?"

Count No Count immediately reached with his long left arm and plucked a card from a loose array of paper detritus on our messy table, hastily wrote on the card, and showed the results first to Pete, then me, and then Augie:

$$a \quad + \quad (-a) \quad = \quad 0, \text{ or a balance}$$
$$\text{Cash} \quad\quad \text{Vardaman}$$

"*Danke, meinen* Professor," bowed Augie from his chair.

"*Bitte, bitte*," acknowledged Boris, with a tight smile denoting a sense of satisfaction for his ability to be of assistance in this literary investigation.

Lifting his copy of AILD from the table, Augie pronounced, "Now we can proceed to the paragraph's third sentence, which, with its explicit mathematical language, logically follows the first two. Quoting here, 'And now he has three children that are his and not mine.'"

I raised my right hand high into the Dibsean atmosphere. "Even I, an arithmetical ignoramus and Faulkner novice, can discern the numbers and names suggested here. Addie totally concedes Darl, Dewey Dell, and Vardaman to Anse; 'not mine'—what terrifying words! And with this sentence she also strongly suggests a converse set of assumptions, which I could summarize in these words: 'I have two children who are mine and not his'—Cash and Jewel. Three plus two equals FIVE! Am I ready to be named to a distinguished chair of mathematics, Boris?"

"An EXtinguished chair, perhaps, Doctor," chuckled our abstract mathematician. "And I agree with your interpretation that Addie's first and third sons are wholly hers, each of them conceived and born when the possibility—but not necessarily the realization—exists of an enduring love with the son's father. I believe that my conclusion systematically develops out of your interpretation, Peter and Augustus."

"True, true," responded Pete, and Augie nodded in concord. The Captain spoke up: "Professor Schuller, please look on page one-seventy-two for further confirmation of your conclusion."

"I will be happy to, when I return from a necessary respite. As Butler Countians are fond of saying, 'I need to go outside.' Dib's has adequate indoor plumbing, but occasionally I enjoy making use of the antique building out back, the one with the quaint half-moon on the door and the Sears catalog hanging by a string attached to the inside wall. *Entschuldigen Sie mir, bitte.*"

Boris arose from his chair and slowly strolled toward the bar, stopping along the way to chat with various other regular patrons of Dib's, to observe a tricky billiards bank shot, and to compliment tavern keeper Dib himself on the quality of tonight's servings of ribs, especially the secret sauce that Dib mixes up in a locked former garage backing onto the swamp some thirty yards from Boris's destination, the outdoor powder room. Any detective foolhardy enough to attempt a clandestine investigation of the ingredients used in the creation of Dib's rich, tongue-tingling sauce would likely find himself peppered with buckshot blown out of the business end of a handy shotgun.

We remaining three self-anointed Faulkner sleuths stood up, stretched, strolled around the evening's restaurant of choice, visited the indoor comfort station, and gratefully accepted refills on our desired beverages from Maureen, the waitress who never stopped moving or ceased chewing the swollen wad of Juicy Fruit gum in her oversized jaw. When Boris reformed our quartet, Augie resumed the analysis of Addie's mysterious paragraph.

"Now, fellows, let me add one more observation to my understanding of the third sentence. Remember that now we are looking at page one-seventy-two and then on to one-seventy-three. By cold-heartedly ceding three of their children to Anse, Addie also fulfills to her own secret satisfaction a tacit pledge that she had once made to her husband. In her rigidly suppressed fury at having become pregnant with Darl, she feels betrayed by life itself, with its empty words, and decides that her father was right when he had told her about living in order to 'get ready to stay dead a long time.' After Darl's birth she begins thinking ahead to her own death, and she implies to Anse that they will have no more children. For the selfish, indolent Anse, the more children the merrier, since he will have more hands to work on the farm, and he replies—look on one-seventy-three—'"Nonsense . . . you and me aint nigh done chapping yet, with just two."' By conceiving and bearing first Dewey Dell and then Vardaman, Addie is able to grant Anse his wish. Until the final two children are born, Anse possesses as his own 'chap' only Darl. But eventually he receives from Addie a total of three who are his, all his—and in Addie's mind in no way hers."

Augie raised his eyes, surveyed his companions, and politely inquired, "Ready for the final sentence now, gentlemen?" Nods all around, and onward proceeded our esteemed leader. "This final sentence now logically follows: 'And then I could get ready to die.' Combining her two primary adult roles of teacher and domestic worker, she has balanced the equation and has finished metaphorically—I'm quoting here from page one-seventy-six—'cleaning up the house,' that is, using her body, or 'house,' to accomplish her final, highly private and determined acts of will."

Augie made eye contact with first Boris and then with me; we both nodded to our ratiocinist in mute and mutual endorsement of his interpretation. When the Captain then looked across the table at Pete, I followed his gaze and noticed that the English professor was squinting fixedly at his copy of AILD and silently moving his lips. Abruptly Pete raised his head, met Augie's eyes, and slowly asked, "Monsieur Dupin, do you find any other meanings in this paragraph? I completely agree with your reading of it and also that Boro has supplied us with the key to the mystery by offering to us the concept of the additive inverse. But your explanation opens up another possibility to me. Everybody please scan the paragraph and take note of these words: 'gave,' 'gave,' 'replace,' 'has,' 'his,' 'mine', 'get ready to die.' Now concentrate: in what type of document, one in longtime and widespread use, would we ordinarily encounter such diction? Anyone, anyone, anyone, care to hazard a guess?"

A word suddenly appeared in large block letters directly in front of my mind's eye. "A will, a legal will," I shouted, drawing turned heads and raised eyebrows from scattered diners, sleekly attired pool sharks, and assorted honky-tonk gals sporting beehive hairdos. Lowering my voice a notch, I surveyed my companions and stated emphatically, "A last will and testament."

Pete jumped out of his chair and punched the air with his fist. "YES!" he bellowed, this time eliciting from our fellow Dibseans assorted murmurs, head shakes, and several twirling index fingers pointed to temples. Loco we might be, but we amateur Faulkner bloodhounds were hot on the trail, noses all a-twitchin'.

The professor was jubilant. "Speck, you are the Snoop with the Poop, the De-Tec-Tive of the Week. Congrats, my good man. In this key paragraph Addie Bundren uses not only certain terms from the discipline of mathematics but also the language of a rudimentary bequest."

Pete plopped back into his chair and looked across the table at Augie.

"Monsieur Dupin, Addie Bundren's private mathematical equation is also her last will and testament. Please notice that this final bequest appears just ahead of the monologue's concluding paragraph, which is an ironic epilogue reiterating Addie's distrust of conventional religion and her rejection of the uselessness of conventional language in comparison to the power of actions, or deeds. Throughout her life Addie temporarily staves off loneliness only through actions: beating the children, having sex with Anse or later with Whitfield, bearing her five children. Significantly, Addie's four sentences that constitute her mathematical bequest express the power of deeds, not words: deeds such as giving Anse three children, keeping two children for herself, and preparing her body and soul for getting 'ready to stay dead a long time.'"

With a warm smile Augie arose, leaned across the table, shook Pete's hand, and proclaimed, "Wonderful thinking, Professor. Your insight solidly augments my theories concerning the meaning of mathematics in these sentences. Let's call this passage by your suggested heading: a 'mathematical bequest,' because it truly is a will as well as an equation."

"Gadzooks, Augie, do we now require the services of a lawyer?" I asked in alarm. "We have been able sneakily to pick Boris's brain for the cost of a ride to Crocodile and a rib dinner, but I shudder to think about subjecting ourselves to legal fees."

Boris threw back his head and roared with laughter. "Yes, Doctor, I worked on the cheap, as your American expression goes—or should I say that I gave you a freebie? But I think that we will not need to consult an actual attorney at law. Am I correct, Captain Augustus?"

Augie balled his left fist and mock-punched me on the right arm. "Pot calling the kettle black anyway, Doctor Fee For Service. If we need a literary legal opinion, I could probably put in a call to my longtime friend Benjy Mitchell at the law school in Little Rock. He owes me a favor or two."

The Captain then picked up the legal pad in front of him. "Thanks again,

Pete, for your flash of inspiration. Fellows, let me now move on to my final two observations, if you will be so kind. We have to wind up our chat here before Dib gives us all the old bar room heave-ho. Do you remember earlier tonight I suggested that we could use our solution to Addie's equation—excuse me, Pete, her equation-bequest—as a way of solving a couple of other mysteries that Addie takes with her to her grave? Let me now move through these quickly. Number one is the question of the identity of the offspring nominated by certain critics to be Addie's favorite child. Some of Addie's neighbors, including the pious and nosy Cora Tull, assume that Jewel is her most beloved child. Look on page twenty-four. Quoting here from Cora's interior monologue, 'Jewel, the one she had always cherished. . . .' Darl once states—page eighteen, and I quote, 'ma always whipped and petted him more—' meaning Jewel. And when Addie is on her deathbed, Dewey Dell claims, "'It's Jewel she wants'"—page forty-seven.

"Apparently basing their conclusions on these statements and on other commentary by characters within the novel, several critics refer to Jewel as Addie's favorite child. Let me see here. . . ." Augie picked up a note card from the table. "I count . . . five who make that claim, and I may have overlooked others, Pete, in the critical material that you selected for me. HOWEVER—we four investigators are aware that Addie actually has not one but TWO favorite children, and each of them is equally important to her, albeit for different reasons. Here is one critic, Pamela Annas, who is correct in her assessment of Addie's inordinate fondness for two of her five offspring: 'Addie feels a special tie to Cash, her first born, and to Jewel, the consequence of an act that had meaning to her.'"

I listened closely to my neighbor's explanation and responded, "Apparently these critics fall victim to a type of error in mathematics, Augie. They automatically assume that if a mother plays favorites with her children, she will designate one as the single most beloved child, not two, each special in an unusual way. Of course, who would expect any mother of five to reject totally three of her biological issue by stating that the children are, egad, 'NOT MINE'?"

"A valid observation, Speck, and one that I appreciate. So—our solution to Addie's equation-bequest demonstrates conclusively Addie's choice of both Cash and Jewel as her favorites. Augie paused here and swiveled his head back and forth, looking at each of his dinner companions once, then twice. "Moreover, our mathematical solution also provides the key to understanding Jewel's unrelenting, consuming jealousy toward Cash."

"Wait, Augie," interrupted Pete. "Are you saying that Jewel is truly envious of his oldest brother? I guess that I must have overlooked that point in my earlier hopscotches through the book."

"Professor," replied our chief detective, "please look at pages fourteen and fifteen, Jewel's only interior monologue in the novel. Surprisingly, critics of AILD have focused almost exclusively on this monologue's last few sentences, in which Jewel viciously expresses his obsessive, confused love for his mother by revealing his desire to be alone with Addie, and I quote here from page fifteen, 'on a high hill and me rolling the rocks down the hill at their faces.' Most of this vitriolic monologue, however, is a diatribe against Cash. Jewel seethes with hatred of his stolid older brother because he, Jewel, wants to be Addie's only favorite child. Look on page fourteen and read along with me as I quote Jewel's intense thoughts:

> It's because he [Cash] stays out there, right under the window, hammering and sawing on that goddamn box. Where she's got to see him. Where every breath she draws is full of his knocking and sawing where she can see him saying See. See what a good one I am making for you. I told him to go somewhere else. I said Good God do you want to see her in it. It's like when he was a little boy and she says if she had some fertilizer she would try to raise some flowers and he taken the bread pan and brought it back from the barn full of dung."

Pete stared at his copy of AILD, finally raised his head and transferred his stare to Augie, and said, "Well, I'll be damned. Jewel wants his mother all to himself and knows that Cash is his chief rival—hell, his ONLY rival—for the status of numero uno among her offspring. But Cash doesn't seem to be envious of Jewel or to treat him harshly."

"Correct, Professor," responded Augie. "Cash and Jewel are both aware that Addie cares deeply for the other son. Cash accepts the situation with magnanimity, but throughout the novel Jewel maintains a seething fury at Cash that is not even alleviated by the placement of Addie's corpse in her desired grave in the Jefferson cemetery. Jewel simply cannot tolerate sharing his mother with one of his siblings. Cash and Jewel belong irrevocably to Addie, as all three persons are aware. Addie and Cash quietly affirm their relationship and mutually benefit from it, but Jewel constantly covets Addie for himself and loathes Cash accordingly."

Pete stood, raised both thumbs level to either side of his face, jabbed his thumbs four times into the air, and announced, "The Captain strikes again. The Dupin genetic strain of genius once more asserts itself. Augie, you have brought clarity to my muddled swampy pit of a brain with AILD just as you have with the first two Faulkner mind benders. How can I thank you enough?"

"Pete, Pete, calm down. The other people in here are watching," modestly replied Monsieur Dupin V. "You have more than repaid me by providing welcome challenges for my stagnating mind during my retirement and especially by introducing me to fascinating people such as Professor Schuller here, who somehow has stayed awake through all of this interminable blather and has not fallen out of his chair in boredom."

"Of course not, Captain Augustus. I have enjoyed myself immensely this evening," assured the Austrian mathematician. "Now I must find time to read this novel and perhaps some of Mister Faulkner's other books. You have whetted my appetite with your titillating talk about coffins, wills, revenge, alienation, and adultery. Especially that last subject. . . . Tell me more about this affair that Addie Bundren carries on with that minister. . . ."

Pete escorted Boris from our table to the bar, where the English professor whipped out his wallet and attempted to press his Visa card into Dib's meaty palm before any of the rest of us could react. But Pete turned out to be several stealthy moves to the rear of the erstwhile Gorgeous George Uehgandt, Squire of Crocodile, Arkansas.

Wiping his hands on his stained apron, Dib reached to the cash register, pushed a button, and extricated a one-hundred dollar bill from a drawer. "George gave me this portrait of Ben Franklin earlier today, boys, and informed me in no uncertain terms that HIS money is viable currency in Butler County and that YORES ain't. I'll give George his change tomorrow. Thanks for stopping in tonight, and y'all come back mighty soon." Dib hurried toward his kitchen and left us Murryvillians no recourse but to ask Boris to thank our benefactor and to tell him, according to Southern etiquette, that we owed him.

As we descended the step from Dib's long porch and crossed the parking lot toward Augie's waiting Oldsmobile, I touched Boris on his lengthy left arm and said, "Count, your earlier emphasis on the word 'adultery' reminds me of an anecdote that my friend C. Y. Hollowell, Senior, father of the current Moffatt student, tells about his grandfather, who established the family's law firm in our town early in this century.

"It seems that when Grandfather Hollowell was a young man, he sat the first time, before he was adequately prepared, for the oral part of the Arkansas Bar examination—a prerequisite to his gaining of his attorney's license. C. Y. says that his granddad was once quite a ladies' man and that the then-youthful Romeo had spent most of his free time chasing women—some single, some married— rather than learning about criminal or civil legal procedures."

We reached Augie's auto and stopped while I completed the story. "During the exam candidate Hollowell was stumbling and mumbling his way through all of the questions, delivering precious few correct answers, when a compassionate white-haired examiner, a venerable judge, took pity on the dismal wretch and asked him to relate a standard legal distinction, one found in several textbooks current to that era. 'Young man, will you please explain to me the difference between fornication and adultery?' Hollowell's face brightened, then clouded up, then brightened again. In a high-pitched voice he replied, 'Yes sir, Judge, yes sir. The difference between fornication and adultery. Hmmmmm. Well, let's see. . . . Uhhh, well, Judge, to tell you the truth, I have tried them both, and I couldn't tell a bit of difference!'"

Chapter Six

The Case of Faulkner's Arch-Villain in *Light in August*

Neatsy Keen

𝔐𝔲𝔯𝔯𝔭𝔟𝔦𝔩𝔩𝔢 𝔐𝔢𝔰𝔰𝔢𝔫𝔤𝔢𝔯

Thursday, September 21, 1995

The Town Tattler
by
Turner Stoneman, Editor

Perry Mason, Jessica Fletcher, and Lieutenant Colombo, move over and get ready for some company. Murryville can now boast about the presence of its own colorful crime-solving sleuths.

Perhaps some of you observant townspeople have noticed that a certain prominent doctor takes early-morning walks with a distinguished retired Memphis police detective. And maybe some of you other folks were in and out of Story's Cafe last May when Doctor Speck Watkins and Captain Augustus Dupree sat and chatted for several hours with young Doctor Peter E. Prefont, a popular recent addition to the English faculty at Moffatt.

But did you know that these three brainy boys have been busy solving mysteries? Informed sources tell the Tattler that our three amateur Sherlock Holmeses so far have closed the files on an assault, an episode of perjury, a burglary, a suicide, and a complex inheritance case. My spies in Crocodile whispered in my eagerly waiting ear about that last one.

No, Doctor Speck has not given up tinkering with people's eyes, and Detective Dupree has not signed on with our town's police department, not in an official capacity, anyway. These two solid citizens of our minor metropolis are assisting Professor Pete in the investigations of crimes and other mysteries in . . . BOOKS. That's right, faithful *Messenger* readers, books—and all by one author, Mister William Faulkner, late of our sister state of Mississippi, where many of you have friends, relatives, or both.

So the next time you see one of these triple threats on our town's streets, stop and ask him to fill you in on his latest investigation of a novel. Maybe Murryville someday will become the location for its own television mystery miniseries!

Cellular phones, fax machines, and the internet are all developments of modern communication that boggle the minds of some of us children of the forties and fifties who can readily remember the local telephone operator, portable typewriters, and the transition from network radio to black-and-white television. But no electronic devices powered by microchips or linked to satellites have yet surpassed the small-town rumor network, whether it is oral or in print, as a means of disseminating information in the most rapid manner imaginable. Within hours of the publication of Turner's column in our local newspaper (sometimes referred to as the "weekly wiper" by those townspeople who find themselves on the receiving end of editor Stoneman's irascible prose fusillades), my telephone (push-button, of course), had rung with at least twenty calls from acquaintances, well-meaning and nosy alike, who hungered for more information about what one caller, my friend W. Christopher Hurdle, attorney-at-law, termed the "Crowder County Private Eye Agency." Yuk, yuk. When after three hours I was finally able to stop fielding calls and place two of my own, I got through to Augie and Pete, who informed me that their left ears were also red and sweaty from continuous physical intimacy with A. T. & T.'s most familiar piece of household hardware. Fortunately, the public clamor soon subsided, and our citizenry returned to conversations concerning the progress of the O. J. Simpson trial, the vicissitudes afflicting the Arkansas Razorbacks football team, and the interminable Republican attacks on our state because of its native son, President Bill Clinton. But Turner Stoneman's "Tattler" column did come to the attention of at least one reader in a town located to the northeast of ours, and the modest fame—or infamy—enjoyed in Murryville by Augie, Pete, and me soon brought to us an invitation to take our moveable investigative feast, for the first time, on the road for a performance that necessitated an overnight stay.

Friday, November 10, 1995, found your feckless narrator, your favorite Arkansas detective of French descent, and your fair-haired, fresh-faced 'fessor ambling amiably over the one-mile distance between the Confederate soldier's statue on the town square in Brookville, Arkansas, and the Confederate States of America memorial arch at the entrance to the campus of Northeast Arkansas Teachers College. It seems that my Moffatt College contemporary, Professor Errol Tedford, now a distinguished professor of language and literature at another college in our fair state, had gotten wind of the September 21 "Tattler" revelation because Tedford's mother lives in Murryville and of course knew of my longtime friendship with her son. Errol was the 1995-1996 president of the Arkansas Literary Association, a group of teachers of English and modern foreign languages, and he had called to invite Augie, Pete, and me to appear at the ALA annual meeting which is always held on the campus of N. E. A. T. C. Errol had told me that one of the conference's sessions would be devoted to scholarly papers on Faulkner's novel *Light in August* and that as the convenor of the session he was particularly eager to hear a presentation from, as he phrased it, "the fabulous Murryville mystery-solving crew." After a series of intense conversations, we three intrepid emissaries from Crowder County consented to the requested diplomatic mission to Whisenhunt County located in the extreme northeastern corner of our state, with the mighty Mississippi River forming the eastern boundary and contributing the unusual name for the athletic teams at Northeast Arkansas Teachers College, the River Rats. In addition to its gleeful embracing of an ordinarily repellent rodent name for its sporting clubs, the local school also has long been affectionately known by a rare nickname, this one formed approximately from its initials. In print the familiar name appears as NEAT-C, and the pronunciation is "Neatsy."

"Pete, Augie, were you aware that for several decades the Moffatt Bulldogs competed against the River Rats in football, basketball, baseball, and track? Indeed, NEAT-C was our chief rival until it grew so much larger than our school and then joined the NCAA Division II, placing its scholarship athletes on a higher level of competition than that of our non-scholarship ones." I lectured to my friends about local sports history as we strolled past an impressively restored antebellum mansion featuring circular white columns, three balconies, a veranda, a surrounding gravel path lined by cedars, and a formal garden built around a massive magnolia tree. College Avenue, which connected the Whisenhunt County courthouse square in downtown Brookville with the campus of NEAT-C, was lined with numerous restored homes that were first constructed before the Civil War in this old river town, once the most bustling center of cotton trading on the banks of the Mississippi north of Memphis and south of St. Louis. Now Brookville thrived as a seat of county government, as the home to a sprawling Hallmark greeting card printing plant, and as the agribusiness mecca of a region comprised of eleven counties in Missouri, Tennessee, and Arkansas. At seven p.m. my sleuthing partners and I arrived in Brookville, 57 miles from home, and after a brief period of settling in at the downtown Holiday Inn, I had suggested a nocturnal stroll to the NEAT-C campus and back as a way of showing my friends some of the highpoints of the town's scenery and history.

As we passed a one-story apartment complex tastefully blended into the dominant Old-South architecture of the neighborhood, next descended a small hill, and then strode up the gradual rise leading toward the College's main entrance, I continued my jabbering about the extinct yet memorable athletic rivalry between my alma mater and NEAT-C. "Julianna's father, who attended Moffatt in the 1930's, took the field or the court numerous times in battles against the River Rats. Pops Murry once told me that the Bulldog supporters could always arouse the ire of the NEAT-C contingent with a derisive cheer that he and some companions had created one spring evening over in Crocodile during a spasm of malt-enhanced inspiration:

> NEAT-C, NEAT-C, Neatsy keen,
> River Rats think you're so darned mean.
> NEAT-C, NEAT-C, fie, fo, fum,
> Bulldogs beat you like a drum.

Apparently the Rat backers would become so angry that they could shout only

'Boo!' or 'Shut up!' in retaliation, but Pops Murry told me that at one football game the NEAT-C group did manage to shout collectively,

> Bulldogs, bulldogs, who are they?
> Little pink poodle pups stuffed with hay.

A lamentably weak riposte, it seemed to Pops, and I certainly agree."

With his hands stuffed in the pockets of his brown suede jacket, Pete chuckled and responded, "I'm amused by the civil tone and content of the yells taking place at those long-ago contests. Speck, Augie, did either of you see the home basketball game that Moffatt played against NEAT-C last December—the one now designated as the final game between the two teams?"

As we walked along, Augie and I glanced at one another with raised eyebrows, shook our heads simultaneously, and turned our attention back to Pete, who finished his explanation. "The authorities at both schools have decided to discontinue playing each other because both student sections became overly rowdy last winter. The River Rats' section periodically broke into this chant:

> Bulldogs, bulldogs, mutt, mutt, mutt;
> Come on, little school, kiss my. . . .

And then all of the students would hop around one hundred and eighty degrees, stick out their posteriors, and shout "Nyaaaaaah!" In response, the public poets of Moffatt College would chant

> Give it up, pack it up, go start the truck;
> Northeast Rat Finks, YOU SUCK!

Quite a degeneration in civility indeed from the cheers popular in the sedate thirties, Speck."

As we entered the NEAT-C campus and passed beneath the Confederate memorial arch, I spread my arms widely and proclaimed, "I for one am sorry that the rivalry between our two institutions has taken on such a major-college tone, Pete. After my own alma mater, I am the fondest of this school, with its harmonious style of architecture, its friendly faculty, and its industrious students, most of whom fan out from here all over our state and become skilled classroom teachers of children from kindergarten age through high school."

Augie spoke for the first time. "Yes, Speck, I understand that this school has maintained its traditional identity and has resisted the widespread trend toward envious emulation of major universities."

"You are correct, Captain," Pete interjected, "and in these times of avid pursuit of television sports' riches, NEAT-C has also retained a sense of balance between academics and intercollegiate athletics. Several members of the Board of Trustees here are trying to push the school into Division One in football and basketball, but wiser heads have so far prevailed, blessedly. My friend Jake Lambert, who teaches here, tells me that two Board members tried in October to get their rapacious hands on the piddly seventy-five thousand dollars that the English Department uses to support this annual literary conference—the one at which we will be speaking tomorrow—and to pay for the publication of the highly regarded quarterly *Journal of the Arkansas Literary Association*. The greedy barons of the Board wanted to add the seventy-five thou to a four-million-dollar proposal that would support a reconstruction of the football stadium. But hurrah for our side. The school's president, Salzburg—or Salty—Lowrey, vetoed the act of sabotage, and both our meeting and the *Journal* are still breathing, even if they are on life-support systems now."

Expressing our dual gratitude for the temporary victory of literary study over subsidized gladiatorial combat, Augie and I maintained our steady pace as we strode parallel to Pete, admiring while we walked the white-stone buildings and carefully landscaped grounds of the NEAT-C campus. Just as Pete was pointing toward Henderson Hall, the site of our scheduled appearance on Saturday, all three of us amblers were startled by the sudden appearance of a young man dressed in an expensively tailored tan suit and carrying a large tumbler of thick amber liquid. This nattily attired male, apparently an undergraduate, staggered with much banging and slamming through the front door of a nearby two-story fraternity house (identifiable by the wooden green Greek letters dominating the front wall). He shouted incoherent fragments of an unrecognizable song as he first swayed unsteadily on the porch and then lurched down the uneven wooden steps at the front of the building, risking with every erratic body movement a crashing fall onto the cement sidewalk or into the bordering shrubbery.

Augie looked leftward at me and then rightward at Pete, hesitating only slightly before he announced, "I think we had better help that reveler before he harms himself. Apparently he has just left a festive gathering of some sort." We three visitors to NEAT-C could all clearly hear a rock-and-roll band inside the fraternity house as it perpetrated serious aural damage to the Eagles' classic song "Take it Easy." Moving in rapid step up the entrance walk to the frat house, we Crowder County Samaritans then observed the original party animal reach the base of the steps, veer with a swoop and a "Whoop!" to his left, and erratically follow the cement walk as it made a semicircle and led to more steps, this set partially hidden from view beneath the porch.

Still singing his indecipherable ditty, the young boozer held tightly to a rail, without sacrificing life or limb reached a basement entrance which was located directly beneath the house's front entryway, and disappeared through a dark-green half-door that swung inward on hinges. Staying tactfully in his lee, our trio of trackers quietly followed our quarry through the door, taking quick notice that he had entered a men's restroom. As we all turned in unison to make our exits, tacitly convinced that whiskey's child was now reasonably safe, Augie glanced back, smothered a laugh, and with a raised right hand silently signaled for Pete and me to stop and to join him in observation of Evan Walker Early Times Jim Beam, Junior.

At top volume now shouting an off-key version of "Delta Dawn" directly into the plaster wall touched by the flattened tip of his red nose, our celebrator carefully placed his whiskey glass on the right half of the porcelain urinal's flat top, with his right hand pulled down the front zipper of his light tan suit trousers, with his left hand shoved the left front corner of his suit coat out of the way, reached with his right hand through the opened front flap of his pants, extricated the right shirttail of his light-blue Oxford button-down, and proceeded to urinate copiously for approximately half a minute down the length of his pants, in the process soaking the crotch area of his pants and turning his sharply pressed left trousers leg a darker, glistening shade of brown. Finishing his adherence to nature's call, he vigorously shook his shirttail, reinserted it inside the flap of his pants, closed his zipper, retrieved his tumbler of whiskey, shrugged his shoulders in an attempt to straighten his coat, stepped away from his personal puddle, and turned with a stumble in our direction. Assuming an erect posture, he widened his eyes, slowly pronounced "Good eve-uh-ning, gin-tull-men," and marched directly across the stone floor past us, taking measured steps, every other one of which elicited a bizarre sound caused by his left foot's pressing of liquid into the interior of his cordovan leather shoe: "click, SQUISH, click, SQUISH, click, SQUISH."

We three vagabonds from Murryville slowly swiveled our heads as we followed the progress of Sir Jack of Daniels across the floor and out through the green door half-door. With a low whistle of admiration, Pete whispered, "Strange things we travelers see!" I was too dumbfounded to speak, but Augie grinned widely and then posed what was for him a typical intellectual challenge to his companions: "Think hard now, fellows. Can you remember any other time when you have observed a breathing human being who was that intoxicated and who was still able to remain on his feet? I have been plundering my memory, and I cannot think of any similar incident to top that one. Anyone, anyone, anyone else offer a nominee for the winner as all-time stand-up drunkard?" After a moment shaking our heads and then both proclaiming "No," Pete and I joined Augie in exiting the restroom, our evening stretch-the-legs walk having reached the place from which it was logical for us to turn back toward our hostelry located in beautiful downtown Brookville, Arkansas.

Head of the Crass

The next morning, Saturday, November 11, found Pete, Augie, and yours truly comfortably ensconced in thickly cushioned theater seats, third row, Hudson Auditorium, NEAT-C campus. We had each enjoyed a night of sound sleep in our rooms at the Holler-Day Inn, undergone a successful foraging expedition to the Inn's bountiful breakfast buffet, and completed another invigorating ramble by foot to the campus and to the ALA conference's morning Faulkner session. By 10:30 we had heard three provocative papers on topics in *Light in August*. The first wrestled with several lingering questions about the novel's complex chronology of events; number two focused on the similarities between a typical 1930's-era Nazi storm trooper and Percy Grimm, the vigilante who kills Joe Christmas, a dominant character in the book; and the third examined closely the final chapter in the novel, with the paper's presenter asserting that Lena Grove finally achieves the status of authentic heroine in the novel because of her series of small victories over various male characters.

Each paper stimulated from the audience several questions or divergent opinions, so the session developed into an invigorating intellectual experience for all who attended, even non-professorial interlopers such as Captain Dupree and your humble ophthalmic servant. My longtime friend Errol Tedford, who was pulling double duty as both ALA prexy and convenor of this session, was particularly pleased by all of the interaction elicited by the morning's presentations. After a short refreshment break Errol reconvened the meeting and began to introduce the upcoming part of the proceedings by providing brief biographical sketches of Augie, Pete, and even insignificant Doctor Me Own Self. As Errol limned our *curriculum vitae*, I leaned leftward toward my co-conspirators and whispered, "Let's hope that he doesn't build us up so much that we wind up falling flat on our haunches while our talk goes over like a pregnant pole-vaulter."

With his extended fingers steepled in front of his nose while his chin lightly rested on his thumbs, Augie had been casually looking around the auditorium, as I also had, at the heavy deep-scarlet draperies covering most of the wall space; at the four elaborate chandeliers, each artfully illuminating its one-quarter of the area's square footage; and at the highly polished Baldwin grand piano sitting next to an ornate harpsichord in a distant corner of the stage. As I babbled nervously into his ear, Captain Cool Guy subtly smiled and whispered in answer, "Still mixing your metaphors, I hear, Speck. Just relax and remember that you and I are fish out of water here, so very little is expected of us. Pete is among his peers, and we need to help him shine. Ready, partner?"

My neighbor finished uttering his quiet words to me just as the assembled group of professors, students, and curious kibitzers broke into polite applause at the finish of Errol's generous introductory remarks. "Ready," I responded to Augie, and then I arose from my aisle seat and led my fellow Murryvillians up three wooden platform steps to the middle of the low stage, on which a heavy oak table and three matching cushioned chairs awaited our august presence. One slender silver removable microphone occupied a black plastic cylindrical holder on the table, and another mike was attached to the front of a contiguous tall lectern behind which any or all of us could exercise the option of standing. The table also served as repository for three Vintage International Editions of *Light in August*, three legal pads, several stacks of note cards, and a lineup of pens and pencils. As I took my seat, I scanned the audience and estimated that a total of approximately one hundred literary junkies, Faulkner voyeurs, or bored Brookvillians had decided to spend a part of a warm, drizzly November Saturday morning finding out just how fully three self-styled book sleuths from Crowder County could keep them all entertained.

Pete bypassed his assigned chair and marched straight to the lectern. Placing his note cards on the tilted surface in front of him, our professor eschewed any further biographical bleatings and plunged directly into the topic at hand.

"Thank you very much, Errol, for the gracious introduction. Ladies and gentlemen, so far today you have heard three outstanding analyses of challenging subjects encountered during readings of *Light in August*. With your kind permission my colleagues and I"—a sweeping gesture by Pete's left arm symbolically gathered Augie and me into this perhaps foolhardy experiment—"want to construct our joint presentation somewhat differently. First, I will provide a brief summary of the process that we have followed in deciding on our topic for today's conference. Next, we will invite from you responses to a specific question relating to the cast of characters in *Light in August*. Third, the three of us on stage will present our commentary on the central problem that we have chosen for close examination. In this third endeavor we hope to be able to prove our case. Finally, we want to solicit responses to a question involving Faulkner's fiction in a broader sense and then conclude with our own argument. We promise to wrap up our presentation in time for the luncheon that Errol has arranged for us."

Dressed in a deeply golden corduroy sport jacket, a starched beige shirt, standard red-gold-black Tabasco tie, dark brown trousers, and polished cordovan dress loafers, Pete presented himself as the very portrait of a conscientious but non-establishment pedagogue on parade. Augie and I had settled on conventional dark-gray suits, white shirts, and patterned red ties for this solemn occasion, but what else would you expect from middle-aged mortgage holders, anyhoo? I was proud to be an associate of neat-guy Pete at this conference, and I concluded that his relaxed yet tasteful attire contributed measurably to the aura of confidence that surrounded him as he lifted a note card from the small stack in front of him, scanned it quickly, and moved on to his enumerated point one.

"In his introductory remarks Doctor Tedford referred to a revelatory item appearing in our local Murryville newspaper. This specific 'Town Tattler' column spilled the once hermetically sealed can of beans concerning certain literary investigations pursued by Detective Dupree, Doctor Watkins, and me. I am proud to confirm the printed rumor: the three of us here on stage actually have closely examined certain passages and episodes in *Sanctuary*, *The Sound and the Fury*, and *As I Lay Dying*. Principally because of the intellectual skills of our veteran detective, Captain Augustus Dupree, we also believe that we have developed plausible solutions to various literary puzzles that we have encountered, some of which include criminal activity and thus logically call for the scrutiny of a veteran professional investigator." At this tribute to his talents Augie modestly lowered his eyes and raised them again only when Pete resumed his oral commentary.

"In sporadic conversations held earlier today, while we all sipped coffee or chomped on doughnuts, several of you"—Pete looked up from his notes and swept the audience with his eyes—"politely, or in some cases actually rather pointedly or even RUDELY"—responsive laughter engulfed us—"asked me about these earlier investigations into Faulkner. Please allow me to postpone commentary on them for the present, since with my partners' permission I am now preparing the first one for possible publication and will move on to the others just as soon as I can."

From the sixth row a tall, balding, bespectacled listener proclaimed quite audibly, "You are about as subtle as a runaway dump truck, Pete. Errol there knows a hint when he hears one, and how could the *Journal of the Arkansas Literary Association* reject your submissions now?"

Pete joined in the general laughter and then responded, "You are quite observant, Ed. Do you think Professor Tedford might need his lawn mowed or his shoes shined, also? Okay, I'll move on. But folks, be certain to check the table of contents of your next issue of *JALA*...." At the resulting laughter Pete waved his right hand in a dismissive gesture and returned to his principal subject.

"When my partners and I were studying *Light in August* in order to determine if we could develop a topic suitable for this conference, we each first read—or reread—the novel carefully, making lists of questions that occurred to us, principally questions focusing on possible violations of the law, since such areas of inquiry point to the reason that the three of us began in the first place to collaborate on what Doctor Watkins likes to call 'this Faulkner bidness.' The three of us got together on several occasions, discussed our questions, and looked at scholarly books and articles pertinent to our searches. In the process we kept returning to one central issue: Joe Christmas's lifelong lack of an identity, a dilemma growing in part out of the seemingly insoluble mystery about Joe's racial heritage. As we dug further into this complicated issue, which many of you have also explored in your own teaching or research, we encountered a startling number of crimes—beatings, kidnappings, and murders, in particular. And naturally, we all began to search for the person or persons primarily responsible for these dastardly actions."

Pete stopped speaking, gripped the edges of the lectern as he straightened his arms and locked his elbows, and again surveyed the assemblage. "I will halt at this point and ask each of you who has read *Light in August* to ponder one central question. Who are the principal villains in this novel? Later, I will ask a follow-up question. But for now: do you people have nominees for the category of 'Characters, comma, Bad Persons,' in the novel before us?"

A bearded gentleman wearing a brown tweed sport coat and clamping his teeth on an unlit pipe shouted from the next-to-last row, "Why, Joe Christmas himself, of course. He slits Joanna Burden's throat in cold blood. Or I guess some readers would call it HOT blood."

Upon hearing this first submission, Pete signaled to me with an extended left index finger, walked to the wall on the west side of the stage, accepted my assistance in carrying a portable chalk board to a position near the lectern, and then picked up a fresh piece of chalk from the board's tray. "All right, Doctor Hendrix. You have nominated Mister Christmas himself," Pete loudly responded to the first contributor. Our chalk man then turned to the portable board, hurriedly printed several capital letters on its green surface, and pivoted back toward the audience. Ripples of laughter greeted this name on the board:

JOE XMAS

"Get right with God, you heathen," shouted a broadly smiling, brown-suited African-American man in an aisle seat halfway to the back.

Arranging his facial features in a perfect Buster Keaton deadpan expression, Pete looked at the board, then back at his challenger, then back to the board, whence he jumped a foot into the air, landed on the stage with a loud WHAP!, rushed to the board, and energetically erased the errant letter "X," replacing it with the six correct ones. Looking completely abashed, Pete protruded his lower lip, rested his chin on his chest, and said, "Sorry, Doctor Stevens. I'll spell the names the long, straight, HONEST way from HERE ON OUT. AMEN!"

The audience seemed to enjoy Pete's little sideshow and to shake off its collective Saturday-morning post-break torpor, because within ninety seconds Pete had listed seven more names (one of them a pseudonym) on the board after his having heard the names shouted, some of them by several nominators, along with accompanying justifications.

"Joe Brown, alias Lucas Burch. He seduces and abandons Lena Grove, and then he squeals on Christmas. What a slimy jerk!"

"Percy Grimm. He not only kills Christmas but also savagely castrates him."

"Simon McEachern, the religious zealot, who beats the teenaged adopted child Joe Christmas for not learning his catechism."

"Then how about Max, the pimp controlling Bobbie Allen, Joe's first sweetheart? Max participates in clobbering Joe until the young man bleeds."

"Could we include Joanna Burden? She tries to force Joe to become what he cannot, a responsible member of the Black race."

"Maybe Gail Hightower, the defrocked minister. He drives his own wife to suicide."

Pete dutifully listed all seven of the proffered names and then faced the audience. "Thank you very much for your nominations, folks. Now let me print up here on the board the title of our presentation today." With his chalk Pete hastily slashed at the board once more, stepped aside, and pointed to these words:

FAULKNER'S ARCH-VILLAIN

After pausing a brief moment to allow everyone to read the title, Pete resumed his parody of a quiz show. Gesturing dramatically toward his two companions on stage, Pete raised his voice and orated in pear-shaped tones, "Captain Dupree, may I have the envelope, please?"

Augie obligingly played his role in this mock drama, walking rapidly to Pete and handing to our man of the moment a sealed white envelope. From his inside jacket pocket Pete produced a gleaming silver letter opener, precisely slit the top of the envelope, and removed a single sheet of paper. He then passed the envelope and letter opener over to Augie. (I had named our trusty assistant "Vanna Baby" during an informal rehearsal at the motel on the preceding night, eliciting a glare and a growl from the Captain). Next, Pete announced, "And the winner is. . .

EUPHEUS 'DOC' HINES."

We had hoped for a modest amount of confusion and consternation, but the audience's reaction exceeded our expectations and pleased us very much. As I intently observed the people in the plush theater seats respond to Pete's surprise nominee, I could pick out a few distinct phrases from the collective murmur that grew into a mixture of rising vocal statements and that finally became a cacophony:

"Who? What name did he say?"

"Hines? Who's that?"

"You know. Joe Christmas's grandfather."

"Who? Oh yeah, that nutty, smelly old guy."

"But isn't he a cuckoo head?"

"Hines? He's a complete whacko."

"How can that shriveled-up old bird be an arch-villain?" What does he do?"

"Huh? What? You say Hines? Doc Hines?"

"Aw hell, Christmas is a lot worse villain than that old Hines is."

"Percy Grimm still gets my vote."

"I'll stick with Joe Brown."

"I'm for Lucas Burch."

"Same guy as Joe Brown"

"WHATEVER!"

Then, overriding all of the intermingled voices came one ringing shout: "PUT UP OR SHUT UP, PREFONT. PROVE YOUR CASE!"

This final statement, bellowed from the back row by Professor Jefferson Hendrix, whom I had cordially met during our recent coffee break, provoked Pete into raising his arms in an unconsciously professorial parody of a pastoral blessing. The patient Doctor Prefont then politely asked the crowd several times for silence. When the restless masses complied, Pete magnanimously replied to his challenger, "Jefferson my good man, with a little help from my friends I sincerely hope to accomplish that very purpose. MOREOVER—Captain Dupree and Doctor Watkins will join me in an attempt to prove that Doc Hines achieves a more infamous status than that of the principal villain in this novel alone. Everyone, please reread the offered title of our presentation." Once more Pete pointed to the chalk board.

From the fourth row a tall woman with shoulder-length brown hair asked Pete, "Do you mean to say that this Hines person is the worst villain in all of

Faulkner's fiction?"

Pete pointed to his inquisitor and proclaimed, "Correct you are, Professor Lucas. My friends and I hope to demonstrate the validity of that very statement, but first please allow me to focus on the role that Hines plays in our session's designated novel for inquiry, *Light in August*. If you kind people will indulge me, I would like to read to you the three introductory paragraphs of our argument and thus set the stage for further presentations by Captain Dupree, Doctor Watkins, and little old me."

Pete returned to the lectern, scanned the audience for visible dissenters, and smiled confidently at overheard comments from the group such as "Go ahead, but this had better be good," and "You've bitten off a big wad of Bull-of-the-Woods this time, Prefont. Jaw away, but don't choke on your plug!" Clearing his throat, Pete moved briskly into his opening argument.

"If you have a copy of *Light in August* with you, please join me in looking at selected passages. As I read my commentary, I will refer to specific page numbers in this Vintage International Edition. This first series of quotation to which I refer can be found on pages one-twenty-six, one-twenty-seven, and one-twenty-eight. Here we go. Chapter Six of *Light in August* begins the novel's lengthy flashback into the tortured childhood, adolescence, and young manhood of Joe Christmas. Set almost wholly in a squalid Memphis orphanage where Joe spends most of the first five years of his confused life, this chapter also contains the novel's initial appearance of an anonymous, enigmatic janitor who usually is found sitting in a boiler room doorway and staring fixedly at young Joe. When confronted about his obsession with Joe and accused of coming, quotation, 'here just to do that, to watch him and hate him,' end of quotation, this, quoting again, 'small, dirty man . . . of forty-five' who lives in 'a backwater suitable for a man of sixty or sixtyfive,' end of quotations, speaks demoniacally of the child as being, quotation, "'A walking pollution in God's own face,'" end of quotation, rants about, quotation, "'womansinning and bitchery,'" end of quotation, and hints darkly about waiting five years, quotation, '"for the Lord to move and show his will,"' end of quotation. When he becomes convinced that Joe will be sent to the orphanage for Negroes, the janitor sneaks out of the building under cover of night and takes the child by streetcar and train to Little Rock, where the two are caught and Joe is returned to the Memphis orphanage.

"This shabby and perverse man is then absent from the book for two-hundred pages (and approximately thirty years of Joe's life), reappearing in Chapter Fifteen during the novel's presentation of the capture of Joe, by this time an accused murderer. Please look on pages three-forty-four and three forty-five. When this now, quoting here, 'frail little old man with the light, frail bones of a child,' end of quotation, hears that Christmas is nearby, he struggles, quotation, 'with the fluid and supple fury of a weasel,' end of quotation, until he confronts the captive, strikes him with his walking stick, and shouts, quoting here, '"Kill the bastard!. . . . Kill Him. Kill him,"' end of quotation. People in Mottstown, Mississippi, know this man as Doc (or Uncle Doc) Hines, and Faulkner soon reveals that Doc's actual first name is Eupheus, that he is the maternal grandfather of Joe Christmas, and that he has lived in a state of suppressed rage at Joe for over thirty years, believing he was keeping in touch with God until he senses that God tells him, quoting here from page three-eighty-six, '""It's that bastard. Your work is not done yet. He's a pollution and a abomination on My earth,"''' end of quotation. In Chapter Sixteen the reader finally learns the sordid and horrifying truth about Doc Hines: he has shot to death the father of Joe Christmas; he has refused to bring a doctor to his own daughter, Milly, while she is giving birth to Joe and has watched her die; and he has stolen the baby Joe away from the care of Mrs. Hines in order to take him to the Memphis orphanage and set into motion a diabolical scheme to punish the innocent Joe, making the child the victim of what Hines calls, quoting here from page three-eighty-three, '"the vengeful will of the Lord,"' end of quotation.

"Despite the nature and extent of the treachery of Doc Hines, critics of

Light in August have consistently underestimated the importance of his role in the novel. The majority of critics consider Doc to be merely one of the book's, quoting here, 'minor characters' or 'subordinate villains,' end of quotations. Several interpreters have been content to categorize him (along with Simon McEachern, Joe's adoptive father, and others) in a group of fiery evangelical zealots, calling Doc something like a, quotation, 'sacrilegious and obsessed preacher,' end of quotation. Other commentary on the novel more accurately assesses the depth of Doc's iniquity. John Pilkington asserts that, quotation, 'Hines . . . has gone beyond religion to become pathologically grotesque,' end of quotation. Cleanth Brooks nominates Doc as, quoting here, 'the worst' of the book's 'fanatical Protestants,' end of quotations. And Debra Moddelmog calls Doc a, quoting here, 'violent, uncompromising extremist,' end of quotation, pointing out that, by the end of Joe's life, the younger man has come to resemble his grandfather quite closely in temperament and behavior. But not even these attentive critics have given Doc Hines enough discredit. He is the principal villain of *Light in August*, the primary instigating force for the pattern of recurring violence and tragedy in the novel. Moreover, the foul nature of his malicious deeds readily qualifies him for a place at the forefront of Faulkner's chief perpetrators of evil. Indeed, when the full extent of his perfidy is examined, Doc Hines might properly be viewed as the most odious character in all of Faulkner's fiction."

When Pete finished reading his preface, a restless silence prevailed in the auditorium. Pete quickly walked over to the oaken table, sat in his chair, leaned into the waiting microphone, and announced, "Captain Augustus Dupree will now continue our presentation." The professor then moved the microphone in front of Augie, leaned back, folded his arms across his chest, and indulged himself in a tight smile of satisfaction.

Our versatile ratiocinist lifted a note card from the small stack in front of him, put on his reading glasses, leaned leftward toward me while whispering "I miss my 'Detective' cap," and pointed his chin toward the expectant audience.

"William Faulkner once eloquently summarized what to him was, quoting Faulkner here, 'the tragic, central idea," end of quotation, of *Light in August*: that of a person remaining forever uncertain of his essential identity. Here I quote Faulkner again: 'Now with Christmas, for instance, he didn't know what he was. He knew that he would never know what he was, and his only salvation in order to live with himself was to repudiate mankind, to live outside the human race. And he tried to do that but nobody would let him, the human race itself wouldn't let him. And I don't think he was bad, I think he was tragic. And his tragedy was that he didn't know what he was and would never know, and that to me is the most tragic condition that an individual can have—to not know who he was,' end of quotation. Ironically, it is Joe's own grandfather who viciously assures that Joe will be doomed to just such a life of incessant torment."

Augie looked out at the audience and said, "Those of you who have copies of *Light in August*: please join us again in looking at some pertinent passages." The Captain raised a legal pad and frequently consulted it during his subsequent remarks.

"Eupheus Hines, approximately thirty-nine years of age at the time, is the foreman of a sawmill in rural east Arkansas in a December of the early 1890's when a circus wagon breaks down near the mill and Hines helps to extricate the wagon from the mud—look on pages three-seventy-three and three-seventy-four. His eighteen-year-old daughter Milly runs away the next night with a circus worker of ambiguous racial origin, and Hines eerily chooses the correct short cut out of a half-dozen possibilities, catches up with the fleeing couple, and, as Byron Bunch later describes, '"Grabbed him by one hand and held the pistol against him and shot him dead and brought the gal back home behind him on the horse."' Byron's quotation appears on page three-seventy-six."

Augie glanced to his right at Pete, who nodded, shifted the microphone in his own direction, shuffled his note cards until he found the correct one, and took another turn. "Here are some helpful comments from critics concerning Doc's first murder. Olga Vickery points out that Doc needed a reason for this murder and that he readily found it: quotation, 'Since Milly's pregnancy is considered an unforgivable sin by Hines, he looks for a scapegoat who will bear the guilt and punishment. By calling her lover a '"nigger,"' he can transform a commonplace seduction into the horror of miscegenation. That is his justification, moral and religious, for the brutally inhuman treatment of his daughter, her lover, and her child.' Hugh Ruppersburg contributes this convincing explanation: quoting here, 'Because Hines believes that God has cursed Negroes and that the boy [Joe] has Negro blood, the word '"Nigger"' signifies to him the boy's damnation,' end of quotation. Both critics underscore the fact that Doc wastes not one moment worrying about whether his murder of Joe's father is legal or is an act of justice. Doc cares nothing for the law and is irrevocably convinced that he attains justice by murdering the man. Lamentably, Doc is later acquitted of the killing of Joe's father, using the questionable testimony of the circus owner that the victim really was part-Negro rather than possibly Mexican to convince the racially prejudiced jury that he was justified in shooting the man." Critic Ruppersburg again is helpful here. I quote, 'Hines apparently used as his defense the contention that he had shot a black man who had slept with his daughter, which would have made the murder '"justifiable homicide"' in the South and other parts of the nation,' end of quotation."

Augie and Pete looked at one another, the two men simultaneously nodded, and then Pete leaned over toward the microphone and said, "Doctor Watkins, who has politely listened all of this time to the ceaseless chatter of his alleged friends, will now continue our presentation." Augie redirected the microphone toward me, and I entered the fray.

"My colleagues and I believe that Doc Hines's second murder is more chillingly frightening and repelling than is the first. When we initially examined Faulkner's depiction of this second killing, we could not decide whether Doc actually intends for his daughter Milly to die. Clearly Doc premeditates the killing of Joe's father, but the second killing raises some questions involving legal definitions. Fortunately, Captain Dupree enjoys a longtime friendship with W. Benjamin Mitchell, Professor of Criminal Procedure at the Arkansas School of Law in Little Rock. Since I had volunteered to be the lead investigator on this particular crime, I telephoned Professor Mitchell, using Augie Dupree's name as my method of introduction, and sought his advice on the matter. Mister Mitchell patiently listened to my questions, asked for time to read the pertinent passages in the novel and to mull them over, and the next day telephoned me with his opinion. Let me read it to you." I raised a note card: "'Eupheus Hines's actions at the time of his daughter's death demonstrate evidence of premeditation and thus could be considered murder under the Arkansas laws of the 1890's. A jury eventually would have to render a verdict, but a prosecutor plausibly could charge Hines with the crime of murder.'"

I paused and looked up from my note card. "Please look with me at pages three-seventy-eight and three-seventy-nine in the novel. When Milly has come to full term, Eupheus Hines pretends to set out for the doctor but instead sits on the outside steps of his house with a shotgun across his lap in order to deter anyone from interfering with his plan. As the long-suffering Mrs. Hines relates, quoting here: "'and he said ""Get back into that house, whore's dam"" and I said ""Eupheus"" and he raised the shotgun and said ""Get back into that house. Let the devil gather his own crop: he was the one that laid it by.""' And I tried to get out the back way and he heard me and run around the house with the gun and he hit me with the barrel of it and I went back to Milly and he stood outside the hall door where he could see Milly until she died.'" Mrs. Hines does not disclose the length of time that Doc stared at his only child while Milly underwent labor, delivery, and death, but even if Milly died quickly the young woman must have undergone severe mental as well as physical torment. With this vile deed Doc has deprived his grandchild of the potential nurturing influence of the second of his biological parents. Hines then considers the possibility of killing the child, but evidently he decides that Joe must suffer for the actions of his parents in another way."

I nodded to Augie, and he shifted the microphone back to the center of the table. "Thank you, Speck." He looked out at the hushed audience. "Ladies and gentlemen, so far we have seen evidence that Doc Hines is guilty of two premeditated homicides, one of them in which his only child is the victim. And now we will move on to Doc's malicious psychological torture of Joe Christmas, the older man's sole grandchild. Herein we hope to demonstrate that Eupheus Hines himself instigates the pattern of recurring violence and tragedy in the novel and thus should be acknowledged as the novel's principal villain."

Glancing right and then left, Augie received nods from Pete and me. Once more focusing his eyes on his legal pad, he continued our triumvirate's tip-toeing through the Hinesean treachery. "Two days before the next Christmas, Hines kidnaps Joe from Mrs. Hines and leaves the baby on the steps of the Memphis orphanage, the institution at which Doc has been employed for two months. After the baby has been taken in and named 'Joe Christmas,' Doc begins his insidious scheme to torture the child psychologically, thus carrying out what Doc believes to be the Lord's own desire for vengeance. As the distinguished Faulkner scholar Joseph Blotner points out, Faulkner is careful to create a, quoting here, 'perception of his [Joe's] role as a victim . . . , particularly in episodes where the helpless child is at the mercy,' end of quotation, of such people as Eupheus Hines. First, Doc slyly suggests to the other children at the orphanage that they call Joe, quotation here, 'nigger,' end of quotation."

"Wait just a minute. I have to interrupt here. Pete, Captain, Doctor, may I?" All eyes shifted to the aisle seat from which Pete's acquaintance Professor James Stevens arose in a half-crouch, waving his left arm while holding in his right hand an opened copy of LNA. (Pete, Augie, and I had adopted this handy acronym, pronounced "ELL, IN, EH," for this Faulkner novel).

Pete quickly responded, "Certainly, Jim, go ahead. Do you disagree with

Augie's analysis here?"

Stevens resumed his seated position and stared at his copy of the novel. "Perhaps I do, Pete, or then I may not fully understand what Doc Hines actually does at the orphanage. I have always thought that Hines expressly did NOT tell the children to call Joe 'nigger' and that the source of Joe's confusion over his own racial makeup cannot be traced back to any one person or particular event."

As Stevens was talking, Pete, Augie, and I were simultaneously nodding our heads quite vigorously. Fortunately, most of the people in the audience were looking at Stevens while he spoke, or we three on the stage might have appeared to be auditioning for roles as Curly, Larry, and Moe, the Three Crime-Solving Stooges. Pete took the lead in responding to this important question. "Jim, in my several readings of the novel I had always thought the same way as you about the source of Joe's racial dilemma—that its origins were forever unknown, because Faulkner, in his typical inscrutable fashion, did not provide sufficient facts for readers to be able to decide the matter for certain. But as I mentioned earlier, when my two friends here and I were plundering our ways through *Light in August* in preparation for today's conference session, we kept banging up against the issues of identity, race, and family history. So we closely examined this very point: why does Joe even begin to think in the first place that he may have Negro blood? The idea must originate somewhere else besides in the mind of a tiny orphan boy who is no older than three or four when he starts to use the word 'nigger' in possible relation to himself; look on page three-eighty-three."

Standing and walking hurriedly to the lectern, Pete waved his copy of LNA toward the audience. "Jim, everyone, let's first look into the assumption that Doc Hines is NOT the person who plants the concept of Negritude into little Joe's innocent and baffled mind. Do you remember that earlier I began our presentation by referring first to Chapter Six, which contains the initial appearance of Eupheus Hines? In Chapter Six Hines is never named but is identified only as the dissolute, solitary janitor at the Memphis orphanage. Please look with me at page one-twenty-seven.

"When the dietitian first seeks assistance from this man whom she knows only as the janitor, she tells Hines that many times she has observed him as the man stares malevolently at young Joe: quoting here, '"watching him and hearing the other children calling him Nigger."' Now flip to the next page, Jim, and anyone else who holds a copy of the novel. Here may appear the source of your assumption that Hines has NOT planted in Joe's mind the idea of the little boy's possibly being, at least in part—I use this abominable word only because Hines so often does—quotation, 'nigger,' end of quotation. Look closely at Doc's demonic language as he speaks to the dietitian: '"You have heard them. I never told them to say it, to call him in his rightful nature, by the name of his damnation. I never told them. They was told, but it wasn't by me."' End of quotation. Explicit language, it is true, but inaccurate and therefore highly misleading."

Stevens raised his hand and spoke. "So Pete, you are asserting that Hines out-and-out lies with these words?"

Still poised at the lectern, Pete responded, "Yes, Jim, I am. But with his perversely twisted sense of logic, Doc apparently can justify to himself that these words are truthful ones. You see, Hines believes—or at least implies that he believes—that GOD, and not Eupheus Hines himself—that God actually places the word 'nigger' into the children's mouths. Look at the next sentence, the one appearing just after we stopped reading a minute ago, on page one-twenty-eight. '"I just waited on His own good time, when He would see fitten to reveal it to His living world."' End of quotation. And later in the novel we learn that in Doc's mind, 'He'—God—reveals 'it'—Doc's conviction that Joe carries Negro blood—by Hines's telling the other children in the orphanage to call Joe 'nigger.'"

From the back of the auditorium Jefferson Hendrix boomed out, "William Faulkner, you sly old fox, you. Throwing us old bloodhounds off the scent again. The feint, the hidden ball trick, the old shell game. Now you see it; now you don't know it."

At our cozy table Augie turned to me and smilingly said, "Doctor Hendrix appears to be your chief rival for the Chair of Metaphorical Mixology."

"Very funny, neighbor. Arf, arf," I replied. "Listen—what is Pete saying?"

"As all of you know from your readings of the novel, Eupheus Hines firmly believes that he and God can converse with one another. So it is not a mental stretch on Doc's part for the man to believe that God, using Hines as God's vessel, medium, intermediary, larynx, ventriloquist's dummy, or whatever you want to call him, speaks directly to the other children in the orphanage. For confirmation of this interpretation, turn with me to Chapter Sixteen, page. . . . Let's see, page three-eighty-two. In this scene Byron Bunch has brought the elderly couple Mister and Mrs. Hines to talk with Gail Hightower in the hope—the hope of Byron and of Mrs. Hines but not of Doc—that Hightower can provide an alibi for Joe Christmas, who at the time is under arrest for the murder of Joanna Burden."

Flip, flip, flip, rustle, rustle of pages, and then everyone apparently reached the designated place in the novel. Pete resumed his explanation. "Here is the key passage. Please allow me to read it aloud. 'It was the Lord. *He* was there. Old Doc Hines give God His chance too. The Lord told old Doc Hines what to do and old Doc Hines done it. Then the Lord said to old Doc Hines "'You watch, now. Watch my will a-working.'" And old Doc Hines watched and heard the mouths of little children, of God's own fatherless and motherless, putting His words and knowledge into their mouths even when they couldn't know it since they were without sin yet, even the girl ones without sin and bitchery yet: Nigger! Nigger! in the innocent mouths of little children. '"What did I tell you?"' God said to old Doc Hines. '"And now I've set My will to working and now I'm gone."'"

From the lectern Pete waved his copy of LNA as he held it high in his left hand, and then he brought the book back to reading level. "Everyone please pay special attention to this sentence: '"The Lord told old Doc Hines what to do and old Doc Hines done it.'" Here is proof of Doc's dogma that God speaks directly to him and, more importantly, THROUGH him. And next let's look carefully at a very syntactically complicated sentence." Pete set his book on the lectern, spread his arms widely, and proclaimed, "Grammar teachers of the world, let us unite and ponder sentence structure together!"

Guffaws, comments such as "Did he say 'grammar?'" or "Oh, what B. S.," and one shouted admonition of "Right on, Peter the Great!" greeted Pete's rallying cry. Emboldened by the positive reinforcement while selectively ignoring any negative comments, Pete plowed forward. "Let's focus our collective minds on the sentence beginning with the words '"And old Doc Hines watched and heard. . . ."' Does everyone find the participial phrase beginning with the words '"putting His words and knowledge into their mouths. . . ."'? Okay, if I may ask you, what noun or pronoun is described by this phrase? In other words, to what word or words is it directly linked, according to the rules of grammar?"

From his front-row seat Errol Tedford, staring at the copy of LNA that he held with both hands directly in front of his eyes, replied, "Pete, I am moving backwards within the sentence, and my first reaction would be to choose 'fatherless and motherless,' or then 'children,' or then 'mouths' as candidates for the described naming word, but no, we can't do that. . . ."

Pete now stood at the edge of the stage, his hands tightly clasped behind his back as he leaned precariously far forward, raising his chin and eyebrows, and asked, "Why not, Errol, why not? Please continue, if you will."

Rattling the book in peevishness, Tedford replied in a snapping tone, "Because, damn it, the 'mouths,' the 'children,' and the 'fatherless and motherless' absolutely cannot, by the rules of logic as well as those of grammar, be 'putting His words and knowledge into their mouths'—meaning the children's OWN mouths—since the end of the sentence reads, 'in the innocent mouths of little children.' The phrase beginning with the word 'putting' can be directly linked to only two possible nouns. . . 'Doc' and 'Hines.' Prefont, you young rabble-rouser, you have just proved false a statement that I have made for more than twenty years to students in my Faulkner course, that we readers of *Light in August* cannot know for certain the ultimate source of Joe's confusion over his racial identity."

"Thank you, Errol; thank you, er . . . , I assume. Just so that we can conclude this line of reasoning, may I follow up on your examination of the sentence?"

"Certainly, Pete," replied Tedford with a disdainful flip of his right wrist. "I have played the court fool long enough."

"Not at all, Errol," said Pete as he walked back to the lectern, "but let me make certain that everyone did hear Errol name the proper noun that is described by the phrase beginning with 'putting His words and knowledge. . . .' As we emulate Errol and move farther backwards in the sentence. . . . Voila! We come upon the proper noun, the name. . . . At least thirty voices took the bait and shouted in near-unison, "DOC HINES." Pete extended both fists into the air, shouted "YES!" and then picked up LNA once more. "If I may paraphrase. . . . We discover Eupheus Hines putting what he believes to be God's words and knowledge into the mouths of innocent orphan children, especially telling these young children to call tiny Joe Christmas a, quotation, 'nigger,' end of quotation. Look at the terrifying end of this key sentence: '"Nigger! Nigger! in the innocent mouths of little children."' We may now safely conclude that in Chapter Six Doc misleads the dietitian AND legions of readers of the novel with his false statement '"They was told, but it wasn't by me."' Doc may implacably believe that God has told the other orphans to call Joe a, quotation, 'nigger,' but we know that the damning words themselves originated in the vocal chords of the one and only Eupheus Hines, railroad brakeman, sawmill foreman, husband, father, grandfather, double murderer, and demonic warper of an innocent tyke's mind." After a dramatic pause, Pete whirled away from the lectern, returned to our central table, and asked, "Augie, will you take over now, please?"

"Happy to, Professor," our chief detective replied, as he slid the microphone into place directly in front of himself. "Doctor Tedford, are we still within our time limit?"

"Oh yes, Captain," replied the sessions's convenor, now fully recovered from his petulant sulk. "We are scheduled to break up by twelve-thirty, and by my watch you have nearly an hour remaining. This is a casual group, and anyone who needs to take a break may certainly leave the auditorium quietly, with no need to request a hall pass or restroom permit."

A few auditors followed Tedford's direction, stealthily exited, and later re-entered the proceedings during the next hour, but for the most part we grateful Murryvillians were blessed with an attentive and actively participating crowd. Consulting his legal pad, Augie resumed our joint presentation. "Peter has just shown us how Doc Hines perniciously plants the seed of racial confusion into Joe's unformed mind. Next, in subsequent months as Joe broods alone on the playground of the orphanage—please look on page three-eighty-three—, Doc reinforces the child's pain and bewilderment over his racial identity with such taunts—these directly from Doc's own mouth—such taunts as '"Why dont you play with them other children like you used to?"' and '"Is it because they call you nigger?"' The Black yardman does not help either, with his caustic and far-reaching statement: '"You dont know what you are. And more than that, you wont never know. You'll live and you'll die and you wont never know"'—page three-eighty-four. This key statement by the yardman represents an ominous prefigurement of Doc's objective to have Joe become a pariah whose life evolves into a ceaseless journey in pursuit of an unattainable sense of self.

"With his manipulation of Joe during the boy's years at the Memphis orphanage, Doc Hines irrevocably establishes the pattern of Joe's dismal life—the 'street' or 'corridor" which eventually leads to the schoolhouse where Joe possibly kills Simon McEachern (page two-oh-five), the bedroom where later he cuts the throat of Joanna Burden (page two-eighty-two), and the rural church where he fractures the skull of Roz Thompson (page three-twenty-five). Although Joe himself, of course, is responsible for these deplorable actions, it is Eupheus Hines who cunningly misshapes the mind of the person confused and desperate enough to commit them. As a five-year-old child Joe instinctively fears Hines. Look on page one-thirty-eight: 'With more vocabulary but no more age he might have thought *That is why I am different from the others: because he is watching me all the time.* But Joe never becomes aware of just how thoroughly Doc Hines has damaged him."

As Augie was winding up this segment of our presentation, I carefully scrutinized the faces of people in the audience whom I selected at random, skipping my eyes from nearby rows to distant seats, back, forth, and around Hudson Auditorium. Despite my inherent tendency toward caution, I could not help but conclude that we had convinced a sizable majority of the group of the validity of our argument. By their pursed lips, slowly nodding heads, and placid expressions, I assumed that many of our listeners now agreed with our contention that Eupheus Hines initiates the pattern of violence and tragedy permeating LNA and thus qualifies as the novel's principal villain. Only a few diehards retained skeptical looks or continued to shake their heads slowly in a signal of disagreement. Augie's next words suddenly jolted me out of my reverie: "Doctor Watkins, please take over for me now."

An inveterate ham at heart, I arose ponderously, swatted at Augie's nearest hand, stalked like a gorilla around my end of the oak table, and growled, "Where is Kid Dynamite? Get back in the ring for this tag-team match, you coward." Surprisingly, a few of the ordinarily reserved academic clientele actually laughed, as my charitable Murryville partners did also, and I thought that more of these ivory-tower girls and boys would have joined in the group chortle if they hadn't been fearful of displaying to their peers their secret awarenesses of the spectacle known as wrestling, or 'rass-uh-lin,' as some of us pronounce the word in the South. Reassuming my tutorial pose, I sat down, perused my legal pad, and orated. "Earlier in this session, when Doctor Prefont first mentioned Eupheus

'Doc' Hines, I overheard some of your responses, and words such as 'cuckoo,' 'whacko,' and 'nutty' were clearly audible. We three presenters must assume that some of you consider Doc Hines to be insane. Correct? And you also conclude that concomitantly he is not fully responsible for his actions. Right? Hmmm?"

From her fourth-row seat Professor Deborah Lucas waved her right hand and spoke in an ironic tone. "You and your accomplices have landed several big fish already today, Doctor Watkins. I'll be the little trout who swallows the hook on this one. In the few times during my classroom discussions of *Light in August* that I have paid any attention to Doc Hines, I have always thought of him as hopelessly mentally ill. Are you now saying that he is normal?"

"Not at all, Doctor Lucas," I quickly replied. "Hines's actions are certainly abnormal, but my colleagues and I submit that these actions emanate from a mind with a highly focused obsession and not one distorted by a definable neurosis or psychosis. We contend that Doc Hines knows exactly what he is doing and is thus fully responsible for his malevolent actions. But it is certainly easy for us readers of *Light in August* to think of Doc as being a hopeless lunatic. Faulkner most definitely nudges us toward such a conclusion."

I lifted my copy of LNA and waved it in the direction of the audience. "Let's all dive back into the book once more. When Doc first appears as the anonymous janitor in Memphis, he is called 'mad'—page one twenty-seven—and 'fanatical'—page one-twenty-nine. Later, when Doc reappears with a name in Chapter Fifteen, such words as 'crazy'—three-forty-one—and 'fanaticism'—three-forty-three—are used in relation to him. When we combine Faulkner's consistent application of these along with many other kindred adjectives and nouns to Doc Hines with the author's descriptions of Doc's disheveled, distracted appearance and his bizarre behavior, naturally we all want to consign Hines to our own imaginary asylums and to write him off as an incurable neurotic or psychotic. But again Faulkner has artfully lulled readers into a false sense of complacency. Here is one more instance of the deceptive complexity of reality as it exists within the

Yoknapatawpha fiction."

I surveyed my listeners, noted no imminent book throwers, took a deep breath, and motor-mouthed onward. "Let me return for a moment to Faulkner's use of such words as 'mad' and 'fanatic' as they apply to Eupheus Hines. In several strategic places in *Light in August*, the author employs similar terminology to refer to persons who, like Doc, are irrevocably committed to a course of action that will have dire consequences. For example, the amorous dietitian, who is terrified that little Joe will disclose her tryst with Charley the intern, becomes 'quite calmly and completely mad'—page one-twenty-five—while she schemes to eliminate Joe as a threat to her job. And Joanna Burden becomes 'fanatical' and 'mad'—page two-seventy-seven—when she decides that she must either bend Joe to her will or else kill Joe and then herself."

Continuing to lean into the microphone, I looked up from my notes. "The dietitian and Joanna are not insane. They are both totally obsessed with achieving a fervently held objective—and of course, so is Doc. The two women may be described by Faulkner as sometimes appearing to be, to quote the author's word, 'mad,' but they do not ever suffer from prolonged states of delusion or hallucination—and neither does Doc Hines. In fact, Doc commits his atrocities—the murders of Joe's parents and the extensive warping of Joe's young mind—while Hines is coldly rational. In each case Doc carefully plans what to do and then acts decisively, continuing a lifelong tradition of brutality."

From the pile of material in front of me I found three note cards, quickly scanned them, and continued my diatribe on Doc. "Mrs. Hines reveals that her husband has always been a man with a penchant for violence. In his youth and young adulthood he often fought other men out of, quoting Mrs. Hines, '"his vanity and pride,"' end of quotation—page three-seventy-two—because he is self-conscious about his shortness. For several months, as he tries desperately to arrange an abortion for Milly, he is arrested numerous times for assaulting physicians and officers of the law—see page three-seventy-eight. But after he allows Milly to die and the baby Joe to live, he directs all of his lethal instincts toward Joe, and he is never again considered a threat to the peace of any community. During the years that he concentrates on first torturing young Joe and then vehemently despising him *in absentia*, he operates from the shadows of society and ironically is assumed to be merely eccentric, becoming quite easy to ignore, both in the orphanage for five years and then later in Mottstown for more than three decades."

I glanced to my right and said, "If Professor Prefont is not comatose by this time, he will carry this marathon's torch for the next few oratorical miles." Then I slid the mike in Pete's direction.

"Thanks, Doctor Double-You. Gentlefolk one and all, let me attempt to summarize what my medical friend here has just asserted. Eupheus Hines is not insane but is the most dangerous kind of villain, one who is able to work with stealth and precision toward the achievement of purposes that are so repugnant as to be incomprehensible to the ordinary rational mind. Please listen to this next description, and when I am through reading it, someone be so kind as to identify its author and source. Now—this category of villains into which we have placed Doc Hines: these people are—and here I begin the pertinent quotation: 'madmen, and of the most dangerous sort, for their lunacy is not continuous, but occasional, evoked by some special object; it is protectively secretive [or] self-contained, so that when . . . most active it is to the average mind not distinguishable from sanity. . . . Toward the accomplishment of an aim which in wantonness of atrocity would seem to partake of the insane, [such a man] will direct a cool judgment sagacious and sound.'"

As Pete read from his note card, I watched the audience and observed numerous people who nodded their heads in recognition, some of them beginning at the time of the first words of Pete's little pop quiz. When our man Prefont finished, he lifted his eyes, swung his head from right to left, and waited only one or two seconds until we three presenters on stage all heard an intermingling of many voices as they responded with several proper nouns: "Melville. *Billy Budd.* Claggart."

Pete quickly announced, "We have a whole host of winners, folks. In his classic novella *Billy Budd, Sailor*, Herman Melville here is describing John Claggart, master at arms in 1797 aboard the British naval vessel the *Bellipotent*. Only we readers have any inkling of the deadly malice that permeates this respected veteran officer's heart and mind. For no rational reason Claggart decides to destroy the innocent foretopman Billy Budd, and the officer's debased scheme ultimately results in Billy's execution by hanging. In Melville's view the evil wrought by such men can be attributed only to a 'depravity according to nature.' Like John Claggart, Eupheus Hines is successful at villainy because he is and always has been thoroughly depraved."

After a moment's silence Errol Tedford waggled his left hand and drew Pete's attention. "So, Doctor Prefont, you are placing Eupheus Hines in league with John Claggart, one of American literature's most abominable villains. And the longer you talk, the more it does appear credible that these two perpetrators of evil have much in common."

Pete responded, "I'm grateful for that comment, Errol, and with your permission and that of the rest of the audience I would now like to move into the final phase of our presentation. Relief truly is soon to occur, folks, as is that tasty luncheon that Errol has promised for us. Since we are now thinking about Doc Hines in comparison to his literary peers in wickedness, let us attempt to place Hines in his rightful place among William Faulkner's roster of A-team bad guys."

Hopping up from his chair, Pete loped over to the neglected chalkboard, snared a fresh piece of chalk, turned to his listeners, and announced, "It is audience-participation time again on the Du-Wat-Pre show, good people. Reignite your thinking machines, and let's compile a list made up of the dishonorees in the Yoknapatawpha Hall of Shame." Pete turned and printed the capitalized words, along with the one preposition, at the top of the green surface area. Walking toward the waiting populace while tossing the piece of chalk from hand to hand, Pete requested, "What are your nominations for Faulknerian characters whose deeds earn them inclusion in this Mississippi rogues' gallery? Who are Mister Bill's most accomplished villains? Let's disregard Doc Hines for the moment and mentally ransack Faulkner's novels and stories for other candidates."

For the next several minutes Pete fielded names from the eager teachers, students, and other readers of Faulkner. At one time seventeen characters' names filled the board, and Pete asked the group for permission to reduce the number to a more manageable number. Vigorous debates ensued, with proponents and opponents of various nominees all being allowed to present their succinct arguments, and then Pete called for an election. The majority of the nominators requested a final total of six, so Pete reminded everyone to vote no more than six times and then ran through the names one by one, asking for a show of hands. Augie and I assisted by tallying up the votes and than writing on our legal pads the names of the winners. Pete erased the board, wrote the words "Dirty Half-Dozen" at the top of the now chalk-smeared surface, and listed these names:

> Anse Bundren
>
> Flem Snopes
>
> Popeye
>
> Thomas Sutpen
>
> Percy Grimm
>
> Jason Compson

Returning to our central table, Pete picked up a thick stack of banded note cards from the pile of litter on the oak surface and held it up in view of the group. "In preparation for today's song-and-dance routine, my cell mates and I compiled our own lists of Faulkner's worst villains and then compared their action with those of Doc Hines. I am proud to say that your six consensus rotten eggs"—Pete waved his extended right arm toward the chalkboard—"are in our selections, as are several more. Give us just a minute to shuffle through these cards, and then we will head this cattle show toward the last roundup."

A few scattered sounds of "Moo," punctuated by other vocal impressions of barnyard and pasture animals, came wafting up from the audience, and we three speakers smiled as we bowed our heads over the stack of cards, scanning them rapidly and in concert separating them into two rough piles. Picking up the larger collection, Pete flipped through its contents, rearranged a few cards, asked Augie and me to check his results, and then with a curt nod returned with his chosen cards to the lectern.

Gesturing toward the chalkboard, Pete stated, "Captain Dupree, Doctor Watkins, and I firmly believe that Eupheus Hines deserves enshrinement at the forefront of this frightening assemblage of malefactors. Indeed, we vigorously contend that Doc Hines has iniquitously earned his place of dishonor at the head of the crass." Pete's pun elicited a cascade of boos and groans, exactly the response that he ardently desired. Flipping systematically through his note cards and speaking with energetic animation into the lectern microphone, Professor Peter E. Prefont vigorously advocated our case.

"Like Anse of *As I Lay Dying*, Doc Hines is totally self-absorbed and consistently abuses other people, particularly members of his own family, in nefarious pursuit of his goals. Like Flem Snopes of *The Hamlet, The Town*, and *The Mansion*, he possesses a ruthless tenacity and the ability to sidestep retribution for most of his mean actions. Like Popeye in *Sanctuary*, he kills quickly and decisively in order to further his obsessive purposes. Like Sutpen in *Absalom, Absalom!*, Hines is consumed by the need to achieve a decades-long 'design,' and he runs roughshod over anyone who attempts to deter him. Like Percy Grimm, also of *Light in August*, Doc relentlessly tracks Joe Christmas and is determined to destroy him, more because of what Joe represents than because of what Christmas may have done. And like Jason of *The Sound and the Fury*, Hines psychologically tortures and warps a close relative, unalterably convinced that he is acting with justice."

Barely pausing for breath, Pete bravely rode his Brahma bull of an argument around the figurative rodeo ring. "Possessing close affinities to Faulkner's other villains, Doc actually surpasses them all. Anse Bundren, Flem Snopes, and Jason Compson never kill anyone, although Flem's amorality contributes to Eula Varner's decision to kill herself in *The Town*. Anse and Jason are content with making miserable the lives of the other Bundrens and Compsons. Thomas Sutpen is guilty of no murders (presumably he kills enemy soldiers in Civil War battles); his denial of his son Charles Bon, of course, leads indirectly to Henry Sutpen's shooting of Charles. Percy Grimm murders and castrates Joe Christmas, but Grimm ironically carries out Doc Hines's most fervent old-age wish—remember Doc's entreaty to '"Kill the bastard!"' Grimm also creates for Joe a fleeting moment of the peace which Christmas has long sought but has never found in life; look on page four-sixty-five. Only the malicious Popeye in *Sanctuary* belongs in proper company with Doc, with the former's outright killings of Tommy and Red and indirect responsibility for the death of Lee Goodwin seeming to match Hines's homicides of Joe's parents and his ceaseless hounding and torturing of Joe. But Doc is able to bask in a kind of savage enjoyment of his accomplishments, while Popeye is not. *Sanctuary* ends with at least a rough sense of justice, as Popeye is executed in an Alabama prison for a murder that he did not commit. Doc, however, lives to see his wicked goals achieved: Joe, having endured a miserable existence, becomes a murderer, is hunted down by members of a vengeful community, and suffers a gruesome mutilation and death."

Exhaling until his shoulders slumped forward, Pete waved toward our table and said in a tired voice, "I now ask Captain Dupree to take the floor. Augie?"

Policeman and professor exchanged places, and Augie quickly consulted the cards that Pete handed him, paused to collect his thoughts, raised his gaze to the audience, and spoke, periodically looking at one of the note cards held in his left hand. "Retribution of sorts occurs to Popeye and to some of Faulkner's other leading villains, but not to Hines. Flem dies at the hands of his vengeful relative

Mink Snopes in *The Mansion*, and Thomas Sutpen is cut down with a rusty scythe by the dishonored Wash Jones. Jason has to suffer both a blinding headache and severe humiliation at the end of *The Sound and the Fury* when his niece Quentin absconds with his hoard of money, much of which he has swindled from her. Only Anse, preening in the company of his new wife, and the vigilante Grimm avoid measures of retaliation for their crimes, as does Doc. But the villainy of neither is a match for that of Hines, and thus their escape from punishment is not as dismaying.

"Doc is last seen at nine o'clock at night on the same day Joe Christmas dies, as attorney Gavin Stevens places Eupheus Hines and his wife on the train from Jefferson back to Mottstown, blithely unaware of the role the now doddering Doc has played in Joe's abysmal life. Speaking to Mrs. Hines, Stevens explains, '"Yes, yes . . . he'll be on the train tomorrow morning. I'll see to it. All you'll have to do is to arrange for the funeral, the cemetery. You take Granddad on home and put him to bed. I'll see that the boy is on the train in the morning"'— page four-forty-five. Presumably, Doc Hines will now be able to gloat inwardly during the meager funeral of his only grandchild."

Augie returned to our table, and Pete glanced at his watch. "Tell your stomachs to wait only a couple more minutes, gracious members of the audience. We are headed for the finish line up here. Okay. One final statement, and the inspiration for these words comes from Captain Caesar Augustus Dupree, whose linkage to a celebrated American nineteenth-century author is. . . . Well, ask him about this subject later, if you wish." From his messy legal pad Pete then read the conclusion to our presentation.

"As Faulkner's most successful representation of malevolence, Eupheus Hines belongs in the company of such memorable villains as Shakespeare's Iago and Melville's John Claggart. But he resembles more closely Edgar Allan Poe's Montresor, the narrator of 'The Cask of Amontillado,' a man who chains his adversary (the ironically named Fortunato) to a wall, builds a stone barrier sealing off the man from the world, and fully half a century later survives to revel joyously in the consequences of his iniquity. Like Montresor, Doc observes the accomplishment of his heinous goal and escapes punishment. Against such diabolical, relentless, and ultimately successful villainy, ordinary rational human beings seem helpless, and readers of *Light in August* can only shudder in revulsion as they contemplate such a masterfully depicted—and unerringly triumphant—perpetrator of evil as Eupheus (Doc) Hines. Thank you for your attention, kind people."

Vigorous applause erupted, and Errol Tedford walked quickly up the steps of the stage, shook hands with Pete, Augie, and me as he briskly adjourned the session, and joined us as we walked up the aisle. We three now pleasantly fatigued presenters were hauling our miscellaneous books and papers toward a storage spot before we heeded the demands of our persistent abdominal growls and started stuffing our faces with cardboard beef, rubber chicken, plastic peas, shotput rolls, mentholatum apple pie, and other standard cafeteria banquet cuisine. Jefferson Hendrix intercepted us as we walked through the auditorium doors, stating enthusiastically, "Guys, many kudos on a terrific presentation. You really enlightened many of us about that novel. I thought that I knew *Light in August* well. But you just showed me that in regard to some subjects I am about as clueless as the beginning physics student who was trying to cram into his resistant brain the definitions of some basic terms such as 'velocity,' 'gravity,' and 'mass.' After hours of futile effort, he threw his physics book across his dormitory room and proclaimed, 'I don't know mass from a hole in the ground.' Well, at least now I know Doc Hines from your average scum of the earth. What a dirtbag that character is." With a round of guffaws and vigorous slaps on several assorted backs, our pack of hungry literary wolves descended on the awaiting feast, unanimously eager to consume a standard week's worth of calories, starch, or fat while remaining collectively grateful that none of us would have to spend any more time that Saturday in the company of one Eupheus (Doc) Hines.

Chapter Seven

The Case of the Infatuated Final Narrator in *Light in August*

Simple and Odd

"Archie, dear, get yourself under control. All of us saw the same play that you just saw, and we are managing to keep our collective composure. Come, now; it's time to stifle the blubbering. What would the voters of this town think if they knew that the Mayor's husband is an old softie who breaks down and cries at the end of a stage drama?"

"Not at the end, Julianna," I wheezed huskily between hiccups and boo-hoos, "just during the scene when we learn that Shelby has died. I had been dreading that revelation for so long.... Oh, hell, here I go again." And I began to bob my head and jiggle the shoulder pads of my dark blue suitcoat in a renewed fit of lachrymose lamentation.

On Friday evening, December 15, 1995, the couples Prefont, Dupree, and Watkins had met at the Hughes Community Theatre for a presentation by the Murryville Players of the contemporary drama *Steel Magnolias*. Lindsey Burnett, a vivacious, very popular English teacher at our local high school, portrayed Shelby, the young woman whose tragic death serves as the play's climax. Lindsey, who coincidentally was one of my patients, proved to be so realistically effective in her role that many members of the audience, yours truly included of course, were overcome by emotion and wah-wahed vociferously, with three spectators needing assistance as they staggered up the aisle and out into the more private environment of the lobby. I had managed to recover sufficiently to join my five fellow playgoers in vigorous applause at the drama's final curtain, but when we all reached the Prefonts' apartment for a planned rendezvous with dessert and coffee, I again thought of Shelby, began to sniffle, and then to weep aloud once more. Understandably, Julianna became short-tempered with her distraught dilettante of a date, particularly when I would nearly close the floodgates on Grand Archibald Dam and then unaccountably open them again.

"Okay, Julianna, I'll quit this childish sobbing," I proclaimed as I straightened my shoulders, dabbed my eyes repeatedly, blew my nose honkedly, and glanced around at my social companions with a look of mixed determination and embarrassment. "I profusely apologize, friends, but now you know just how much of a sucker I am for a genuinely touching story. The untimely deaths of young people seem to affect me the most severely. Thank goodness I practice a medical specialty in which patients rarely expire while under my direct care—at least expire of eye disease, I mean."

"Yes, Archie," Julianna said, shifting her tone from remonstrative to supportive now that I had clamped the leaking ocular faucets, "I have always thought that you chose ophthalmology in part because many of your patients do not suffer from any illness but usually are seeking improvements in their vision. And blessedly, you rarely are forced to bury one of your slip-ups."

Soon the conversation turned to more pleasant topics, such as how well Ellie's contact lenses were improving her vision and how Augie's father in Memphis was planning to come to Murryville in January so that I could operate on a cataract in his left eye that had been ripening for more than eighteen months, followed by questions concerning the health and welfare of various members of assorted families. During this time I allowed myself the luxury of slowly gazing around the Prefonts' living room and admiring the holiday decorations that Ellie and Pete had recently placed on walls, tables, windows, and the front door. Wreaths, mistletoe, candy canes, framed Christmas scenes in both needlepoint and brushstroke, a stuffed Santa doll, a large Rudolph wind-up toy, and a heavily ornamented and tinseled five-foot-tall Scotch pine in the northwest corner combined to express an avid joy for the festive season that once more had sneaked up so rapidly on us. The apartment smelled enticingly of fresh evergreen and of baked sugar. The Duprees and the Watkinses had each contributed a large potted poinsettia to the Prefonts' seasonal decor, and Ellie's richly frosted, moist, and nutty carrot cake proved to be so delicious that I could not resist my customary second helping. All in all a most convivial occasion, and certainly reason enough to prevent me from crying again, which I began to do promptly at the instant that I swallowed my final bite of the superb carrot cake.

"Why, Archie. . . ." Julianna looked as if she were ready to stamp my forehead with a giant "VETO," but I waved my right hand in an attempt to deter her from further expressions of disapproval.

"I'm all right, sweetheart. These brief tears dropped out because for some reason I just now thought of Allison's ninth-grade play. You remember, don't you, the time when she played Juliet in that abbreviated death scene and did such a believable job that all of us once-beaming parents found our tear ducts transformed into thunder clouds?"

"Archie, I hadn't thought of that silly junior-high play in years. My goodness, our daughter was a ham then, and she still overacts in whatever she does, whether on stage or not," Julianna replied, shaking her head gently as she remarked on our spirited, vagabond only child.

It now occurs to your faithful narrator that I have prattled on heedlessly for lo these many pages without even once mentioning Ms. Allison Carol Watkins, age 23, the delight of my life and occasional sword in my side, on whom I had laid nary an eye for more than eighteen months. Allison, or A. C. as I sometimes called her (she adamantly refuses to let me any longer use my favorite childhood nicknames for her, "Ace" or "Acey-Deucey"), graduated from Moffatt College as a language major and then set out for Europe in order to extend her fluencies in German, Spanish, and French while she immersed herself in stimulating foreign cultures. So far she had used her Eurorail pass to travel some 5,000 miles all over the continent, with stops for work or extended play in Munich, Berlin, Salzburg, Bern, Barcelona, Nice, and Hamburg. Rather than returning home last summer as previously planned, she had journeyed to Minsk, Belarus, to stay in a classmate's apartment while the girlfriend worked for an international investment company, and consequently now our daughter was adding Russian to her linguistic repertoire. Julianna and I both missed Allison very much, but we were also proud of how successfully she had managed to learn so much about life in foreign countries and to make legions of international friends. Long ago we had concluded that our only offspring, hopelessly infected with wanderlust, would likely spend most of her life away from Murryville and her perplexed parents.

Mary Alice had diplomatically avoided displaying any recognition of my immature sniffling or Julianna's petulance, and now our favorite school principal turned to my wife and asked with enthusiasm, "Julianna, do you know when Allison will arrive for Christmas? Last week you told me that she would be coming home for the holidays, but you knew no definite date of arrival."

The Mayor and I simultaneously shook our heads in mutual exasperation. "Our darling daughter was supposed to come home for Christmas last year, if you remember, Mary Alice," Julianna replied, "but she called on December twenty-third from Rauris, Austria, and said that she simply couldn't refuse a friend's invitation to join a skiing expedition. So Archie and I will believe that she is actually in Murryville when we can reach out and touch her in the flesh instead of having our hands on only another of the scores of photos that she has sent to us. Right now she is working as a translator in Minsk, but she has solemnly promised to be here by Christmas Eve."

From the contiguous kitchen, where she was storing the remaining section of the significantly shrunken carrot cake, Ellie raised her voice and spoke. "I really look forward to meeting Allison. When she gets to town, please have her call me. She will probably be glad to spend some time with . . . uhhh, I mean . . . let's see. . . ."

"To get away from us boring, doddering senior citizens, you mean, young Miss Ellie," I replied, rising from the orange couch, strolling three steps forward, and leaning around the wide opening into the kitchen until I caught the eye of our hostess.

Ellie held up both palms, waved them toward and then away from one another, and insisted, "No, no, Speck. I meant to say . . . well. . . ." Ellie stamped her foot, abruptly dropped and raised her right fist, jerked her chin down and up, and stated firmly, "Yes, you are right, venerable Doctor, sir. Allison assuredly will thrive in the company of her matriarchal female gender person, but if she is forced to hang around you too much, then she will be crying at the end of every sit-com or soap opera on television. Better send her over here to me for some stimulating association with a peer."

At that moment Pete entered the kitchen, balancing six crumb-bestrewn plates and an equal number of forks smudged with the remains of vanilla frosting. "Go easy on Doctor Double-You, Ellie. We have finally coaxed a smile or two out of him on this pleasant evening. Speck, I need to lead you back into the safe and comforting world of novels once again. Exposure to live drama seems to tug at your emotions much too drastically."

From the front room Julianna piped up. "Oh no, ladies. Did you hear what the Professor just slyly said? I suspect that he is trying to start the ball rolling again toward yet another of those demented literary investigations. Cease and desist, Pete! Mary Alice, tell him to leave your husband alone. Ellie, come out here and help us. Please put a muzzle on your frisky Doberman."

Having placed all plates or utensils in the dishwasher, Pete circled back into the living area, holding up both arms at head level in a gesture of surrender as he spoke. "Don't worry, Mayor Watkins. I won't drag your husband or Monsieur Dupin into any more adventures in page turning. They have already helped me more than I deserve, and as we speak I am blessed with five cases to summarize in preparation for my submitting them to academic journals. Captain Dupree's solutions to the crimes, mysteries, or puzzles in *Sanctuary, The Sound and the Fury, As I Lay Dying,* and *Light in August* should help me immeasurably here at the raw beginnings of my scholarly career. No, no, I couldn't POSSIBLY expect any more help from my dear friends Augie or Speck with ONE particularly nagging question that keeps nipping away at the edges of my curiosity. . . ."

Pete slowly lowered himself onto a reversed straight chair, dangled his right wrist from the top of the chair's back while he held his left fist in front of his mouth, each of his guests as well as with his wife, who had left the kitchen and had seated and slowly rotated his head several times from left to right, making eye contact with herself in the middle of the orange couch. An ominous silence filled the room. The four guests plus Ellie all looked around at one another, raised or lowered their eyebrows, turned up various palms, and carried on this mime contest until the predictable person, my little chickadee, shattered the silence. "Oh, goose feathers. Go ahead and ask your Faulkner question, Pete, you dirty dog. You know damned well that you have aroused the instinctive nosiness of all five of us over here on this side of the room. Ellie, Mary Alice, say 'Bye, bye' to your hubbies again. These three secret Faulkner agents will be going under deep cover once more, but let's hope for not too lengthy a tour of duty this time."

Mary Alice sat back in her chair and folded her arms across her chest. "Just think, Julianna. They could as readily be falling off bar stools at some tacky gambling den over in Tunica, Mississippi. At least if they are talking about a book we will know that they are wearing clean underwear, drinking town water, and avoiding the company of besmirched women."

Ellie crossed the left leg of her elegant emerald pants suit and spoke. "I agree, ladies. But aren't you two as jealous as I am of all the fun that these guys are having? Don't you feel left out?"

Julianna banged her right fist into her left palm. "Yes, Ellie, yes. At first I thought that all of this literary talk would be about as exciting as watching crabgrass grow. But the boys seemed to have had so much fun with it that I, for one, am VERY envious." The Mayor pointed her right index finger at Pete and, in a laudable imitation of a childish tantrum, whined, "Professor, this time may we girls play, too? Huh? MAY WE? PLEASE?"

Mary Alice then firmly stated, "Count me in too, girls," and Pete quickly recognized that he was seriously outnumbered. Phooey fuzzy! Any single one of

Pete slowly lowered himself onto a reversed straight chair, dangled his right wrist from the top of the chair's back while he held his left fist in front of his mouth, and slowly rotated his head several times from left to right, making eye contact with each of his guests as well as with his wife, who had left the kitchen and had seated herself in the middle of the orange couch. An ominous silence filled the room. The four guests plus Ellie all looked around at one another, raised or lowered their eyebrows, turned up various palms, and carried on this mime contest until the predictable person, my little chickadee, shattered the silence. "Oh, goose feathers. Go ahead and ask your Faulkner question, Pete, you dirty dog. You know damned well that you have aroused the instinctive nosiness of all five of us over here on this side of the room. Ellie, Mary Alice, say 'Bye, bye' to your hubbies again. These three secret Faulkner agents will be going under deep cover once more, but let's hope for not too lengthy a tour of duty this time."

Mary Alice sat back in her chair and folded her arms across her chest. "Just think, Julianna. They could as readily be falling off bar stools at some tacky gambling den over in Tunica, Mississippi. At least if they are talking about a book we will know that they are wearing clean underwear, drinking town water, and avoiding the company of besmirched women."

Ellie crossed the left leg of her elegant emerald pants suit and spoke. "I agree, ladies. But aren't you two as jealous as I am of all the fun that these guys are having? Don't you feel left out?"

Julianna banged her right fist into her left palm. "Yes, Ellie, yes. At first I thought that all of this literary talk would be about as exciting as watching crabgrass grow. But the boys seemed to have had so much fun with it that I, for one, am VERY envious." The Mayor pointed her right index finger at Pete and, in a laudable imitation of a childish tantrum, whined, "Professor, this time may we girls play, too? Huh? MAY WE? PLEASE?"

Mary Alice then firmly stated, "Count me in too, girls," and Pete quickly recognized that he was seriously outnumbered. Phooey fuzzy! Any single one of these formidable women is more than a match for any of us weakling male gender cave persons, and all three of our wives together—Oooo wheee; give it up, pack it up, go start the truck. Pete stood and rapidly said, "Whatever you say, ladies. Let me grab my notes, and I will gladly pose the question to all of you." He then spun on his heel and bounced toward the back bedroom of the apartment, which doubled as a storage area for the collected papers of the teachers Prefont.

Emerging from his private archives, Pete waved a copy of LNA (ELL, IN, EH) in our direction and announced, "I am somewhat vexed at myself, ladies and gentlemen, because this question that keeps annoying me did not seem at first to be a difficult one—odd, perhaps, but not difficult. I might even call it a simple question, but I can't seem to put my finger squarely on the answer."

"Simple and odd," said Captain Dupree, nodding his head once while he held his left index finger studiously in front of his extended lower lip.

"Why yes, Monsieur Dupin, the problem appears to be both odd and simple, strangely enough. But I must admit to being quite baffled by this question."

"Perhaps it is the very simplicity of the question which puzzles you," said Augie with a meditative expression on his face.

Pete asked, "What did you just say, Augie?"

"Perhaps this mystery is different from the other Faulknerian challenges that we have tackled together," was the Captain's retort. "Maybe the solution to this one is a little too plain."

With a widely opened mouth and narrowed eyes, Pete stared at our ratiocinist and replied, with stunning profundity, "Huh?"

"A little too self-evident," Augie stated with emphasis on the hyphenated adjective.

"Ha, ha, ha," Pete laughed nervously, "I admit to being totally clueless concerning the meaning of your string of riddles, Monsieur Dupin. May we start over?"

In reply Augie merely waved his left hand in a gesture of dismissal and gently stated, "All of this murky verbiage will likely resolve itself into meaningful clarity once we have wrapped up the case, Pete. Now, will you tell all of us here just what is the matter at hand? In other words, will you articulate the major question before us?"

While Augie and Pete were exchanging their mumbo-jumbo riddles, the remaining four of us had sat in puzzled silence. Finally Coach Ellie spoke up. "If the rest of this little oral tennis match makes no more sense then this first set, then I for one will unstring my racket and make a bee line for the clubhouse."

Augie stood, walked to Pete's side, and placed his right hand on our host's left shoulder. "I apologize for my temporary flight of fancy there, Pete. Now—hit us with your inquiry."

Patting Augie's resting hand with his own right paw, Pete said, "Thanks, Captain. Okay, here is where I could use some help. Gentlemen, you will remember well the concluding chapter of LNA. Ladies, I know that you may not have read this novel yet"—three feminine nods confirmed Pete's assumption—"but your respective husbands later can summarize for you the novel's main events, and then you can each, at your leisure, read this brief chapter. It is only fourteen pages in length. Okay by you, my fair damsels?"

"Yeah, yeah, Sir Galahad. Keep on with your lipping. We three reformed airheads are paying very close attention," replied my tart-tongued turtle dove from her nest on the orange couch. "Even bimboes can handle a rip-roaring total of a gigantic fourteen pages, especially if we can trace the big words with our little-bitty fingers."

As Julianna tossed her barbed witticisms in Pete's direction, the professor slid into his customary habit of pacing while he simultaneously meditated and conversed. Concentrating on a page in LNA, he didn't seem to hear the Mayor's reply, or if he did her sarcasm pierced his armor of oblivion not in the slightest. "Speck, Augie, you will remember last month, at the ALA conference, when we listened to the paper arguing that Lena Grove achieves heroic stature in the novel's final chapter because of her several triumphs over various male characters. Last week I was looking back through the ending of LNA, stewing over that hypothesis about Lena, when a big question hit me, and I have been mentally chewing on it ever since."

"Stewing and chewing," I quietly said, instantly cutting short any further sarcastic remarks in reaction to a sharp mayoral toe that vigorously met my left ankle. Pacing to and fro, waving his book, addressing us five social companions at times and at other moments delivering his remarks to an assortment of walls, windows, or doors, Pete moved into high oratorical gear.

"In earlier sections of the novel the important character Byron Bunch demonstrates uncommon selflessness, courage, loyalty, and honor in such actions as his care for the pregnant Lena in the face of Jefferson's calumny toward her, his attempts to help Joe Christmas and Joe's grandmother by asking Gail Hightower to provide an alibi for Joe, his crucial role in sending Hightower to assist in the delivery of Lena's baby, and his arranging for the odious Lucas Burch, or Joe Brown, to see Lena and the child, followed by his stoic acceptance of the inevitable beating when he confronts Burch, the biological father of Lena's baby."

Pete halted his pacing, looked at his audience, and announced, "Here I am reading from page four-thirty-nine in the novel. 'It does not last long. Byron knew that it was not going to. But he did not hesitate. He just crept up until he could see the other, where he stopped, looking at the crouching and unwarned figure. '"You're bigger then me,"' Byron thought. '"But I dont care. You've had every other advantage of me. And I dont care about that neither. You've done throwed away twice inside of nine months what I aint had in thirtyfive years. And now I'm going to get the hell beat out of me and I dont care about that, neither."'"

When he finished reading the passage, Pete resumed his pacing. "Byron Bunch certainly emerges as an unlikely hero in the novel, but he is definitely depicted as a plucky, determined, and resourceful individual who rises above his nondescript, colorless origins and becomes a sympathetic, successful defender of fragile moral values that are under attack in these perilous times. At least Byron seems to grow in this way until the book's final chapter. In this conclusion Byron appears to degenerate into a hapless buffoon. He is pathetically unsuccessful in his attempt to force himself romantically upon Lena Grove, and all of his other actions also seem foolish or inconsequential. Byron is even described as '"the kind of fellow you wouldn't see the first glance if he was alone by himself in the bottom of a empty concrete swimming pool'"—page four-ninety-five. And here is another negative description of Byron: '"He looked like except when he was at work, he would just be something around. I just couldn't imagine anybody, any woman, knowing that they had ever slept with him, let alone having anything to show folks to prove it'"—page four-ninety-six."

In the middle of his living room Pete stopped and flamboyantly scratched his head. "My question: what happens in the novel to make Byron degenerate into a wimpish dunderhead? I am truly troubled by this disparity in the characterization of Byron between his appearances in earlier chapters and those in the book's conclusion. What am I missing? Do there exist some subtle clues pointing toward Byron's descent into his final role as a hopeless nerd, some signals that I have overlooked? WHAT? AAARGH!"

By this time Pete was gripping his copy of LNA tightly in his left hand while with his right he grasped a clump of his thick, sandy hair and pulled vigorously on it. Fearful that next he would revert to his previous habit of pounding himself on his forehead, I arose and moved toward him, but Augie had already reached his side. "Okay, Pete," the Captain spoke soothingly, "I believe that we all have gained a clear picture of the problem. Tell you what. I will drop by the Moffatt Library and search for some pertinent scholarship on this curious development—or I should say 'regression'—of Byron as a character in the final chapter of LNA." Turning toward the wives, Augie continued, "Ladies, please read Chapter Twenty-One of your husband's copy of the novel."

"We have a joint property law in this state, Mister Detective," acerbically spoke Her Honor, although she ended her statement with a faint glimmer of a smile on her lips.

"Your MARRIAGE'S copy of the novel, then. I stand corrected, Mayor Watkins," Augie responded, concluding with a bow worthy of Rhett Butler at his most gallant.

Augie then walked to his wife's side, bent over and whispered in her ear, arose as he nodded simultaneously with Mary Alice, and said, "We would be delighted if you fine people would come to our house for dinner on Saturday, December twenty-third—one week from tomorrow. Mary Alice will be baking a holiday ham, and we have been intending to try to find a time when we could celebrate the holiday season with the four of you, our dear friends. So—how about it?"

Rapid consultations showed that the Prefonts and the Watkinses most assuredly would be delighted to attend, so the first act of Monsieur Dupin's final investigation of a Faulknerian mystery came to a satisfying conclusion. Simple, odd, and to be continued.

Gets Around, Gets Around,
A Body Gets Around

On Wednesday morning, December 20, the first winter storm of the season hit northeast Arkansas with a bitter vengeance. Winds gusting as high as thirty miles per hour brought all the way from Canada an Alberta clipper that combined with abundant moisture from the Gulf of Mexico and generated an inch of treacherous ice coating all of the exposed surfaces in the region. On Wednesday evening four inches of heavy, wet snow fell out of the leaden skies. Temperatures plummeted to a low of ten degrees Fahrenheit, and the citizenry of Murryville and outer Crowder County collectively hunkered down for a period of intimate acquaintance with cabin fever.

Arriving in her office at Town Hall just as the storm was beginning to dump frozen precipitation all over her municipality, Julianna set up a command post and remained on duty for nearly sixty straight hours, dining on delivered pizza or snacks from vending machines, napping on a cot that she kept stowed in a closet, and rarely leaving her desk with its array of telephones which she constantly used to deploy our town's skeleton army of emergency snow equipment—two plows and one truck that spread road salt. The Mayor also kept tabs on numerous elderly shut-ins, coordinated a squadron of volunteer shovelers of snow who cleaned downtown sidewalks, and sent physicians in police cars with tire chains on several errands of medical mercy. Fortunately the storm blew through our area very quickly, and by late Friday evening the main roads and sidewalks were passable enough that my feisty chief executive was able to telephone me at my office and ask me to pick her up. My Explorer features reliable four-wheel drive, so I was easily able to transport Julianna back to our blissful cottage on Summit Avenue, where upon arrival she walked directly into our bedroom and proceed to collapse fully clothed onto our queen-sized Sealy Posturepedic mattress, gently firm model.

By late Saturday morning my wife-mate had revived sufficiently to join me in a brunch of waffles and bacon ineptly prepared by Chef Boy-Archibald-Me. After a few phone calls had reassured her that travel and commerce were once again humming along at nearly normal speeds in Murryville, Julianna relaxed enough to check our home calendar and to remind me that we had promised to have dinner that very evening at the Dupree domicile next door. Immediately I telephoned Augie to make certain that the dinner plus Faulkner session was still on tap, received assurances that the ham was baking while Dupin brain cells were operating at full power, and called Pete and Ellie to offer them taxi service to the festivities. The Prefonts promised me that Herbie Junior was a veteran at surmounting obstacles such as semi-frozen streets, considering the upper Midwestern origins of his owners, so Julianna and I settled down in our sunroom for an afternoon's review of principal events in LNA followed by dual slow, deliberate readings of the novel's final chapter.

At seven p.m. Mary Alice and Augie greeted their guests with cups of potent eggnog served in front of a cheerfully roaring fire, and the promised feast that soon followed surpassed the expectations of all our taste buds: succulent ham steaks glazed with cherry sauce, sugary candied yams, green beans with slivered almonds, fresh buttery rolls, and a superb Liebfraumilch that tinglingly dissolved on the tongue. Dessert was a diverse assortment of freshly baked Christmas cookies, the aroma of which had been teasing our appetites since our first arrivals at the Dupree home.

By the time we were seated in the paneled and book-lined den, enjoying our coffee and liqueurs, all six of us were lounging, sipping, digesting, and lollygagging in corporate placidity following the survival of the storm's challenges and the consumption of an epic holiday banquet. Five of us would have been content to allow the evening to drift along in small talk, carol singing, or admiration of the Duprees' majestic six-foot decorated Douglas fir Christmas tree which reigned in front of the den's picture window. But NO-OHH-OHH. Professor

Obsessive-Compulsive himself, Peter Edward Prefont, had to shatter the evening's mellow, soothing mood by clapping his large hands together sharply and yammering, "Time to dive into Faulkner, kiddies. Let's get this Byron Bunch show on the road! Is everybody ready to tackle the mystery in the final chapter?"

From the waist-high cabinet shelf where she was raptly admiring Mary Alice's elaborate collection of Dickens Village miniature Victorian buildings, figurine characters from *David Copperfield* and *Oliver Twist,* and the small-scale backdrop of lampposts, trees, fences, plus a pioneering locomotive engine, Ellie poutingly replied, "Oh, Pee-tur! Do we have to? It feels so good to relax now that both our Moffatt semester and this snowstorm are behind us. I'm ready for Christmas break. Let's postpone the literary quiz for tonight."

Julianna hopped up from her seat deep within a richly cushioned green armchair. Her bright red sweater depicted a snowy mountain scene on the front and featured bells that softly jingled when she moved her arms or torso. "Now, Ellie; let's not let these arrogant men-folk get the best of us. Remember that we three girls asked to be included, so rally your energies and let's show our husbands that our meager brains are also capable of solving a Faulkner puzzle."

Mary Alice walked into the den, carrying a tray of liqueur glasses as she seconded Julianna's motion. "I recollect that you two ladies helped to get the guys started on their Faulkner wild-goose chases last spring when you both thought of answers to questions about Poe. So we have all been involved in this literary game since its beginnings, although we genteel lady-folks have graciously allowed our virile cavemen to be the clan's principal hunter-gatherers."

With a loud sigh Ellie turned away from the Dickens Village display and retreated to her seat on the sofa near the picture window and the Christmas tree. "I am clearly outvoted," she said in a resigned tone, "so I'll be a good little Brownie Scout and play along. But I would still prefer to talk to Julianna and Speck about Allison. The more I learn about her, the more intriguing she becomes. I hope that she gets home soon so that I can talk to her. Speck, since you told me that she has seen the German women's national futbol team play in Hamburg, I can't wait to pick her brain."

From my sprawled position in a corner armchair I replied, "Well, Ellie, she may not have much of value to tell you, since she went to the contest primarily as an excuse to get ready for the post-match beer party. But Julianna and I will be grateful when we finally hear from her and learn of her projected date of arrival. So far all we know is that sometime late this week she is scheduled to catch flights from Minsk to Frankfurt to New York and then eventually connect to Memphis. I am ready to hop in my car and speed on Interstate Forty-Eight to the Bluff City just as soon as we receive a phone call or a page on my beeper from her."

Augie arose from his chair and said to me, "Yes, Speck; Mary Alice and I are grateful to know that Val and Gus will both be getting home on Christmas Eve. I am confident that you will hear from Allison soon." He then spread his arms widely, looked around at his other guests and his wife, asked if we would mind rearranging the seating, supervised the shifting of the three women to the couch while the men all assumed seats in nearby armchairs, grasped his hands together in front of him in a modified prayerlike fashion, and initiated the evening's Faulkner session. "Let us quickly review the problem at hand, my fellow participants. Pete has asked all of us to examine the perplexing changes in the stature of Byron Bunch, who seems to degenerate in the final chapter from an unassuming hero into a blithering bumbler. Is my summary accurate, Professor?"

"Yes, Monsieur Dupin," answered Pete, "and I do appreciate everyone's help tonight. Let's see if we can untangle this Faulknerian-Gordian knot, and then we can all celebrate the holiday with no cumulus clouds of ambiguity enveloping and choking us."

"Nifty gaseous metaphors there, Pete," Augie said with an ironic smile. "You've been hanging around old gas passer Speck too much, I suggest. All right, folks. Does everyone remember when Pete first posed this question last week, and also when I suggested that the solution might be so apparent we all could be looking right at it and still not see it?"

Five nodding heads affirmed our unanimous memories of Augie's rhetorical riddles, and our chief detective continued his introductory remarks. "Pete, let's examine your original assumption. Throughout the novel's first twenty chapters, Byron gradually becomes an admirable character whose impressive accomplishments are achieved through courage and sacrifice, but in Chapter Twenty-One he appears to be one of life's sorry losers, certainly no hero but merely a dim-witted dunce. Is my statement accurate?"

"Right on, Captain Dupree. You have summarized succinctly the cause of my perplexity. My question, then, is—WHY? How can we make sense of this incongruity? And are you suggesting, Augie, that the answer is apparent? If so, then I must need another eye examination, Doctor Double-You, because I shore as hay-yull cain't see hit." With his concluding dependent clause Pete lapsed into the drawl of a Crocodile, Arkansas, honky-tonk regular barstool patron.

"Let's retreat to a close examination of the text then, Pete," amiably suggested our leader. "Everyone please turn to four-ninety-four in LNA, the first page of Chapter Twenty-One. Read the first few sentences silently, ponder the information contained therein, and then tell me what crucial fact we have all been overlooking." Tactfully, Augie did not emphasize that only Pete so far had failed to see the forest for the mighty oaks or little acorns—or however that aphorism goes.

Julianna held up her right hand and asked our interlocutor, "May we girls confer, O grand and glorious inquisitor? After all, we regard ourselves as a unified team."

"Certainly, Madame Mayor," Augie replied in a tone of magnanimity. "Confer to your hearts' and minds' content."

The three Eurocentric female-gender humans quickly formed a lopsided circle, with Ellie in the middle and the older women leaning left and right directly in front of her. Frantic whispers issued forth from their urgent huddle, while we men-folk each sat marooned in solitude. Augie leaned the back of his head on his chair and gazed at the top of the Christmas tree, Pete stared with a deep frown at his copy of LNA, and I scanned the two pages in front of me, totally incapable of deciphering this solution that must have been so obvious to Augie.

Black, gray, and blonde hairdos parted company, our wives' faces became visible again, and Ellie looked directly at first Pete and then Augie before she spoke. "We have a guess, Sir Quizmaster," Ellie said in a hesitant voice. "All of us think that the sudden appearance of this chapter's new narrator must furnish one of the pieces to this puzzle. I am referring to the 'furniture repairer and dealer' mentioned in the first and second lines of the chapter. Are we somewhere close to being correct?"

As Ellie spoke, a smile stole slowly across Augie's calm face, and when she concluded her offering, our chief detective clapped his hands together sharply— CRACK!—and proclaimed, "Wonderful insight, Ellie. Yes, yes, my fair ladies, you have gone straight to the heart of the confusion about Byron. In three words: 'Consider the source!' Pete's uncertainty about this last chapter apparently occurs not because Byron himself degenerates as a character but because this new narrator depicts Byron unfairly and erroneously. Therefore, this investigation should focus on a SIMPLE examination of an ODD point of view."

Smiles of triumph beamed forth from the residents of the couch, and the three wise women patted each other's backs, gripped hands, and bounced up and down in glee once or twice each. Pete stared at the celebrants, shifted his gaze to Augie, and said in a tone of wonderment, "Well, I'll be ding-dong-damned. You are right, Captain. All along I HAVE been overlooking the obvious reason, and it was staring me directly in my uncomprehending face. What an airhead I am. AAARRRGH!"

Five people rose a few inches off their seated positions and stared raptly at Pete's long right arm, which stretched forward slowly, reached its full extension, and then . . . fell to Pete's side. With a unanimous exhalation of breath—

"Whoosh!"—Pete's volunteer potential rescuers resumed their seats and leaned back, all of us quite grateful that we did not have to leap forward and prevent another bashing of his cranium.

From the centered coffee table Augie lifted a legal pad and resumed his analysis. "Ladies and gentlemen, please allow me to read a summary of my initial findings about this new narrator, who appears only in this novel's concluding chapter. I conducted some research in the Moffatt Library—before the storm hit us—and discovered that several Faulkner scholars have contributed some helpful thoughts about the traveling furniture man. Does anyone mind if I read to you a couple of paragraphs of my purple prose? In preparation for last month's ALA conference I developed this helpful habit of writing out some of my observations, theories, and interpretations."

Still flushed with their initial success, the women all urged Augie to proceed, and Pete and I added our encouragement to the offer. Clearing his throat, Augie straightened his reading glasses, with a proud smile picked up his blue "Detective" cap from the floor beside his chair, set the good-luck headwear firmly into place, and read to us the words scribbled on his legal pad.

"The four quotations that I will include all appear on page four-ninety-four of the novel. Ahem. At the beginning of the final chapter of *Light in August,* Faulkner introduces a new character, identified only as, quoting here, 'a furniture repairer and dealer,' end of quotation, who makes a journey by truck from eastern Mississippi into southwestern Tennessee. The man later returns home with, quotation, 'some old pieces of furniture which he had bought by correspondence,' end of quotation, and, while relaxing in his conjugal bed, suffused with a postcoital contentment, he recounts to his wife, quoting here, 'an experience which he had on the road,' end of quotation. Having stopped to purchase gasoline for his tank, the furniture man had obligingly offered rides to a woman, a man, and a baby, who are soon identified by readers as Lena Grove, Byron Bunch, and Lena's three-week-old son. During the ensuing trip lasting about eighteen hours, this new narrator had become so captivated by the activities of his companions Lena and Byron that he later, quoting here, 'considered [their story] amusing enough to repeat,' end of quotation, and he proceeds to fill the novel's concluding chapter with an improbable tale, delivered in country vernacular, of doggedly persistent courtship, humiliating romantic failure, and fumbling reconciliation resulting in a continuing journey.

"Several critics have examined the strategic narrative role of the furniture repairer and dealer in the entertaining and artistically effective conclusion of LNA. H. C. Nash explicates the fragments of conversation between the furniture man and his wife and asserts that these, quoting here, 'exchanges . . . project a natural intimacy' while they 'help to restore a *normal* continuity and stability (in social and sexual terms) critical to the novel's knitting up,' end of quotations. Another interpreter, Ronald Wesley Hoag, points out that in the final chapter, quotation, 'the furniture dealer/narrator offers to his wife a whimsical valentine,' an 'affirmation,' end of quotations, that is closely connected in theme and characterization with its two preceding chapters in what Hoag calls the book's 'triptych conclusion': Chapter Nineteen, which recounts the pursuit and killing of Joe Christmas, and Chapter Twenty, which contains the lengthy introspective reverie and closing epiphany of Gail Hightower. Both Nash and Hoag cite pioneering commentary by Cleanth Brooks, the first Faulkner scholar to discern the structural and thematic significance of the furniture dealer's narration in LNA. Brooks characterizes the last chapter as a type of, quoting here, 'social comedy,' end of quotation, and he views the furniture man as one in a series of voices of, quoting, 'the community . . . the powerful though invisible force that quietly exerts itself in so much of Faulkner's work,' end of quotation.

"All three of these critics react favorably to the appealing qualities of the furniture repairer and dealer himself. Nash finds, quoting here, 'essential decency and warmth' end of quotation, in him, and Hoag calls him, quoting, 'a symbolic marriage broker' with a 'benign presence,' end of quotations. Brooks ascribes to the man even greater stature, calling him, quoting here, 'the anonymous, earthy, genial, experienced, tough-minded representative of a corporate body of values, insights, and beliefs,' end of quotation." Looking up from his notes, Augie surveyed his listeners and politely asked, "Is everyone with me so far?"

The women and I all produced smiles of affirmation and assorted nods, but Pete retained on his visage a look of concentrated frustration. "Augie, I agree with you that this new narrator offers a fresh perspective on the events in the novel and represents a divergent voice from the ones that we have heard in the first twenty chapters. But I still don't understand why the furniture dealer portrays Byron as unsympathetically as he does."

Augie dropped his legal pad on the nearby coffee table, held up his right index finger, and said, "Precisely my next point, Pete. Although the furniture dealer possesses all of the admirable characteristics ascribed to him by critics Nash, Hoag, and Brooks, the man also discloses through his narration that he is not flawless. Indeed, I hope to demonstrate to you that this furniture dealer is not even totally trustworthy."

Picking at his upper lip as he listened to Augie, Pete responded, "So you are saying that the furniture dealer deliberately does not tell us the truth here? Is he lying to his wife as well as, uh, laying with her? Yuk, yuk."

Ellie stamped her right foot and said with vehemence, "Pete, you zip your nasty lip right now. Leave it to you to toss in a sexual pun."

"Oh, lighten up, Coach Ellie," I interjected, a grin spread across the folds of my cheeks. "Remember that you asked to be included in this male bull session, so you'd better be prepared for some coarse locker-room humor."

Ellie raised her eyes in their sockets, shook her head in exasperation, and muttered, "Men! What little boys they really are." Her admonition was greeted with mumbled words of agreement from Mary Alice and Julianna.

Augie jumped back into the lead. "No, Pete, the furniture man is not deliberately telling his wife any falsehoods. Instead, I suggest to you people that this final narrator suffers from a distinct and pervasive bias, one that powerfully warps his observations and assumptions."

Pete hopped to his feet and launched into his habitual trot. "Bias, bias," he repeated loudly, "a distorting bias. Augie, are you saying that this bias directly shapes the narrator's portrayal of Byron? Could you define this bias more fully?"

"Pete, the word 'Yes' is the answer to both of your questions," Augie replied, shifting in his seat as he reclaimed his legal pad from the table. "The furniture dealer's bias is indeed the key to Byron's apparent—let's see, I believe that you used the word 'degeneration' several times—Byron's apparent degeneration, which I hope to be able to show you is not a change in character at all. Within the framework of the novel's narrative Byron definitely does not become less heroic. He remains selfless, determined, and courageous, just as you described him earlier, Pete. As Chapter Twenty ends and Twenty-One begins, what DOES change is the DEPICTION of Byron. Now, as for your second question, the one asking for a more complete definition of this bias I have mentioned—here I would appreciate the able assistance of Ellie, Julianna, and Mary Alice again."

Consulting his legal pad, Augie continued his presentation. "Ladies, please allow me to read a series of comments made about Byron by our new acquaintance, the furniture repairer and dealer. By the way, for the sake of convenience let's give ourselves the option of calling this man by a shortened title. How about F. D. (EFF DEE)? All right? Good. Now, let me remind you that several times F. D. describes Byron in unflattering terms. Last week Pete read to us a couple of these descriptions, the one about how no one would notice Byron if he was by himself in the bottom of an empty swimming pool, and the remark that no self-respecting woman would admit to having slept with Byron.

"F. D. particularly relishes telling about Lena's rejection of Byron's sexual advances, claiming that Lena had picked up the pathetic suitor and, quoting here from page five-oh-three, '"set him back outside on the ground like she would that baby if it had been about six years old, say, and she says, 'You go and lay down now, and get some sleep. We got another fur piece to go tomorrow,'" end of quotation. F. D. greatly enjoys rubbing some figurative salt in Byron's wounded pride. Quoting here from page five-oh-four: "'But I knew about how I would have been standing and feeling if I was him. And that would have been with my head bowed, waiting for the Judge to say, 'Take him out of here and hang him quick,'" end of quotation. In his final description of Byron, who is, quoting here, '*Standing there . . . hangdog and determined,*' end of quotation, F. D. smugly concludes that Byron's fate with Lena will be determined fully by Lena herself. Quoting here from five-oh-six, "'And her looking at him like she had known all the time what he was going to do before he even knew himself that he was going to, and that whatever he done, he wasn't going to mean it,'" end of quotation."

Augie rambled purposefully onward. "In contrast to his descriptions of Byron, throughout the final chapter F. D. depicts Lena Grove in consistently flattering terms. I have compiled a short list of only a representative few of these comments.

1. On first observation Lena is a '"young, pleasantfaced gal"'—page four-ninety-five-and a '"young, strapping gal"'—page four-ninety-six.

2. Later he says that she is '"placid and calm"'—page five-oh-one, '*a big strong gal*'—five-oh-three, and '"a goodlooking country gal"'—five-oh-four.

3. Although Byron does most of the talking for the pair, F. D. soon concludes that Lena is actually in charge of plans for the traveling trio. From page five-oh-one: "'And so I heard him talking to her, about how they might travel on like this from one truck to another and one state to another for the rest of their lives . . . and her sitting there on the log, holding the chap and listening quiet as a stone and pleasant as a stone and just about as nigh to being moved or

persuaded.'"

4. The true extent of Lena's command of the situation is soon revealed in her firm yet tactful refusal of Byron's maladroit effort at sexual union. Page five-oh-three: "'and then I heard one kind of astonished sound she made when she woke up, like she was just surprised and then a little put out without being scared at all, and she says not loud neither: 'Why, Mr. Bunch. Aint you ashamed. You might have woke the baby, too.'"'

5. On page five-oh-six, he begins a concluding hymn of praise about Lena with these words: "'Yes, sir. You cant beat a woman.'"'

During his meditative strolling Pete had already meandered around the den numerous times, and as Augie paused in his presentation the professor abruptly stopped, leaned his right elbow on the edge of a bookshelf, and spoke directly to our lead investigator. "You're right, Augie. F. D. does consistently disparage Byron while he praises Lena. But I'm still confused as to why his appreciation of Lena would make him describe Byron as such a zero of a guy."

"We are all getting closer to the solution of our mystery, Pete," Augie responded. "At this point once again I humbly solicit the expert assistance of our feminine contingent." The wifely trio sat expectantly on the front edges of the couch cushions, poised in eagerness for further detective duty. Augie continued, "Ladies, you are all acknowledged experts in the inexact science of understanding masculine behavior. Please confer for as long as you wish, and then inform us less mentally agile males of your interpretation concerning the primary reason motivating F. D.'s commentary about both Byron and Lena."

Julianna responded immediately. "We do not need to confer, Augie. The solution occurred to all three of us as you were just now reading that summary of F. D.'s commentary."

Pete jerked his body into an erect posture, a look of incredulity spread across his eyes and mouth. "But how could you have reached such a unanimous opinion, Mayor Double-You? Only Augie has been talking, except when I just did."

Mary Alice calmly placed her hands into her lap, sank backward into the couch cushions, and replied, "Oh, Pete. You have been married such a short time that you apparently haven't yet caught on to the fact that women often can communicate with each other through hand gestures, facial expressions, and other body language. While you have been staring at your book or at Augie, we three Jane Marples. . . . Sorry, Ellie, I can't think of a young female detective—oh, wait. How about Kinsey Milhone for you? ANYWAY—we three female detectives have reached a unanimous opinion. Ask those two tamed tough guys there who have been married for more than twenty-five years apiece."

Nods of affirmation from Augie and me confirmed the validity of Mary Alice's statement, and Pete gave up. "Obviously I have MUCH to learn about many subjects—Faulkner, French detective families, females, particularly females—so I concede the point. Now, ladies: what is this theory, the one conceptualized and shared by empathic feminine telepathy?"

Julianna whistled and gave Pete a look of mock admiration before she turned toward Pete's wife. "Elegant diction coming from the mouth of a mere assistant professor, right, Ellie? Coach E, you tell these dudes our solution, okay?"

"Certainly, Mayor, I'll be happy to. In short, the furniture dealer has the hots—the BIGTIME HOTS—for Lena Grove."

Pete flopped backward as if he had been hit in the chest by a rifle shot. Staggering while he attempted to regain his balance, Pete grabbed hold of the rounded top of a nearby dining room chair, steadied himself, stared at his wife in astonishment, and shouted, "What? He WHAT? Oh, bullsh. . . . I mean, bull roar, Ellie. You mean to tell me—us—that this narrator is sweet on Lena? You say that he is drooling for her body? Huh? How can that be?"

During Pete's tirade the three women had calmly watched the slapstick routine, subtly shaking their heads in wonderment at this display of masculine naiveté. I felt compelled to defend my fellow man-child.

"Don't feel completely alienated, Pete. I have read this chapter several times now, and this interpretation certainly has never occurred to my dim brain, drowned as it seems to be in pints of cloying testosterone. But I can discern that Augie must have come up with this solution a long time ago."

Our ratiocinist had been observing the actions of his five fellow investigators, and with a calm nod he again took charge of the proceedings. "Yes, you are correct, Speck. Once I decided that I should consider the source of the derogatory commentary on Byron, I began to notice a pattern of parallel favorable words from F. D.'s mouth concerning Lena. Remember, please, that F. D. is telling this comic tale to his wife as they lie in bed together, in the dark, following an episode of conjugal sex. This latter-day, poor-man's Odysseus is smug with the satisfaction of his physical reunion with his own Mississippi Penelope. Look on page four-ninety-nine: *'I just showed you once. You aint ready to be showed again, are you?'* Probably he is not even aware just how much he has grown to admire Lena. I believe that his fondness for Lena is not consciously apparent to him but reveals itself only in the zesty diction of his traveling salesman's story."

Ellie now took her turn. "You are exactly right, Captain Dupree. As you read us those quotations earlier, it became apparent to us three sitting here on the couch that F. D. does not himself know just how extensively he brags about Lena while he deliberately dumps unwarranted abuse on poor Byron."

Augie again picked up his legal pad. "Here are my notes on this theory. Let's see . . . ahem. At the time that the furniture dealer recounts his travel story, the man is still so strongly attracted to the beauty and character of Lena Grove that, inadvertently and probably temporarily, he has become infatuated with her. Obviously, he never openly avows to his wife his nascent crush on Lena, but his comments about his recent female acquaintance reveal, subtly and mostly unconsciously on his part, his uncommon admiration for her." Raising his eyes and locking them on Pete's face, Augie firmly stated, "F. D.'s pervasive bias, then, Pete, the unconscious attitude that powerfully shapes all of his observations and assumptions, is, in a word, INFATUATION."

Mary Alice waved her left hand and jumped into the conversation. "That's an accurate term for F. D.'s feelings, dear. Presumably F. D. loves his wife and is faithful to her—the final chapter presents no evidence to the contrary—but as he tells her his story he still tingles emotionally from a brief episode of puppy love for a young, attractive woman. Crushes like F. D.'s on Lena are a not uncommon affliction besetting many married men. Right, fellows?"

Silence—a tense, total absence of sound—greeted Mary Alice's confrontational question. Unable to allow any auditory void to persist for long, even a perilous one such as this, I bleated, "We plead the Fifth Amendment on this question and on all other unconstitutional invasions of our sanctuaries of male fantasy. Shall we now move on with this inquiry—PLEASE?"

Augie recrossed his legs, hurriedly replaced his legal pads with a note card taken from a stack on the coffee table, and followed my interrogatory with verbiage of his own. "Harrumph. Yes, let's continue. Good idea, Speck." He held the note card in front of his reading glasses and spoke rapidly. "F. D.'s admiration for Lena is implied throughout his narrative, but one specific passage contains the most persuasive evidence that his esteem for her has become at least an embryonic fondness. As the narrator describes Byron's bumbling attempt to have sex with Lena, he claims that, as a witness, he was worried about whether he should attempt to become Lena's rescuer or should simply remain uninvolved. Quoting here: '"But I ought not to worried. I ought to have known that from the first look I taken at her and him,"' end of quotation. Everyone look on page five-oh-three, please. Ladies, again I especially seek your help with the interpretation of a key passage. What is your opinion of the wife's motive as she makes the following statement: quoting here, '*I reckon the reason you knew you never had to worry was that you had already found out just what she would do in a case like that* the wife says,' end of quotation?"

Mary Alice, Ellie, and Julianna all looked at each other, and Ellie said, "Mayor Double-You, tell these hard-headed men what you are thinking."

"Certainly, Ellie, I will be glad to," my dear wife replied, with a brisk bobbing of her carefully coifed hairdo. "The wife, who has been patiently listening to her longwinded husband's drawn-out story, finally becomes irritated by his string of compliments devoted to Lena and by his tone of superiority toward Byron, and she interrupts his prattling with this sarcastic challenge. In other words, she is revealing to him that she certainly knows what may have been on his mind when he was in the company of Lena and Byron. F. D.'s thoughts could be summarized in this way: 'Hmmm. I wonder how this babe would look unclothed and in the sack awaiting my virile presence?'"

"Right, Julianna, right," yelped Ellie. "That is exactly the thought that she is communicating to her loudmouthed husband."

"Wait, wait a minute, please," entreated Pete, waving his left arm in a frantic gesture of alarm. "Are you saying that she actually thinks her husband has tried to get Lena to roll in the hay with him?"

"No, no, Mister Dumb and Dumber," groaned Ellie, who turned with rolling eyes to her couch companions. "I apologize for the blocked cranial synapses of my dear hubby, girls. Give me a few more years, and I will train him to think with more than one brain cell at a time." She then returned her gaze to her crestfallen mate and gently said, "Pete, the wife assumes that her husband likely made no overt move on Lena Grove. But she is also covering all of her bases with her shrewd statement. She is warning him that he had better be disclosing the full truth about his adventures with Lena during the journey."

Mary Alice touched Ellie on the arm and politely interrupted. "And the wife, with the barbed query beginning 'I reckon,' is also communicating to F. D. her inference that he has revealed more information than he realizes about his hidden thoughts concerning Lena—his secret fantasies about this young babe, who obviously is no virgin."

Staring intently at the novel, Pete suddenly blurted, "By God, you girls are right. Look on five-oh-three at F. D.'s response. '*Sho* the husband says. *I didn't aim for you to find that out. Yes, sir. I thought I had covered my tracks this time,*' end of quotation. In this startled retort I now sense a false bravado. F. D. actually reveals that his wife has truly surprised him with her perception, her reading of the thoughts that are not fully formed even in his own consciousness. Yeah. . . . During his time with Lena and Byron he thought lasciviously about Lena, buried his fantasies in a supposedly safe mental compartment, and now has accidentally let them leak out. His wife catches on, because without being aware of what he is doing, he blabs on and on about Lena. . . . Yeah, yeah." Setting the novel on a handy shelf and then steadily rubbing his hands together, Pete started his rambling amble once again.

Augie announced, "Let me conclude this part of our inquiry. Significantly, with her warning now effectively delivered, the wife lets her blustering husband off the hook with these words: '*Well, go on. What happened?*' Although she was happy earlier to match her garrulous mate's sexual requests—look at page four-ninety-nine at her words '*I reckon I dont mind if you dont*'—she has by now grown understandably testy with his hymn of praise to Lena. Folks, I came across one critic who asserts that the wife is only teasing her husband here. What do you think?"

"Teasing? No, it's more than that innocent act," replied Julianna. "She is subtly but unmistakably putting him on warning. Here is the message that she is communicating to him: I know that you had secret thoughts about taking Lena to the sack, and that's okay, because you didn't actually try to bed her. But quit yapping about Lena so much, especially when you have just had your lustful way with me and seem to want to again. Your chance to score again, Buster, depends on how soon you stop being a one-song Lena-my-love bore."

"Yea verily, my sister! Right on! Righteous statement, Mayor Julianna!"

Ellie arose quickly, raised both of her arms, and bestowed a double high-five on the awaiting palms of the triumphantly smiling Julianna. As she plopped back onto the couch, Ellie beamed at Augie and asked, "How are we girls doing so far as amateur detectives, Monsieur Dupin?"

Augie smiled graciously and replied, "Better than the published commentary on LNA, Miss Ellie, at least the ones whose remarks I have been able to unearth. I just mentioned that 'tease' comment, and . . . here . . . let me look again at my notes." Up legal pad; Augie scoped his scribblings. "Apparently the critics of LNA accept the furniture dealer's disparaging words about Byron as truth. None of them takes exception to the speaker's vigorous and snide denunciation of him. One Faulkner scholar does lament that Byron appears to be, quoting here, 'insignificant' and 'puppetlike,' end of quotations, in this final chapter, but the scholar fails to point out that such a startling change in Byron's character is brought about largely by the narrator's slanted commentary about him rather than entirely by Byron's own actions. Another critic objects to the, quoting here, 'cuteness,' end of quotation, and the sniggering tone of the novel's final chapter, but this critic fails to attribute this objectionable tone to F. D.'s all-consuming bias, his infatuation with Lena.

"Critics Brooks, Nash, and Hoag do help us out significantly by stressing the links which the furniture repairer and dealer forges between Chapter Twenty-One and the preceding chapters in the novel. Brooks nominates the man as one of several spokesmen for the community. Nash views him as Faulkner's way of ending the book with echoes of, quoting here, 'sentiment, humor, and poignancy,' end of quotation, all qualities of tone which are important in certain earlier chapters. And Hoag stresses the, quotation, 'underlying parallels and contrasts,' end of quotation, which F. D. develops between the novel's final passages concerning Lena and Byron and those focusing on Christmas and Hightower. Another critic claims that the final chapter seems to be, quoting here, 'tacked on' and 'foreign to much of the text,' end of quotations. But I believe that at least one other strong linkage exists between the furniture dealer and some earlier characters and modes of narration in the novel."

Augie paused and held out both palms in a gesture of placation. "Patient friends, I would like to cover only one more major point, and then we can wrap up this investigation before Christmas Eve itself arrives unbeknownst to us jabberers—to me primarily, I of course refer. ANYHOW—with this final mode of inquiry I will again appreciate knowing the insights of the Feminine Brigade. Please allow me to refer to my notes again, and I will call for help from our highly capable wives in a few minutes. Satisfactory with everyone?"

No dissenter voiced an objection, and Augie began the disclosure of his final interpretive argument. "In several strategic places within LNA Faulkner employs a first-person narrator who possesses only a partial awareness of crucial facts or who may be burdened with some sort of distorting prejudice. These speakers always disclose their thoughts and opinions to another character in the novel. Byron himself serves as one such narrator, conversing at length with Gail Hightower in the bulk of Chapter Four. Byron here explains his own highly personal decision to serve as protector of Lena and also pieces together the bits of information he has picked up around Jefferson concerning three important occurrences: the discovery of Joanna Burden's corpse; the arrest of Lucas Burch; and Burch's indictment of Joe Christmas as, quoting here, 'nigger.'

"Another first-person narrator appears in Chapter Fourteen, a Black messenger from a rural church who informs the sheriff of the perplexing and violent appearance of Joe Christmas at a worship service. Mrs. Hines, Byron Bunch again, and the despicable Eupheus Hines alternate as speakers in part of Chapter Sixteen, collectively disclosing to the increasingly horrified Hightower some of the sordid details of the conception, birth, and early life of Joe Christmas. The closest parallel in mode of narration to the furniture dealer is Gavin Stevens, who presents to his professor friend in Chapter Nineteen a deceptive mixture of fact—the observed actions of Mrs. Hines at the jail and courthouse and of

Christmas when he attempts to escape—and racist speculation—ascribing parts of Christmas's behavior to either, quoting here, 'white' or 'black blood,' end of quotation. Like Stevens, the furniture dealer also merges credible observation with dubious opinion, the latter becoming especially significant in his depiction of Byron as, in Pete's words, a wimpish dunderhead.

"The primary achievement of Faulkner's use of the biased furniture dealer/narrator is the resulting challenge to readers to continue to search for the multiple meanings of this complex novel. All of Faulkner's first-person narrators in LNA, and especially Gavin Stevens and F. D.—and here I quote from the critic Irving Howe—'draw the reader[s] into a more direct and perilous relation to the happenings of the story' and make them 'active collaborators in the working out of the Yoknapatawpha saga,' end of quotations. At the end of LNA Lena and Byron continue to travel, and readers must also continue to try to interpret the actions of key characters, especially when such actions are only partially disclosed or prejudicially presented. As Ronald Wesley Hoag states, 'The novel thus ends without stopping, in motion and dialectic contention, true to the dance of life,' end of quotation. One example should demonstrate the success of Faulkner's implicit challenge to readers to remain actively involved in the search for meanings in LNA."

Augie paused for a sip of his praline liqueur, and Mary Alice offered everyone else refills on liquid refreshments. Our hostess soon filled three cups with fresh chicory coffee and two small glasses with Swiss Cherry Chocolate liqueur, and we all settled down for Augie's final comments and queries. "The smitten furniture dealer takes great delight in telling his wife of Byron's failure to impose himself sexually upon Lena, that 'goodlooking country gal.' Our biased narrator floats two hypotheses concerning Lena's motives for rejecting Byron, and then F. D. settles on his preferred conclusion. First, he speculates that Lena might have been teasing Byron, stringing him along so that she can exploit his dog-like devotion. Quoting here from page five-oh-two: '"Maybe she knew he had just gone off by himself to get himself worked up good to what she might have been advising him to do all the time, herself, without saying it in out and out words, which a lady naturally couldn't do; not even a lady with a Saturday night family,'" end of quotation. But then F. D. decides not to depict Lena as a selfish flirt. Quoting from the same page, '"Only I don't reckon that was it either,'" end of quotation. His second hypothesis is more plausible. Also on five-oh-two, '"Or maybe the time and place didn't suit her, let alone a audience,'" end of quotation. Certainly no 'lady' would want to surrender herself romantically to any earnest suitor while a witness is reposing a few feet away, emitting what F. D. terms a '"fetched . . . snore or two'"—see the same page. F. D. finally decides, of course, that Lena rejects Byron because she considers him to be the world's worst excuse for a romantic partner, quoting here from page five-oh-three, a *'durn little cuss [who] looked like he had reached the point where he could bust out crying like another baby,'* end of quotation. Given his own fondness for Lena, F. D. understandably portrays his rival Byron as the most inept Romeo whom he has ever encountered.

"We readers of LNA are challenged to comb carefully through the scattered facts that F. D. presents in Chapter Twenty-One and also to recall earlier episodes in the novel in order to draw the most logical conclusion for Lena's rejection of Byron, an interpretation not included in the direct reiteration by the vagabond furniture man to his wife during their pillow talk. The narrator does disclose that Lena eases Byron's embarrassment as he rejoins the pilgrimage by telling him—look on page five-oh-six—""'Aint nobody never said for you to quit,"" end of quotation. Moreover, earlier in the novel Hightower has concluded that Lena will eventually marry Byron; see page four-oh-six. And on page four-twelve Lena cries 'with a patient and hopeless abjectness' while she complains openly to Hightower that Byron, quotation, '"is already gone. I will never see him again,'" end of quotation."

Augie looked up from his notes. "We can plausibly infer from Lena's own comments that Byron at least has a decent chance in the future to win Lena's hand in marriage. Here I ask you three female detectives for some more opinions. Can you piece together these clues and perhaps others that I may have overlooked and then supply our group with your keen insights? The principal question before us can be stated as follows. Why does Lena spurn Byron's romantic advances that night in the back of F. D.'s truck?"

Mary Alice was the first to respond. "Augie, just a couple of minutes ago you mentioned two theories that F. D.—'floats' was your word, I believe—that F. D. floats before he decides that Byron is an absolute loser as a lover boy. The second of those theories, the one about time and place. Could you repeat that one?"

"Certainly, dear," replied C. A. Dupin V, shuffling rapidly through the pages of his legal pad. "Ah, here we are. F. D. speculates to his wife, '"Or maybe the time and place didn't suit her, let alone a audience"'—from page five-oh-two."

"Thanks, honey," said Mary Alice, nodding as she consulted the Dupree copy of LNA. "As you explained earlier, the parked furniture truck as a potential seduction spot offers little privacy, since F. D. reclines on a blanket nearby. But let's also remember that Lena has already experienced sex outside of marriage, with the result that we all know about—her little bundle of joy. On foot and by wagon she pursues Lucas Burch—alias Joe Brown—across several counties and parts of two states, she delivers a son out of wedlock, and she confronts Burch-Brown with their baby only to have him abandon mother and child again. My point? I believe that Lena will be glad to have sex with Byron eventually, but only on her terms—within the bonds of marriage, in an actual bed with only Lena and Byron present, and possibly with the assistance of some form of birth control, since I would be surprised if she is ready to bear another child just yet."

Bouncing with excitement on the central cushion of the couch, Ellie began to speak immediately upon the cessation of her soul sister's final syllable. "Yes, yes, Mary Alice. You're right, I believe, and let me add a thought to your comments." Holding herself regally erect on the edge of her cushion, with her hands placed firmly on her tightly pressed knees, the Coach looked at Augie and said, "Captain, you referred to the advantage we readers have over F. D. in that we have access to earlier evidence in the novel. Pete, toss me our copy of LNA."

WHOOSH! SPLAT! Literary forward pass complete for a three-yard gain. Ellie hurriedly flipped pages, stopped, scanned a page rapidly, and shouted, "Aha!" Everybody look on page eighty-two. I thought I remembered a relevant passage that I came across when I was reading the novel last week, a chapter or two at a time whenever I could sneak a few minutes of Faulkner fun into my days or nights."

Pete moved to a spot next to my armchair and shared a look at my copy of LNA. Ellie stated, "The pronoun 'He' in this partial sentence refers to Gail Hightower, in whom Byron often confides and therefore the only other person who logically might possess this kind of private information. I quote: 'He remembers only that Byron is still young and has led a life of celibacy and hard labor. . . .' Now go back to page forty-seven. Quoting again, 'If there had been love once, man or woman would have said that Byron Bunch had forgotten her." Okay. My point is that Byron Bunch is still a virgin, and Lena probably knows that fact, or at least strongly suspects it. Understandably Lena will want to introduce the totally inexperienced Byron to the joys of sex only in the right place—a private one—and at the right time—presumably after they are married. As Mary Alice just pointed out, Lena has already had sex with an experienced lover—Lucas Burch—and if she is fated to have Byron as the next waltz partner on her dance card, then SHE, and only she, will determine the time, place, and circumstances for the grand deflowering of the Bunch man."

Augie commented, "Excellent points, both of you. Ellie, as you were talking I found a comment by a critic that supports your interpretation. Let me read from this note card. Hugh Ruppersburg agrees with you when he writes, 'Lena would probably be Byron's first lover.' You have proven to my satisfaction that Ruppersburg's adverb 'probably' should be changed to 'assuredly.'"

Julianna then waved her hand and announced, "My turn to play, kiddies." She turned to her right. "Girls, you are both directly on target, and I want to add another observation that just occurred to me as I was listening to your commentary. Let me suggest one more reason why Lena rejects Byron's fumbling advances during that fateful night as she dozes with her baby on the blankets in the back of F. D.'s truck. Everybody please take note of the chronology of the novel. On page four-ninety-six, we learn that Lena's baby is three weeks old. So we can assume that Lena, Byron, and the baby leave Jefferson and begin their journey toward southwestern Tennessee as soon as Lena believes that she and the wee one are strong enough to travel. Look now . . . three weeks. . . ."

Pete stared with open mouth at Julianna. "I'm not grasping your meaning, Mayor Double-You. What is so important about these references to a time period of three weeks?"

Julianna quickly looked at her couch companions, acknowledged with eye contact and head bobs that all three women functioned on the same mental wave length, surveyed Augie and me in search of similar unspoken assurances (which she duly received). cleared her throat, and replied in a gentle tone to the perplexed professor. "Pete, can you tell us if F. D. and his wife have any children?"

Pete walked to the couch, received from Ellie's outstretched hand the Prefont edition of LNA, flipped to the final chapter, hurriedly scanned several pages, and said without taking his eyes from the book, "I don't remember a reference to children. Let's see. . . . Is there any mention of kids?"

Julianna replied, "No, Pete, not a specific reference. However, on four-ninety-six"—rustle, rustle, rustle of pages—"F. D. reveals that he possesses some impressive knowledge of babies when he says to Lena, '"You aint had that chap no eight weeks. . . . Not if I know color."' F. D. means that the baby's reddish skin color reveals an age less than eight weeks, the length of time that Lena says she has been traveling away from Alabama. F. D. and his wife may be parents, or he may have picked up this unusual information from friends or from within his own extended family. We cannot tell if Mrs. F. D. has ever given birth to a child. If she had, then F. D. should know. . . ."

Julianna ceased talking, shot a glance at Mary Alice, and glared at Augie and me. "Help me out here, proud long-married citizens of middle age. How can I phrase this concept delicately? Uhh. . . ."

Augie intervened. "Let's all remember that we know F. D. and his wife are either young or middle-aged. Look on page four-ninety-four: 'he and his wife are not old either.' I would guess that they are closer to the age of Byron—thirty-five—than to that of Lena—twenty-one. Despite F. D.'s presumed maturity, the man does definitely overlook an important fact about Lena here. Shall I continue, Julianna?"

Detective Dupin V was rescued from the necessity of pursuing this delicate subject by a loud exclamation of "AW, MAN! OF COURSE! Finally I get the picture. Color me clueless again, fellow investigators." Pete walked rapidly to and fro in the open spaces of the den, at several intervals barely avoiding collisions with tables, chairs, and walls. "Lena delivered her baby only three weeks before this night when she beds down in the back of F. D.'s truck. She is not physically ready to participate in sex again. Right?"

Julianna stood, quickly stepped across the room to a position directly in front of Pete, and shook the pedagogue's extended paw. "Very good, Pete, very good. You said it well. Please remember that Lena on this night would still be recovering from the rigors of her first childbirth. And look at the conditions under which she delivers her little boy. No doctor is present, or even a midwife or a nurse. Hightower ably fills in, of course, and Mrs. Hines attends to some of Lena's basic needs for water and nourishment, but Lena bears the child with no trained medical assistance available. And she certainly is not an obstetrics patient in Johns Hopkins Hospital or at the Mayo Clinic, either. She delivers the babe while lying on a cot in the dilapidated cabin behind Joanna Burden's burned-out house."

I cleared my throat and spoke up for the first time in many moments. "Let me present a medical opinion here, one that I remember from my days as a general intern. Sexual intercourse is theoretically possible for a woman in Lena's postpartum condition but understandably would not be an appealing prospect for her."

Julianna bestowed upon me a warm look of gratitude. "Thank you, sweetheart. You did pay attention to the lectures of your attending physicians at University Hospital, I am glad to see. Pete, our friend the furniture dealer may not be aware from personal experience in his own marriage that in such circumstances three weeks would be a perilously short time to elapse after childbirth before a woman's resumption of sexual relations. Lena clearly refers to her obstetric condition when she warns Byron that he, quoting here, '"might have woke the baby, too."' Look on five-oh-three."

Augie spoke up. "Please permit me to add this observation, Julianna. F. D. appears shrewd enough to draw the correct conclusion, but he is still so smitten with Lena that he prefers to present Byron as a total dunce and not to realize that Lena likely wants to have sex with NO man at this particular time in her life. So once again F. D.'s pervasive bias distorts his thought processes and consequently the content of his narration."

Everyone except Pete took a seat again, and Augie held his left hand, palm inward, at eye level as he used his right index finger to enumerate the major points of his summary. "Just as Faulkner has demanded, we have all become active participants in solving this part of the final chapter's comic mystery. Mary Alice, Ellie, and Julianna have assembled various clues and, assisted by Pete and Speck, have provided us with the logical combination of reasons for Lena's denial of Byron's romantic overtures. First is her understandable reluctance to make her initial trysting place with virginal Byron the housed-in cargo space of a truck owned by a snoopy witness pretending to be asleep nearby. Reason number two is the medical reality of her postpartum physical condition, including her awareness that pregnancy may be unlikely at this time but is still biologically possible. And third is a theory suggested by F. D. himself on the final two pages of the novel, five-oh-six and five-oh-seven. The key sentence reads as follows: "'And so I think she had just made up her mind to travel a little further and see as much as she could, since I reckon she knew that when she settled down this time, it would likely be for the rest of her life.'"

"In summary, dear friends, we can now all be aware that Lena and Byron are last observed in LNA by a raconteur whose commentary, witty and incisive as it may be, makes up only a part of the truth. For the remainder of that truthful picture, we must depend upon our own skills as literary detectives so that we can supplement F. D.'s highly entertaining but biased narrative with our own more fully informed interpretations. If we do, perhaps we can sense some of the same pure pleasure of discovery expressed by Lena Grove in the novel's closing words as she basks in the spontaneous joys resulting from her travels. On page five-oh-seven: '"My, my. A body does get around. Here we aint been coming from Alabama but two months, and now it's already Tennessee."'"

Augie stood and spread his arms. "Kind compatriots, we have been investigating William Faulkner's novels for about nine months now. We have 'gotten around' in Mister Bill's books far more rewardingly than I could ever have imagined that we would, and now I for one believe that, my, my, it is time for us to rest from our literary indulgences. Let the Christmas celebration begin!"

Only two hours later, when the rushes of adrenaline fully subsided and our heartbeats had returned to their regular rates, did Julianna and I gain the opportunity to interrogate the participants in the evening's joyous conspiracy and to learn how they all managed to surprise Doc and Mayor Watkins so totally. It seems that a long-distance phone call reached the Crocodile plantation home of our longtime friends the Uehgandts, and a brave journey by four-wheel-drive truck to the Memphis airport allowed George Uehgandt and Boris Schuller to pick up the most coveted present on the Watkins wish list for this particular Christmas and to bring this present safely over slushy, sometimes icy roads back to Murryville. Eventually Julianna and I learned that the Duprees and the Prefonts were also major players in the conspiracy, with George secretly contacting Augie so that the Crocodile Express could make its clandestine delivery to the proper address in Murryville. We never did learn all of the details of the scheme, but no matter. The careful planning achieved its intended result: absolute, exhilarating, unalloyed joy. For just as Augie invoked with his final spoken words the true beginning of the Christmas season, George and Boris together stepped out of the Duprees' kitchen and into the den, with huge grins spread across their faces. Later I would swear that the ends of Boris's moustache at that instant were curling and uncurling. These two overcoated giants gradually moved apart to reveal standing behind them the petite, teary-faced, pixie-haired, heavily ski-jacketed-and-capped shouter of the sweetest words that I heard that entire holiday season: "My, my. A body does get around. Here I ain't been in Europe but eighteen months, and now it's already Murryville. Mother! Dad! I'M HOME! WHOOOPEEE!"

Epilogue

Late July, 1996

Seven months have passed since that Christmas blessing arrived for Julianna and me, and Allison now resides in Graz, Austria, where she pursues graduate studies in German literature. Boris Schuller, who returned to his native country when he completed his appointment at Moffatt, recommended our daughter for admission to the University of Graz, and he is now serving as A. C.'s gracious tour guide and surrogate papa while she lives in Austria. George and Karen Uehgandt plan to fly to Europe in October, once the soybeans, rice, and cotton have been fully harvested in Crocodile, and a visit to Graz appears at the top of their itinerary.

During 1996 Pete has been working steadily on preparations of prospective Faulkner articles. His essay on the Memphis lawyer in *Sanctuary* will appear next spring in a prestigious journal published in western Illinois, and he plans to send the commentary on niece Quentin's second-story job in TSAF to Errol Tedford in hopes that the *Journal of the Arkansas Literary Association* will accept it. In May, while at Pete's request I was proofreading his draft of the burglary essay, I decided that straightforward academic prose cannot capture the thrill of the chase or the sheer pleasure of discovery that developed out of these six investigations by Augie, Pete, and me own humble self. So with the permission of my colleagues I have been spending the past two weeks—some of it vacation time—talking into my Dictaphone, working from notes, outlines, memory, and consultations with my friends the detective and the professor, in an attempt to reconstruct faithfully and accurately our collaborative adventures in literary sleuthing. Our three noble and long-suffering wives, each of whom continues to flourish in her chosen profession, have also supplied many helpful details to my erratic attempts at piecing together a summary of our analytical Faulkner readings, as ably led by Cesar Auguste Dupin V.

May Ellen Adair, my stalwart office manager, has promised to transcribe these rambling words, and perhaps a publishable manuscript may eventually emerge. Augie is aware that news of his linkage to the ratiocinist made immortal by Edgar Allan Poe may bring unwanted intrusions into the cherished private life of the couple Dupree, but Augie has never kept his Dupin heritage a secret, avoiding only any exploitation of it. Captain Dupree has decided to refer any future media inquiries to Turner Stoneman of the *Murryville Messenger,* and Pete has agreed to converse or correspond with Poe or Faulkner scholars who may come a-calling. If this manuscript does find its way into print, my fondest wish is that, to paraphrase the words of the Mississippi Master himself, I hope you will read it and tell your friends and I hope they will read it too.

Notes

Chapter One

Page 39   Poe scholar Thomas Ollive Mabbott has provided the most useful commentary on Poe's choice of the name "Dupin" for the keenly intellectual solver of puzzling crimes. Poe, *Collected Works* II, 524-525.

Pages 39-42   In the matter of the fictional or actual existence of the character Cesar Auguste Dupin, the reader is kindly requested to engage in a willing suspension of disbelief as a necessary part of this extended experiment in blending literary criticism into the framework of a narrative.

Page 40   Siegel (8) points out the absence of the word "detective" in Poe's three seminal detective stories. Other scholars who provide helpful insights into Poe's inspired creation of Dupin are Bittner (155), Symons (222-225), Quinn (310-311), Weiner (33-37), Panek (12-13), Gilbert (xii-xv), and Crisman (215-229).

Page 42   "The Murders in the Rue Morgue," Mabbott edition, II 531.

Page 43   "The Mystery of Marie Roget," Mabbott edition, III 725.

Chapter Two

Page 55   Cleanth Brooks (118) attributes this insight to Andre Malraux: "*Sanctuary* is not only a gangster novel; it is, as Andre Malraux has suggested, something of a detective novel, in that the meaning of certain events is not revealed until the end, and the author builds suspense, complicates his plot, and presents the reader with sudden and surprising developments."

Page 55   Nishiyama 235.

Page 56   Wilson 443.

Page 58   Of the several analyses of the actual sequence of events in *Sanctuary*, the most complete and cogent appears in Brooks's *William Faulkner: The Yoknapatawpha Country*, 118-127 and 387-391. In a collection of critical essays on the novel, *Twentieth Century Interpretations of "Sanctuary,"* J. Douglas Canfield calls an attempt to learn the facts of the plot a "great red herring of criticism on this novel. . ." (5). But interest in the subject has always been high. Virtually every chapter on this novel in the books of criticism of Faulkner's works at least touches upon the facts of the plot, and some go into the subject in great detail, for example Materalli (145-148). In addition, articles continue to appear that attempt to trace what actually happens in the novel: see Brown (1-13), Nishiyama (235-243), Urgo (435-444), and Boon (40-49).

Page 59   Parker 82.

Page 59   Fiedler 88.

Jay Watson writes that "the 'Memphis jew lawyer' who hovers behind the scenes of the Goodwin trial is a silent, shadowy puppetmaster impervious to legal or moral strictures, a further, ominous reminder of the law's indifference to, and effacement of, individuals in *Sanctuary*" (76).

Pages 62-63   Brooks 125-126.
              Pilkington 132.

Page 64   Volpe 383-387.

Page 69   Brooks 387-391.

Page 70   *"Sanctuary": A Concordance to the Novel* (ed. Polk) lists only these two appearances of the word "spine" in the entire text of *Sanctuary* (468).

Page 73   Dr. Paul L. Weygandt, Sr., orthopedic surgeon, has been kind enough to furnish this explanation concerning the act of sitting on the spine.

Chapter Three

Page 123   Gidley 97, 99.

Pages 123-124   Blotner 460, 234, 432, 627, 545.

Page 125   Brodsky 387.

Page 129   Vickery 44, Williams 87.

Page 138   "Interviews in Japan" 146.
              Faulkner in the University 84.
              "Interview with Cynthia Grenier" 225.

Page 143   In the "Compson Appendix" Faulkner presents the construction history of the house (227). Critic Arthur Kinney provides a photograph of the Thompson-Chandler house in Oxford, an edifice generally acknowledged by Faulkner family members and Faulkner scholars to be the prototype for the Compson house (23). In this picture the second-story windows have ledges that appear to be at least fifteen feet from the ground.

Page 144   "Appendix" 224.

Page 145   Cowley 36.
"Appendix" 235.

Page 145   Not only was Faulkner unconcerned about the inconsistencies between the 1929 edition of the novel and the material in the "Appendix," but also he wanted very much to add the new information about the Compsons to all subsequent printings of the novel. In a letter (dated February 4, 1946) to his editor at Random House, Faulkner vigorously advocated that future editions of TSAF should include the "Appendix" and that the new Compson material should be printed at the very beginning of the volume:

> When you reprint THE SOUND AND THE FURY, I have a new section to go with it. I should have written this new section when I wrote the book itself, but I never thought of it until Malcolm Cowley let me help him getting together his portable Faulkner volume that Viking has.
>
> By all means include this in the reprint. When you read it, you will see how it is the key to the whole book, and after reading it, the 4 sections as they stand now fall into clarity and place. . . . When you issue the book, print the sections in this order, print this appendix first, and title it APPENDIX. This will be anachronic

but no more than the other sections. . . . Be sure and print the appendix *first*. . . . (Faulkner, *Selected Letters* 220-221; emphasis Faulkner's).

Random House acceded to Faulkner's wishes, and in 1946 the "Compson Appendix" appeared at the beginning of the "Modern Library double volume of *The Sound and the Fury* and *As I Lay Dying* which contained, on the title page, the misleading statement 'With A New Appendix As A Forward By The Author'" (Dickerson 253). When the Vintage paperback reissue of the 1929 text of the novel came out in 1962, the "Appendix" was moved to the end of the volume (Dickerson 253). In 1984, when textual scholar Noel Polk established the Corrected Text of *The Sound and the Fury*, he did not include the "Appendix" as a part of the novel proper.

Page 145   "Appendix" 228, 236.

Page 146   Cowley 90, 45-46.

Pages 146, 147, 149, 150   "Appendix" 235.

Page 151   Linscott 38.
The Mansion 322.
"Interview with Cynthia Grenier" 222.
"Interview with Jean Stein Vanden Heuvel" 244-245.

Page 151   *Faulkner in the University* 6.

Because Faulkner was always so devoted to Caddy, it is logical to assume that he would transfer some of his ardor to Quentin, her daughter, especially since both females share the stigma of becoming victims of the treachery of Jason. Within the novel itself Faulkner establishes very early a link between Caddy and Quentin during Benjy's encounter with "*Miss Quentin and her beau in the swing yonder*" (Luster's words), an event occurring on April 7, 1928, but one that causes Benjy to move immediately in his mind to a strikingly similar incident that involves Caddy and a suitor named Charlie as they neck in the same swing when Caddy is approximately fourteen (46-48). The characteristic of age provides another parallel between Caddy and Quentin. Caddy is seventeen when she enters into the passionate love affair with Dalton Ames that leads to her eventual removal from her childhood home, and Quentin is seventeen when she takes the money from Jason and escapes from the same house. Critic David Minter stresses that the stories of Caddy and Quentin are really one continuing saga of sadness: "Deserted by her mother, Miss Quentin is left no one with whom to learn love, and so repeats her mother's dishonor and flight without knowing her tenderness. If in the story of Jason we observe the near-triumph of all that is repugnant, in the stories of Caddy and Miss Quentin we observe the degradation of all that is beautiful" (98).

Other parallels in the novel between Caddy and Quentin are more subtle. Faulkner disclosed to Jean Stein Vanden Heuvel that TSAF began with a mental picture: "I didn't realize at the time it was symbolical. The picture was of the muddy seat of a little girl's drawers in a pear tree where she could see through a window where her grandmother's funeral was taking place and report what was happening to her brothers on the ground below" (245). Critics Gladys Miliner (71), Boyd Davis (28), and Mimi Reisel Gladstein (16) all point out various meanings of the structural and thematic connection in the novel between Caddy's climbing up a tree when she was seven years old and Quentin's climbing down a tree (possibly the same one) some thirty years later. As Miliner summarizes, "The girl Quentin is the obverse image of her mother. The story that began with the image of the girl Caddy climbing up the tree of knowledge ends with her daughter climbing down to escape with bitter knowledge" (71). David Williams discovers another discreet link between Caddy and Quentin (89). The symbolism of the muddy underwear that predicts Caddy's eventual promiscuity appears again in pieces of feminine clothing found by Jason in Quentin's room the morning after she has vanished: "On the floor lay a soiled undergarment of cheap silk a little too pink, from a half open bureau drawer dangled a single stocking" (TSAF 282).

Page 152   "Appendix" 235.

Chapter Four

Page 164   Samway 111-136.

Page 165   In the "Genealogy" that appears at the end of *Absalom, Absalom!*, under the heading "QUENTIN COMPSON," Faulkner states, "Died, Cambridge, Mass., 1910" (309). As early as 1936, when *Absalom, Absalom!* was published, Faulkner had remembered incorrectly that Quentin dies within Cambridge itself.

Page 166   Patrick Samway speculates that Faulkner visited Boston in the spring of 1918 (136), but Samway presents no evidence to support this theory. In a recently published edition of Faulkner's early letters, James G. Watson cogently argues that Faulkner actually made creative use of his extensive visits to another Ivy League city, New Haven, in 1918 and 1921: "Insistent attempts to demonstrate that by 1928 Faulkner knew Cambridge and Harvard well enough to write about it in detail have so far produced no hard evidence of his having been there. His letters from New Haven, conversely, testify to the extent of his imaginative extension of personal into fictional experience, and support the contrary view that Quentin's Harvard is Faulkner's Yale" (29).

Page 167   Lawrance Thompson (40), Melvin Backman (27), John Longley (42-43), and John Pilkington (65) all refer to the suicide bridge but do not mention its location as being either within Cambridge or outside the city. Joseph Blotner correctly identifies "a small town outside of Cambridge" (214) as the place in which Quentin spends part of June 2, but Blotner does not locate the bridge near this town.

Page 172   Samway 134.

Page 182   "Appendix" 229.

Page 182   Geffen 250.

Page 183   Brylowski 78, Matthews 56, Feldstein 4.

Page 184   Samway also states that "Today [1986], a small bronze plaque on the bridge commemorates this tragic event" (134). Cleanth Brooks presumably refers to the Anderson Bridge with this statement: "On one of the bridges spanning the Charles River in Cambridge, there is a small plaque commemorating Quentin's death on June 2, 1910. It was placed there several years ago by three admirers of *The Sound and the Fury* for whom Quentin's death in the river had become a real happening" (*First Encounters* 60).

By the summer of 1993, this plaque had disappeared from the Anderson Bridge. John Seiler, architect, Harvard professor, and resident of the Cambridge area, was gracious enough to scour the Anderson Bridge "from every angle" (as he relates in a letter), "even checking the parts of the bridge which are normally viewed only from the river." Seiler found no plaque with any references to Quentin Compson, TSAF, or William Faulkner. Just to be safe, Seiler journeyed to nine other bridges that span the Charles, all of them in the Boston-Cambridge area, and trained his experienced architect's eyes on them. He found no such plaque as described by Samway and Brooks. Seiler did notice that some faces of concrete panels on the Anderson Bridge appear to have been re-cemented, and he speculates that perhaps the plaque may have been removed from one of these faces in recent years.

Page 189   Thomas Monson, M. D., Professor of Medicine at the University of Arkansas for Medical Sciences, has been kind enough to furnish this expert information.

Page 192   Volpe 377.

Chapter Five

Page 209   Olga Vickery asserts that the child must be Jewel, the son of Addie and Whitfield: "She consciously and deliberately gives Anse Dewey Dell to 'negative' Jewel and Vardaman to replace him (55). Sally R. Page (118) and Robert Kirk (50) agree with Vickery. Andre Bleikasten (*Faulkner's "As I Lay Dying"* 93), John Pilkington (107), and Donald Kartiganer ("Faulkner's Art of Repetition" 43), believe that Cash is the unnamed child. As Bleikasten concludes, "Dewey Dell was the child Addie gave her husband to 'negative' Jewel, Vardaman the one to replace Cash" (93). Richard Godden proposes that "the calculation has two answers: either Dewey Dell and Jewel are removed (Vardaman replacing them, to bring Anse's total to three—Cash, Darl, and Vardaman) or Dewey Dell and Vardaman together make up the sum of the princeless [sic] Jewel, who remains Addie's child" (112). And Joseph Gold decides that no specific child is represented in Addie's thinking: "Addie herself has calculated her child-production with devilish exactitude, 'giving' Anse Dewey Dell to negative Jewel and Vardaman 'to replace the child I [had] robbed him of,' that is the one he would have had, had Whitfield not taken his place" (66).

Page 234   Watkins and Dillingham conclude that Vardaman is six to eight years old at the time of the principal events of AILD (248). Since Dewey Dell is seventeen at this time, Vardaman is between nine and eleven years younger than Dewey Dell, meaning that Addie became pregnant with Vardaman some eight to ten years after she bore Dewey Dell. This chronology also agrees with the assessment of Patten (8).

Page 235   Hays 191.

Page 237   Bleikasten, Pilkington, and Kartiganer are all correct in naming Cash, although none of these critics provides the reasoning that led him to his conclusion.

Page 238   Sally R. Page 118.

Page 238   This definition appears in *The McGraw-Hill Dictionary of Physics and Mathematics* (501).
   Dr. Robert Eslinger, Fausett Distinguished Professor of Mathematics at Hendrix College, has been kind enough to furnish a very thorough explanation of the additive inverse.

Page 239   Bleikasten 93.

Page 249   Swiggart (113, 118), Page (121), and Williams (103) all refer to Jewel as Addie's favorite child. Brooks (*First Encounters* 81, 83) also calls Jewel her favorite child, although he judiciously avoids this description in *The*

Yoknapatawpha Country. Andre Bleikasten first states, "With Jewel, he [Cash] is Addie's favorite" (*Faulkner's "AILD"* 85), but later in the same book he claims that "Jewel is Addie's favorite" (92).

Page 249   Annas 88.

Page 251   Jewel's jealousy of Cash finds further expression in Cash's description of the family's preparation for the carrying of Addie's corpse in her coffin out of the house and into the wagon. Cash is justifiably concerned that the coffin "wont balance" (96); Jewel's response is to curse his oldest brother harshly: "Pick up! Pick up, goddamn your thick-nosed soul to hell, pick up!" (96). Thirty-nine pages farther on, Darl's narration in retrospect of Jewel's purchase of the horse affirms that Addie has special, but different, relationships with both Cash and Jewel. Addie knows that Jewel has purchased the horse partly as psychological compensation for his failure to possess all of her love: "'Jewel,' ma said, looking at him. 'I'll give — I'll give . . . give. . . .' Then she began to cry. She cried hard, not hiding her face. . ." (135). But it is Cash who first defends Jewel's right to purchase the horse: "'So I dont reckon that horse cost anybody anything except Jewel'" (135). And Cash knows how to comfort his mother in her distress: "'You go on to the house,' Cash said. 'This here ground is too wet for you. You go on, now.' She put her hands to her face then and after a while she went on, stumbling a little on the plow-marks" (135). During the trip to Jefferson, when the family tries to transport Addie in her coffin across the swollen river, Jewel continues to curse at Cash, even challenging his brother's courage: "'By God, if you're afraid to drive it over. . .'" (145). But Cash is unperturbed" "'We'll get it over,' he says" (145). Almost drowning in the process, he joins Jewel in trying mightily, but failing, to get Addie's body across.

Chapter Six

Page 274   The chronology of events in LNA is difficult to determine. Four of the most complete studies of this subject all conclude that the setting in time of the principal events appears to be August, 1932. See Hungerford (192), Meats (227), Fadiman (190), and Ruppersburg (305). Fadiman discusses in detail the numerous discrepancies of chronology resulting from Faulkner's revisions of the manuscript and points out, for example, that the actual age of Joe Christmas can never be determined with accuracy because of direct contradictions in dates of important events (53). Fadiman, Meats, and Ruppersburg all helpfully recommend that readers of the novel not be overly concerned with precise dates when examining Christmas's past.

Page 274   D'Avanzo explains that this unusual first name is probably an alternative form of "Euphues" and may have been chosen by Faulkner as an allusion to the principal character in several of John Lyly's Elizabethan works (101-106).

Page 275   "minor characters"—Pitavy, *Faulkner's "LNA"* 58.
            "subordinate villains"—Minter, *Twentieth Century Interpretations of "LNA"* 6.
            "sacrilegious"—Burroughs 35.
            Pilkington 146.
            Brooks, *First Encounters* 186.
            Moddelmog 22.

Page 276   *Faulkner in the University* 72, 118.

Page 277   Vickery 69.

Page 277   Ruppersburg 210, 212

Page 278   W. Dent Gitchel, Professor of Law at the University of Arkansas at Little Rock, was considerate enough to furnish this explanation of the Arkansas legal code.

Page 279   Blotner 301. Bleikasten (*Ink of Melancholy* 394) and Kartiganer ("'What I Chose to Be'" 302-303) concur with Blotner in pointing out how the innocent child Joe becomes the unwitting victim of Eupheus Hines.

Page 289   Melville 76.

Page 291   Cleanth Brooks lists these men as "the half-dozen of Faulkner's most accomplished villains" (*The Yoknapatawpha Country* 339). Other readers of Faulkner's fiction might nominate the cruelly manipulative L. Q. C. McCaslin of *The Bear* because of his sexual exploitation of the slave woman Eunice and his subsequent incest with their daughter Tomasina; or the squalid Grumby of *The Unvanquished,* a brigand who viciously murders the frail but plucky Rosa Millard and then tries unsuccessfully to kill her vengeful fifteen-year-old grandson, Bayard Sartoris, and his companion Ringo; or even Simon McEachern of LNA itself, the Calvinist farmer who adopts Joe and systematically tries to whip, beat, and pound fundamentalist religious doctrine and practices into the boy. But the consensus of Faulkner's leading critics ratifies Brooks's six choices.

Chapter Seven

Page 317   Nash 529.
          Hoag 684, 688, 675.

Brooks 74, 52, 73.

Page 326   Ruppersburg 302.

Page 327   Pitavy, *Faulkner's "LNA"* 35, 118.
            Berland 101.

Page 327   Brooks 73.
            Nash 531.
            Hoag 684.
            Clarke 103.

Page 329   Howe 838.
            Hoag 685.

Page 332   Ruppersburg 300.

Page 333   Ruppersburg helpfully explains that "The baby's reddish skin-color shows it to be much younger than eight weeks" (300).

Page 334   On page 439 of LNA Byron reveals his age to be thirty-five. On pages 4 and 5 of the novel we learn that when Lena is twelve years old she goes to Doane's Mill, Alabama, to live in the house of her brother McKinley, and eight years later she enters into the love affair with Lucas Burch that results in her pregnancy. Approximately one year later, accompanied by her baby, the furniture dealer, and Byron Bunch, she reaches southwest Tennessee.

Works Cited

Annas, Pamela, "The Carpenter of *As I Lay Dying*." *Notes on Mississippi Writers* 8 (1976): 84-99.

Backman, Melvin. *Faulkner: The Major Years*. Bloomington: Indiana UP, 1966.

Baum, Catherine B. "'The Beautiful One': Caddy Compson as Heroine of *The Sound and the Fury*." *Modern Fiction Studies* 13 (1967): 33-44.

Berland, Alywyn. *"Light in August": A Study in Black and White*. New York: Twayne, 1992.

Bittner, William. *Poe: A Biography*. Boston: Little, Brown, 1962.

Bleikasten, André. *Faulkner's "As I Lay Dying."* Revised Edition. Trans. Roger Little. Bloomington: Indiana UP, 1973.

-----. *The Ink of Melancholy*. Bloomington: Indiana UP, 1990.

Bloom, Harold, ed. *Caddy Compson*. New York: Chelsea, 1990.

Blotner, Joseph. *Faulkner: A Biography*. One-Volume Edition. New York: Random House, 1984.

Boon, Kevin A. "Temple Defiled: The Brainwashing of Temple Drake in Faulkner's *Sanctuary*." *The Faulkner Journal* 6 (1991): 33-50.

Brodsky, Louis Daniel. "Reflections on William Faulkner: An Interview with Albert I. Bezzerides." *Southern Review* 21 (1985): 376-403.

Brooks, Cleanth. *William Faulkner: First Encounters*. New Haven: Yale UP, 1983.

-----. *William Faulkner: The Yoknapatawpha Country*. New Haven: Yale UP, 1963.

Brown, Calvin. "*Sanctuary*: From Confrontation to Peaceful Void." *The Novels of William Faulkner*. Ed. R. G. Collins and K. A. McRobbie. Winnipeg: U of Manitoba P, 1973.

Brylowski, Walter. *Faulkner's Olympian Laugh.* Detroit: Wayne State UP, 1968.

Burroughs, Franklin G. "God the Father and Motherless Children: *Light in August.*" Pitavy's *Casebook* 35-51.

Canfield, J. Douglas. *Twentieth Century Interpretations of "Sanctuary."* Englewood Cliffs, NJ: Prentice-Hall, 1982.

Clarke, Deborah. *Robbing the Mother: Women in Faulkner.* Jackson: UP of Mississippi, 1994.

Cowley, Malcolm. *The Faulkner-Cowley File.* New York: Viking, 1966.

Crisman, William. "Poe's Dupin as Professional, The Dupin Stories as Serial Text." *Studies in American Fiction* 23 (1995): 215-229.

D'Avanzo, Mario L. "Doc Hines and *Euphues* in *Light in August.*" *Notes on Mississippi Writers* 9 (1976): 101-106.

Davis, Boyd. "Caddy Compson's Eden." Bloom 26-28.

Dickerson, Mary Jane. "'The Magician's Wand': Faulkner's Compson Appendix." Kinney 252-267.

Fadiman, Regina. *Faulkner's "Light in August": A Description and Interpretation of the Revisions.* Charlottesville: UP of Virginia, 1975.

Faulkner, William. *Absalom, Absalom!* The Corrected Text. New York: Vintage International, 1990.

-----. "Appendix/Compson, 1699-1945." *William Faulkner: "The Sound and the Fury."* Ed. David Minter. New York: Norton, 1987.

-----. *As I Lay Dying.* The Corrected Text. New York: Vintage International, 1990.

-----. *Faulkner in the University.* Ed. Frederick L. Gwynn and Joseph L. Blotner. New York: Vintage, 1959.

-----. "Interview with Cynthia Grenier." Meriwether and Millgate 215-227.

-----. "Interview with Jean Stein Vanden Heuvel." Meriwether and Millgate 237-256.

-----. "Interviews in Japan." Meriwether and Millgate 84-198.

-----. *Light in August.* The Corrected Text. New York: Vintage International, 1990.

-----. *The Mansion.* New York: Vintage, 1959.

-----. *Requiem for a Nun.* New York: Random House, 1950.

-----. *Sanctuary.* The Corrected Text. New York: Vintage International, 1993.

-----. *Selected Letters of William Faulkner.* Ed. Joseph Blotner. New York: Random House, 1977.

-----. *The Sound and the Fury.* The Corrected Text. New York: Vintage International, 1990.

Feldstein, Richard. "Gerald Bland's Shadow." *Literature and Psychology* 31(1981): 4-12.

Fiedler, Leslie. "Pop Goes the Faulkner: In Quest of *Sanctuary.*" *Faulkner and Popular Culture.* Ed. Doreen Fowler and Ann J. Abadie. Jackson: UP of Mississippi, 1990. 75-92.

Geffen, Arthur. "Profane Time, Sacred Time, and Confederate Time in *The Sound and the Fury.*" Kinney 231-251.

Gidley, Mark. "Elements of the Detective Story in William Faulkner's Fiction." *Journal of Popular Culture* 7 (1973): 97-123.

Gilbert, Elliot L., ed. *The World of Mystery Fiction.* Del Mar, CA: U of California San Diego P, 1978.

Gladstein, Mimi Reisel. "Faulkner." Bloom 15-18.

Godden, Richard. "William Faulkner, Addie Bundren, and Language." *The University of Mississippi Studies in English* 15 (1978): 101-123.

Gold, Joseph. "Sin, Salvation and Bananas: *As I Lay Dying.*" *The Novels of William Faulkner.* Ed. R. G. Collins and Kenneth McRobbie. Winnipeg: U of Manitoba P, 1973. 55-57.

Hays, Donald. *The Dixie Association.* New York: Simon and Schuster, 1984.

Hoag, Ronald Wesley. "Ends and Loose Ends: The Triptych Conclusion of *Light in August.*" *Modern Fiction Studies* 31 (1985), 675-690.

Howe, Irving. "William Faulkner." *Major Writers of America.* Vol. II. Ed. Perry Miller. New York: Harcourt, Brace and World, 1962. 825-841.

Hungerford, Harold. "Past and Present in *Light in August.*" *American Literature* 55 (1983): 183-198.

Hunter, Edwin R. *William Faulkner: Narrative Practice and Prose Style.* Washington: Windhover Press, 1973.

Karl, Frederick. *William Faulkner: American Writer.* New York: Weidenfeld and Nicolson, 1989.

Kartiganer, Donald M. "'What I Chose to Be': Freud, Faulkner, Joe Christmas, and the Abandonment of Design." *Faulkner and Psychology.* Ed. Donald M. Kartiganer and Ann J. Abadie. Jackson: UP of Mississippi, 1994. 288-314.

-----. "Faulkner's Art of Repetition." *Faulkner and the Craft of Fiction.* Ed. Doreen Fowler and Ann J. Abadie. Jackson: UP of Mississippi, 1989. 21-47.

Kinney, Arthur, ed. *Critical Essays on William Faulkner: The Compson Family.* Boston: Hall, 1982.

Kirk, Robert W. and Marvin W. Klotz. *Faulkner's People.* Berkeley: U of California P, 1963.

Linscott, Robert. "Faulkner without Fanfare." *Esquire* July 1963: 36-42.

Longley, John L. "'Who Never Had a Sister': A Reading of *The Sound and the Fury.*" *The Novels of William Faulkner.* Ed. R. G. Collins and K. A. McRobbie. Winnipeg: U of Manitoba P, 1973. 31-53.

Materalli, Maria. *I Romanzi di Faulkner.* Rome: Edizioni Adete, 1968.

Matthews, John T. *"The Sound and the Fury": Faulkner and the Lost Cause.* Boston: Twayne, 1991.

McGraw-Hill Dictionary of Physics and Mathematics. New York: McGraw-Hill, 1978.

Meats, Stephen. "The Chronology of *Light in August.*" Pitavy's *Casebook* 227-235.

Melville, Herman. *Billy Budd, Sailor.* Ed. Harrison Hayford and Merton M. Sealts. Chicago: U of Chicago P, 1962.

Meriwether, James B. and Michael Millgate, eds. *Lion in the Garden: Interviews with William Faulkner 1926-1962.* New York: Random House, 1963.

Millgate, Michael. *The Achievement of William Faulkner.* New York: Random House, 1963.

Milliner, Gladys. "The Third Eve." Bloom 68-72.

Minter, David L. *Twentieth Century Interpretations of "Light in August."* Englewood Cliffs, NJ: Prentice-Hall, 1969.

-----. *William Faulkner: His Life and Work.* Baltimore: John Hopkins UP, 1980.

Moddelmog, Debra. "Faulkner's Theban Saga: *Light in August.*" *The Southern Literary Journal* 18 (1985): 13-29.

Nash, H. C. "Faulkner's 'Furniture Repairer and Dealer': Knitting up *Light in August.*" *Modern Fiction Studies* 16 (1970-71): 529-531.

Nishiyama, Tamotsu. "What Really Happens in *Sanctuary.*" *Studies in English Literature* 42 (1966): 235-243.

Oates, Stephen. *William Faulkner: The Man and the Artist.* New York: Harper and Row, 1987.

Page, Sally R. *Faulkner's Women: Characterization and Meaning.* Deland, Florida: Everett-Edwards, 1972.

Panek, LeRoy Lad. *Probable Cause: Crime Fiction in America.* Bowling Green, OH: Bowling Green State U Popular P, 1990.

Parker, Robert Dale. *Faulkner and the Novelistic Imagination.* Urbana: U of Illinois P, 1985.

Patten, Catherine. "The Narrative Design of *As I Lay Dying.*" *William Faulkner's "As I Lay Dying": A Critical Casebook.* Ed. Dianne L. Cox. New York: Garland, 1985. 3-29.

Pilkington, John. *The Heart of Yoknapatawpha.* Jackson: UP of Mississippi, 1981.

Pitavy, François. *Faulkner's "Light in August."* Trans. Gillian E. Cook. Bloomington: Indiana UP, 1973.

-----. *William Faulkner's "Light in August'" A Critical Casebook.* New York: Garland, 1982.

Poe, Edgar Allan. "The Cask of Amontillado." *Collected Works* III 1252-1266.

-----. *Collected Works of Edgar Allan Poe.* Ed. Thomas Ollive Mabbott. Volume II: *Tales and Sketches 1831-1842.* Cambridge, MA: Belknap, 1978.

-----. *Collected Works of Edgar Allan Poe.* Ed. Thomas Ollive Mabbott. Volume III. *Tales and Sketches 1843-1849.* Cambridge, MA: Belknap, 1978.

Polk, Noel and John D. Hart, eds. *"Sanctuary": A Concordance to the Novel.* Ann Arbor: UMI Research P, 1990.

Prior, Tracy. "Faulkner's Caddy Compson: A Reassessment." *Publications of the Arkansas Philological Association* 12 (1986): 45-57.

Quinn, Arthur Hobson. *Edgar Allan Poe: A Critical Biography.* New York: D. Appleton-Century, 1941.

Ruppersburg, Hugh. *Reading Faulkner: "Light in August."* Jackson: UP of Mississippi, 1994.

Samway, Patrick. "June 2, 1910: An Historic Day." *Faulkner and History.* Ed. Javier Coy and Michel Grisset. Salamanca: Edicions Universidad de Salamanca, 1986. 111-136.

Siegel, Jeff. *The American Detective: An Illustrated History.* Dallas: Taylor, 1993.

Swiggart, Peter. *The Art of Faulkner's Novels.* Austin: U of Texas P, 1962.

Symons, Julian. *The Tell-Tale Heart: The Life and Works of Edgar Allan Poe.* New York: Harper and Row, 1978.

Thompson, Lawrance. *William Faulkner: An Introduction and Interpretation.* New York: Barnes and Noble, 1963.

Urgo, Joseph R. "Temple Drake's Truthful Perjury: Rethinking Faulkner's *Sanctuary.*" *American Literature* 55 (1983): 435-444.

Vickery, Olga. *The Novels of William Faulkner: A Critical Interpretation.* Baton Rouge: Louisiana State UP, 1964.

Volpe, Edmond L. *A Reader's Guide to William Faulkner.* New York: Farrar, Strauss, and Giroux, 1964.

Watkins, Floyd C., and William B. Dillingham. "The Mind of Vardaman Bundren." *Philological Quarterly* 39 (1960), 247-251.

Watson, James G., ed. *Thinking of Home: William Faulkner's Letters to His Mother and Father, 1918-1925.* New York: Norton, 1992.

Watson, Jay. *Forensic Fictions: The Lawyer Figure in Faulkner.* Athens: U of Georgia P, 1993.

Weiner, Bruce. "'That Metaphysical Art': Mystery and Detection in Poe's Tales." *Poe and Our Times: Influences and Affinities.* Ed. Benjamin Franklin Fisher IV. Baltimore: The Edgar Allan Poe Society, 1986.

Williams, David. *Faulkner's Women: The Myth and the Muse.* Montreal: McGill-Queen's UP, 1977.

Wilson, Andrew J. "The Corruption in Looking: William Faulkner's *Sanctuary* as a Detective Novel." *Mississippi Quarterly* XLVII (1994): 441-460.